Victoria HarbourCats

Ten Years and Counting

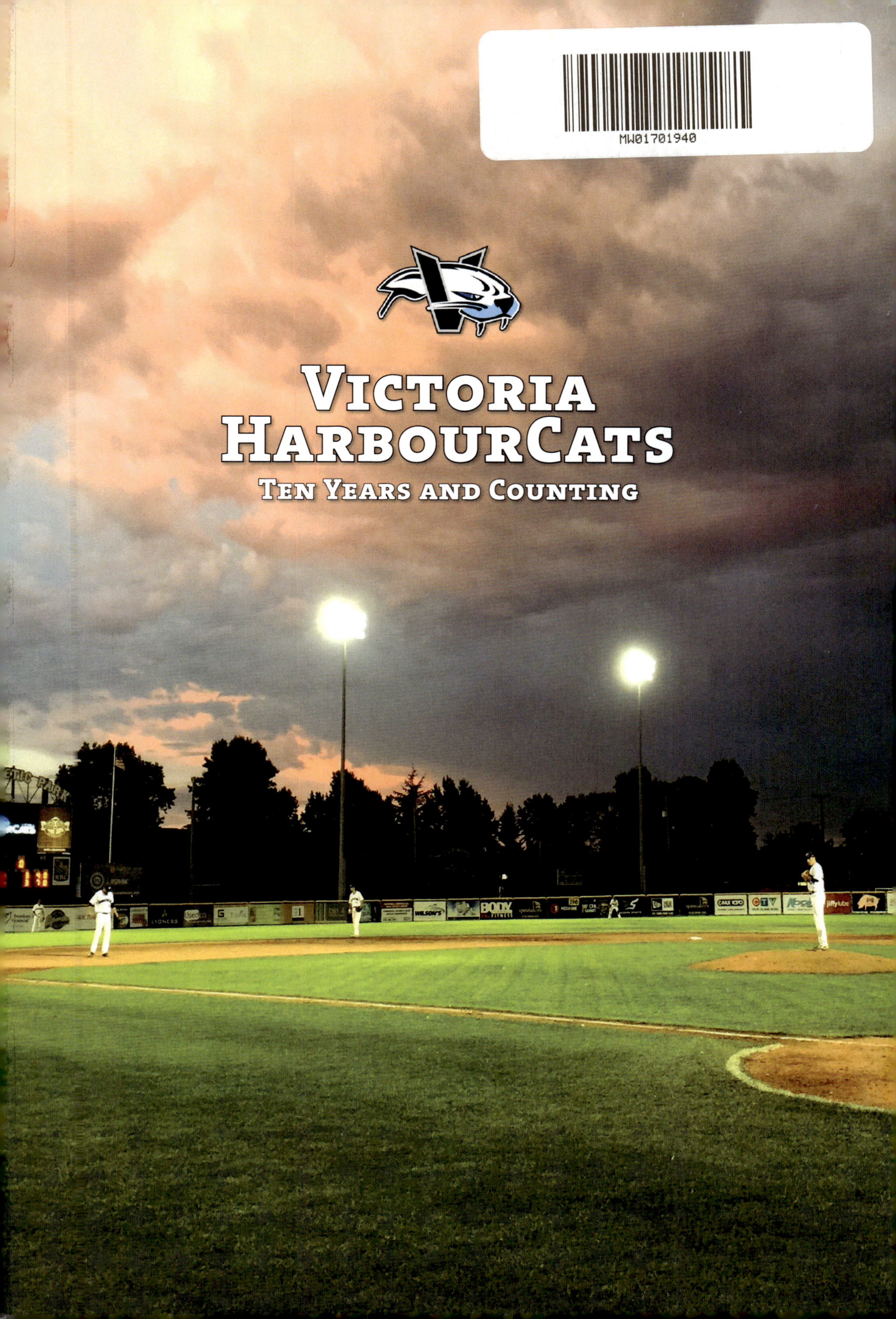

LEKWUNGEN TERRITORIES

The author acknowledges that the land on which these stories occurred is the traditional territory of the Coast Salish peoples, and specifically recognizes the Lekwungen-speaking people, known today as the Songhees and Esquimalt Nations, and that their historic connections to these lands continue to this day.

Victoria HarbourCats

Ten Years and Counting

Helen Edwards

Edwards Heritage Consulting
VICTORIA, BRITISH COLUMBIA, CANADA
2024

BOOKS BY HELEN EDWARDS

The Winter House: Ross Bay Villa, co-authored with Jennifer Nell Barr and Mary Doody Jones, 1998 (re-published as *Ross Bay Villa: A Colonial Cottage* in 1999).

The History of Professional Hockey in Victoria, B.C., 1911–2011, 2019.

Dutchy's Diaries, Life as a Canadian Naval Officer, In His Own Words: 1916–1929, 2020.

Dutchy's Decades: Life as a Canadian Naval Officer, 1930–1950, 2022.

The Heritage Detective, Volume One: The hidden stories of ordinary Victorians who did extraordinary things, 2023.

The Heritage Detective, Volume Two: The hidden stories of ordinary Victorians who did extraordinary things, 2023.

The History of Professional Hockey in Victoria, BC, 1911–2011, second edition, 2024.

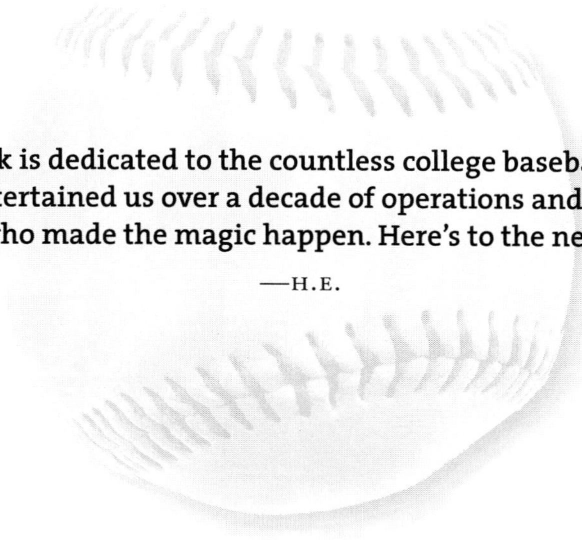

This book is dedicated to the countless college baseball players who have entertained us over a decade of operations and to the coaches and staff who made the magic happen. Here's to the next ten years!

—H.E.

ISBN 978-1-7388726-6-4 (paperback)
ISBN 978-1-7388726-7-1 (electronic book)

FIRST PUBLISHED IN 2024 BY
Edwards Heritage Consulting
Victoria, British Columbia, Canada

For further information or more copies of *Victoria HarbourCats: Ten Years and Counting* please write to heritagelady@gmail.com

Book design by Arifin Graham, Alaris Design
All photos taken by Christian Stewart unless otherwise noted

PRINTED AND BOUND IN CANADA BY DIGITAL DIRECT PRINTING LTD.

CONTENTS

FOREWORD

Local sports teams are not just about a game; I believe that they play an important role in our communities. In a world that can sometimes feel divided, they bring us together.

On a beautiful summer night in June, thousands of residents from all walks of life gather for one common purpose: to cheer on our home team and enjoy some great baseball. You run into co-workers in line for some delicious food from one of the local food trucks. Suddenly, you find yourself high-fiving a perfect stranger with each scoring run. By the end of the game, you have made new friends as you discover you have more in common than just a love for baseball and beers. At the end of the night, everyone leaves with a sense of hometown pride after another big win.

Community is at the heart of local sports teams. It is what inspired our ownership group to bring this idea of togetherness to Greater Victoria by creating the Victoria HarbourCats baseball organization. The unwavering support we have received from you, our community, keeps us coming back year after year and has made us the longest-reigning baseball organization in Victoria's history. This is our story, and it's because of you.

Victoria HarbourCats Baseball...for the love of the game and our home.

Let's go, HarbourCats!

John Wilson

PRESIDENT, C.E.O. OF THE WILSON'S GROUP OF COMPANIES

INTRODUCTION

I have been a baseball fan since my Dad, who loved the game, took me to my first game at Royal Athletic Park when I was about three years old, to watch the Victoria Athletics. Dad told me he had invested some money in the team, but I have never been able to confirm this (it does make a good story). So, although I didn't understand the game at the time, the seeds of fandom were set back then.

As I grew older, Dad and I listened to games on the radio, and once we got a television set in the 1960s, everything came to a halt on Saturday for the Game of the Week. Wanting to follow baseball more often, I saved up my babysitting money to buy a transistor radio and spent many happy hours listening to Vin Sculley call Los Angeles Dodgers games. To celebrate my twentieth birthday, I travelled to Los Angeles on the bus – it took three days – and saw six games at Dodger Stadium and then nine in Anaheim.

There has been professional baseball in Victoria for decades, but no team has been very successful or long-lasting. Plagued largely by unstable leagues and precarious finances, Victoria's teams have come and gone over the years. The Victoria Mussels lasted two years, and the Victoria Blues, one year in the short-season Northwest League. The summer of 2003 saw the emergence of the Victoria Capitals of the Canadian Baseball League, but that team ended when the league folded partway through the season. The Victoria Seals of the Golden Baseball League were very popular with local fans. Still, they only lasted from 2008 to 2010, when they were disbanded due to the instability of the league and issues with the park.

My first foray into sports ownership was as a shareholder of Northwest Sports Enterprises, the then-owner of the Vancouver Canucks. I had really wanted to join the ownership group of the Victoria Cougars Junior Hockey Team, but their owners did not want a female in their group, so I looked to Vancouver. When Arthur Griffiths needed to have a larger percentage of ownership to operate the Vancouver Grizzlies NBA team, he had to buy minor shareholders out to do so, and my ownership of a sports team ended.

I was excited when the Victoria HarbourCats were announced as a college-level baseball team playing in the flourishing West Coast League. However, the question at that time was, would this team survive? Given the history of the game in Victoria, fans were right to wonder. However, the team has been an enormous success both on the field and with the fans. They are the first Victoria-based team to last for more than two years since the late 1940s.

I attended a few games in the first year of operation, decided I liked the product and became a season ticket holder the following season. In 2015, the first four members of the current ownership group acquired the team, and from then on, there has been nothing but success. I convinced my husband to join me at the games, and he became a devoted fan, attending even when his health was failing.

In February 2020, he died, and I could think of no better way to honour his memory than investing in the team we both loved. I was thrilled when I was accepted into the ownership group, and even the pandemic could not dampen my enthusiasm. I am committed to this team and will do whatever it takes to bring a championship to Victoria. In the meantime, I enjoy watching "our boys" make their way up the baseball ladder, with some reaching the pinnacle of the major leagues.

I was thrilled when we set up the Golden Tide team for students at Camosun and UVic. Finally, there would be a place for promising young athletes to play here at the local level. I then invested in the training facility, which we named in honour of my late husband, determined to get the best training for our players. It will be a great source of pride when one of our players makes it to the "show."

As an author, I am always looking for a new project. So, I am pleased to write the history of the Victoria HarbourCats' first 10 seasons. It's been a ton of fun and never seemed like work.

In my private life, I have four children and five surviving grandchildren. I have lived in the same house for more than 50 years, conveniently a short walk to the ballpark. I enjoy billeting players in the summer and encourage them to walk everywhere. I am famous for my chocolate chip cookies, which have proven popular on road trips. I can be seen at all the home games – and some road games – with my trademark red hat and my red jersey signed by the players who have billeted with me.

I will do just about anything for kids and have become a benefactor of the Canucks Place Children's Hospice. I am donating all the proceeds of my book sales to this organization, which does so much good in our province.

As Victor Kiam once said in a famous Remington ad, "I liked the product so much, I bought the company." Well, I liked the HarbourCats organization so much that I joined the ownership group. It has turned out to be one of the best decisions I have ever made. We are here for the long term. Go Cats! Go Golden Tide!

About the Author

Helen Edwards has been a baseball fan since the day her Dad, a rabid baseball fan, took her to her first baseball game at Royal Athletic Park when she was about three years old. While she might have been more interested then in what the vendors were selling, the idea of the game took hold, and she has been hooked ever since. Since girls weren't supposed to play baseball in those days, she played pickup games in a local parking lot with her friends and had hours of unsupervised fun.

She was born and raised in Victoria and has never lived anywhere else, giving her a personal perspective on its history. She has written two books on her father-in-law, who served in the Royal Canadian Navy for 38 years, and a series entitled The Heritage Detective, which tells stories about buildings in Victoria and the people who lived and worked in them. The second edition of her book on early hockey in Victoria was launched on live Canadian TV during Scotiabank Hockey Day in Canada in January 2024.

Helen has been writing since elementary school, when she penned plays for her classmates to perform. She loves the "thrill of the chase" of research and writing stories. Writing this book has been a labour of love, as it combines her passion for history with her love of writing. She is thrilled to share the stories of a very successful college baseball franchise with the world.

Helen is an active supporter of Canuck Place Children's Hospice, and all profits from book sales will be donated to this worthwhile charity.

For more information about Helen and her work, visit https://helenedwards.ca/

Acknowledgments

I am deeply grateful for the invaluable contributions of many individuals, without whom this book would not have been possible.

When I joined the ownership group of the Victoria HarbourCats in 2021, I was told that, as an author, I could write the history. As no other baseball team has survived in Victoria for more than a few years, marking a decade of the franchise seemed appropriate. At that time, we were still not playing due to the COVID-19 pandemic, a challenge that many teams would not have survived. Yet, we persevered. I had time to begin my research. When operations resumed in the 2022 season, I started interviewing people who could help me tell the story.

I am indebted to the former players, coaches, and other members of the organization, as well as West Coast League baseball in general, who agreed to be interviewed. Without them, I would have no idea of the stories behind this successful franchise. Special thanks to the franchise's original owner, John McLean, and former Victoria Mayor Dean Fortin, who provided invaluable details on the franchise's early days.

Every author needs an editor, and I had one of the best. Jim Swanson reviewed my words with a fine-tooth comb and made several suggestions. He has an encyclopedic knowledge of the team and its operations and has forgotten more about the team than I have ever known. The staff at the City of Victoria Archives responded to my request for old baseball photos, which make the history of the sport meaningful to today's readers. Thanks to Christian Stewart, General Manager of the HarbourCats, for allowing me access to the thousands of photos of the games over the decade. Images bring the story to life. Christian took all photos in this book except as noted in the captions. I could never have been published without the work of Arifin Graham of Alaris Design. He takes my words and pictures and transforms them into a magical production.

In the last two years, I have done a lot of writing while on road trips with the team. I am deeply grateful to the players and coaches who tolerated my constant questions and encouraged me to get the job done. To my billets, thanks for educating me on what it takes to be a college baseball player. I learned so much from you.

Through baseball, I have made so many friends who have given me the confidence to write about our team. It will be a pleasure to share their stories with you.

Finally, a special thanks to my amazing family. Your unwavering support and understanding of my passion for this project have been crucial. You have stood by me, supporting your 'crazy' mother in whatever she wanted to do. Someday, I might just write about each of you!

1

In the Beginning

On June 5, 2013, Victoria native Nick Pivetta threw the first pitch for the Victoria HarbourCats, but the recorded history of baseball in Victoria goes back much farther. In the early 1860s, John C. Keenan moved here from Sacramento. He was an Irish immigrant born about 1831 in Ireland, who served as a Texas Ranger and then followed the lure of gold to Sacramento, where he established the Fashion Saloon. By 1858, he had itchy feet again and moved to Victoria to take advantage of the gold rush in British Columbia, leaving his wife Roseanna to manage the Sacramento operations. Here, he operated the Fashion Hotel on Yates Street. In July 1865, he sold the California operations, and Roseanna came north with a "small fortune in bills and gold," along with seven "soiled doves" likely for duty in the hotel. The steamer *Brother Jonathan* struck a rock off Crescent, California, and sank, taking Roseanna and the girls with it. Like many Irishmen of the day, Keenan was keen on sports and was determined to bring the new game of "base ball" to the West Coast. He had played cricket in his home country, and baseball came easily to him. He organized a baseball team, the Fashion Club, which played against local cricket clubs. He was also known as the chief of a volunteer firefighting company in Victoria. About 1865, he sold his business and moved back to Sacramento, where he died of a heart attack at age 49. He was buried in the Exempt Fireman's Plot in the Old Sacramento Cemetery.

A later mention of organized baseball in Victoria dates to September 13, 1866, when a Base Ball Club (note the unusual spelling) was formed under the name Olympic. An archival article in the *Colonist and Chronicle* tells us the details:

BASE BALL CLUB.—At a meeting of Base Ball players, last evening, at the Gymnasium Hall, a club was formed under the name of the Olympic. Mr Gillon was elected President; and Mr E. McQuade, Secretary; Messrs T. Fowler, J. Davies, and R. H. Adams, jr., were elected Directors. The club is limited to thirty members—and the names of twenty-four are already booked. The playing rules of the National Base Ball Association of New York were adopted.

COLONIST AND CHRONICLE, SEPTEMBER 13, 1866, PAGE 2.

By November 3, 1866, we learn that the "deciding match between the 1st Nine and the 2nd Nine of the Baseball Club will be played on Beacon Hill today at 2:30 p.m. The winning Nine will play the cricketers on the 9th inst." The club continued to play local matches and then moved to the international stage, with teams from Seattle and Portland coming to Victoria. In July 1885, it was reported that "the cost of maintaining a first-class baseball club is about $65,000 a year."

The Victoria Amity Baseball Club was organized on April 26, 1895, as a strictly amateur operation. According to newspaper reports, they had trouble finding pitchers. The team was another short-term club. Team names changed over the years as one team morphed into another.

AMITY BASEBALL CLUB, 1878. COURTESY CITY OF VICTORIA ARCHIVES

BASEBALL IN BEACON HILL PARK, MAY 24, 1890.
COURTESY CITY OF VICTORIA ARCHIVES

Gradually, baseball diamonds were established in other areas of town, including Oak Bay.

In 1908, local baseball clubs applied to the Directors of the Royal Athletic Association as they felt the Oak Bay grounds they were currently using were just too far from the centre of the city.

When the 1911 professional baseball season began, a team called the Victoria Bees, playing in the Northwestern League, was featured in a two-page spread in the local newspaper with small stories on each of the twenty-four men on the roster. Leonard A. Wattelet was the first general manager. In 1914, he left baseball and was responsible for the baseball operations for the 40,000 men at Camp Lewis,

BASEBALL TEAM AT OAK BAY PARK, 1910.
COURTESY CITY OF VICTORIA ARCHIVES

Washington. He died on October 28, 1914. The manager was Eddie Householder. He played pro baseball from 1897 to 1911 and died of cancer in 1924. Playing at Royal Athletic Park, which had been established in 1908 as a site for field lacrosse, the team had moderate success but never won a championship. Even having the legendary Lester Patrick of hockey fame join the ownership group could not save the franchise.

Victoria had its first championship when the Victoria Capitals (also called the Victoria Islanders) played the 1920 season on a new baseball field constructed on lands behind the Empress Hotel, on what is now the site of the Crystal Garden. Playing in the Pacific International League, which had teams from Seattle, Tacoma, Yakima, Spokane, and Vancouver, they won 69 games while losing 46. Opening day, May 18, 1920, was well attended despite inclement weather and a Pathfinder II flew over the site, dropping baseballs for players to catch; nobody was successful. Mines Minister Bill Sloan threw the first pitch to Victoria Mayor Robert Porter in front of 4,207 rabid fans.

Over 9,000 fans viewed the final series of that season. The team played again in the 1921 season and finished third in the standings. The league folded in the following year, and teams joined the Western International League. The Victoria Bees played in this league for one season, after which it, too, folded. The Crystal Garden pool was built on the west of the site by 1926, with the Canadian Pacific Lawn Bowling and Crochet Club established to the east of the site in 1923.

Plagued largely by unstable leagues and precarious finances, Victoria's teams have come and gone over the years.

From 1946 to 1951, the Victoria Athletics were a Western International League baseball team. They were affiliated with the New York Yankees from 1947 to 1949. They played their home games at Royal Athletic Park. Gil McDougald, who would become the 1951 American League Rookie of the Year, played for them. From 1952-1955, the Victoria Tyees played in the Class A level Western International League. But they, too, folded. The Victoria Mussels played in 1978 and 1979, and the Victoria Blues, the next year, in the short-season Northwest League. 2003 saw the emergence of the Victoria Capitals of the Canadian Baseball League, but that

When the first hint of a college-level baseball team playing during the summers at Royal Athletic Park surfaced in February 2012, locals were curious but wary.

BASEBALL GAME ON OPENING DAY OF THE VICTORIA MEMORIAL STADIUM, MAY 18, 1920.
COURTESY CITY OF VICTORIA ARCHIVES

team ended when the league folded partway through the season. The Victoria Seals of the Golden Baseball League were very popular with local fans. Still, they only lasted from 2008 to 2010, when they were disbanded due to the instability of the league and issues with the park.

When the first hint of a college-level baseball team playing during the summers at Royal Athletic Park surfaced in February 2012, locals were curious but wary. However, that league differed from any other league that had a team in Victoria as they were a very stable and successful league with no fear of folding. The West Coast League was founded in 2005, and then known as the West Coast Collegiate Baseball League. The name was changed to its current one in 2008. The league was designed to develop college talent, with only current college-eligible players allowed to participate. The West Coast League has produced dozens of professional players, including several major leaguers. Founding members were the Aloha (Ore) Knights, Bellingham (Wa) Bells, Bend (Ore) Elks, Kelowna (BC) Falcons, Kitsap (Wa) BlueJackets, Spokane (Wa) RiverHawks and Wenatchee (Wa) AppleSox. The announcement contained an announcement from WCL President Ken Wilson that "teams in the WCL operate like pro clubs on a for-profit basis with all the promotions fans would expect in a minor-pro setting. Each team plays 54 games from June through August, with 27 at home. The league currently has nine teams—five in Washington state, three in Oregon and one in BC – the Kelowna Falcons."

The eventual owner of the franchise, John McLean, grew up in Moncton, New Brunswick, and had played multiple sports. When he went to University, he majored in Sports Administration but spent his career in finance, travelling on airplanes

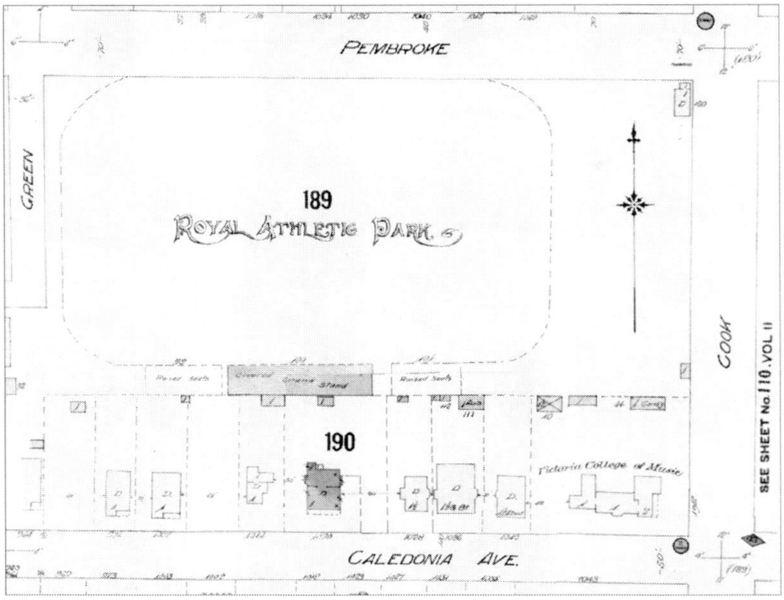

1911 FIRE INSURANCE MAP SHOWING ROYAL ATHLETIC PARK

for 26 years. He was tired of this lifestyle and moved to Vancouver in 2001. He had always loved baseball and considered it a civilized game. The beauty of baseball is that you can be down six nothing with two out in the bottom of the ninth inning and it is possible to come back and win. This rarely happens in football and hockey. It is also a game where you can socialize during the game as a spectator as players socialize with each other in the dugout, and they even socialize with each other on the bases. When he arrived in Vancouver, the Vancouver Canadians were for sale, but their operation did not make sense from a financial perspective. At this time, he became aware of college summer baseball but had not yet heard of the West Coast League. He also considered the Canadian Baseball League, which had a franchise in Victoria – The Capitals – and had discussions about placing a West Coast League college ball franchise in New Westminster, but there were issues that made it unworkable. However, when the Canadian Baseball League folded after two months of operations in 2003, he then turned his focus to Victoria and discussed possibili-

Success would be measured by attendance and local support. Next came a meeting with Mayor Dean Fortin, who was very supportive of placing a West Coast League franchise in Victoria.

The team's name, HarbourCats, was revealed on October 12, 2013. More than 600 submissions were received from the community.

ties for a West Coast League team with Ken Wilson, the commissioner at the time. They visited Royal Athletic Park and, after preliminary discussions with the city of Victoria, felt that the summer college baseball model could work.

Success would be measured by attendance and local support. Next came a meeting with Mayor Dean Fortin, who was very supportive of placing a West Coast League franchise in Victoria. He felt that a good product would help define Victoria as a capital city, and he loved Royal Athletic Park because it's close to town and it feels like part of the community. There were further discussions with the mayor, and he led community negotiations. He felt it was important to speak with the local community and deal with any concerns they had. Mr. McLean was able to work out a deal with Daktronics and the city to take over the scoreboard that had been installed by the owners of the Victoria Seals. Then it was time to negotiate a contract for the lease and to see what could be done to upgrade the field to West Coast League standards. Once those details were settled, it was time to find coaches as they are the ones who have the relationship with the colleges to send players. The owner decided to hire Dennis Rogers, who had been the manager of the Vancouver Canadians when it was a minor league team for the Oakland Athletics, as the head

ROYAL ATHLETIC PARK, 1940S. COURTESY CITY OF VICTORIA ARCHIVES

coach and left the recruiting of players up to him. Next on the agenda was the hiring of a general manager. Under the recommendation of the general manager of the Corvallis Knights team, Holly Jones, who had worked as an assistant general manager in Corvallis, was hired. At the press conference revealing the name of the first general manager of the team, everyone was asking who the "guy" in that position would be. There were several looks of surprise when she was introduced. However, she was highly qualified to do the job and would win accolades at the end of the season. Needing office space, they found a location near the ballpark, ironically, the same building on Vancouver Street in which a larger office for the HarbourCats is located. Holly Jones hired Brad Norris-Jones to run the ticketing operations, and he later added sponsorships to his responsibilities.

The team had not been named, and it would be up to the fans to select a name in a contest. On June 14, 2012, the team owner, John McLean, was introduced to the city in a press conference at Royal Athletic Park with WCL Commissioner Wilson and Mayor Dean Fortin in attendance. WCL average attendance the prior season had been 1,113, but the owners expected to draw over 1,500 per game. The players, being NCAA students, were not paid and would be billeted with local families to reduce costs. The team's name, HarbourCats, was revealed on October 12, 2013. More than 600 submissions were received from the community and included names from the past, including Tyees, Athletics, Mussels, Blues, Capitals, and Seals, but the owners wanted something new. The team colours were blue with grey trim with a stylized blue "V" on the cap.

When the city that had been granted the All-Star game was unable to make arrangements, Mr. McLean told a league meeting that Victoria could do it. He had not consulted Holly Jones or the City of Victoria but reached out to Pat Gillick, former general manager of the Toronto Blue Jays, Philadelphia Phillies, and Seattle Mariners, who lent his support and his name and took part in the festivities. The event would begin with the All-Star Game Kickoff Event on Monday, July 22, with Pat Gillick as a speaker. Major League Scouting Bureau representatives, league executives, team executives, Victoria business partners, and selected media would be attending. It would put Victoria on the map as a college baseball franchise. The all-day event ticket available to the public for July 23 included the All-Star Game, the post-game fireworks, and the Home-Run Derby. The team advised that tickets would go on sale on December 3rd from the team's office at 103-1814 Vancouver Street.

2

2013: The First Season

The year 2013 began with news of the signing of players for the inaugural season of play. As of January 15, 2013, the team had signed Nick Pivetta, Connor Baits, Austin Russell, Connor Russell, Casey Schroeder, David Shucknecht, Brandon Smith, Will Ballowe, Josh Cushing, Anthony Hermelyn, and Brett Urabe. By February 8, 2013, the team had signed an additional 21 players, including MLB draft picks Alex Real, David Olmeda-Berrerra, and Jack Graham.

On the business side of operations, the team signed a soft drink deal with Coca-Cola, a hotel deal with Accents Inns as the official hotel for the inaugural season, and sponsorship with Spinnaker Gastro Brewpub to provide the official beer. General Manager Holly Jones announced the team's office staff including Christian Stewart, director of communications and photography: Helen Welch, sponsorship sales director; Gareth Gilson, ticketing and technology operations manager; Jakki Corrigan, merchandise and design coordinator; Mike Wysiecki, marketing and game night operations manager; Karen Russell, billeting and player transportation coordinator; Alex Sessa, equipment and operations coordinator; Brad Norris-Jones, ticket sales director; John Shah, sponsorship and operations coordinator; and Christina Grimm, sponsor-relations director.

Fans were invited to name the new team's mascot with a contest running until February 24, 2013. Entrants had to explain in 50 words or less why they chose the name they did. The winner would receive two season tickets with two runner-up prizes of 10-game ticket flex packs. Harvey the HarbourCat was introduced to the world on March 29, 2013. In preparation for the all-star game to be played on July

Just before the first game of the season, the team revealed its uniforms. There were three styles: white, dark blue, and a light-blue third jersey.

23, the all-star logo was revealed in April. At the same time, the Yates Street Taphouse was announced as the presenting sponsor of the game.

Just before the first game of the season, the team revealed its uniforms. There were three styles: white, dark blue, and a light-blue third jersey. The home uniform had front lettering reading "HarbourCats," and the away jersey and 3rd jersey had lettering reading "Victoria." One cap featured a basic "V," and the other combined the letters "H" and "C" in a logo that is still used today." The initial reaction to the jerseys was that they looked like major league uniforms and the players would be proud to wear them.

The HarbourCats made deals with local sponsors to provide goods and services to the team. Accent Inns was named the official hotel, Spinnakers Gastro Brewpub would provide the official beer, and Wilson's Transportation and Ambrosia Catering combined to provide the Wilson's Transportation Group Deck, a premium seating section of 102 seats where fans could select from grill items or a buffet.

The *Times Colonist* featured a full-page insert that introduced Victorians to the team, complete with headshots so citizens could recognize the players. Included on that page were 26 players and three coaches. Also noted was the new era of co-operation between the City of Victoria and the baseball team, with improvements having been made to Royal Athletic Park to enhance the fan experience, including moving home plate 15 feet closer to the grandstand. A portable fence-on-wheels was purchased to delineate the outfield boundaries and could be moved much more easily than previous fences, and changes were made to the dugouts, bullpen, and dressing rooms. All was ready for the season to begin.

On June 5, 2013, Victoria pitcher Nick Pivetta was given the start for the inaugural game. Although it was noted that he might be selected in the upcoming Major League draft and might have to leave the team, he was determined to enjoy his time here. The Lambrick Park grad was thrilled to be able to pitch in his hometown. The team behind him on opening day was nowhere complete, as many of the signed players were still playing in the NCAA tournament. However, several Canadian college players were signed to 10-day contracts to supplement the lineup, gaining valuable experience.

An opening night crowd of 3,026 waited patiently for the first pitch, delayed

NICK PIVETTA IN ACTION. DAVE NICHOLSON PHOTO

until 8 pm due to the late arrival of the Kelowna Falcons, whose team bus suffered a flat tire. It was through the influence of John Wilson of Wilson's Transportation, that BC Ferries agreed to hold the ferry until the bus arrived at the Tsawwassen Terminal. Nick Rutckyj of Langley became the first batter in team history and recorded the first hit in the third inning. Chris Lewis from Sacramento State University hit a double to drive home Rutckyj for the first run in franchise history. Catcher David Schuknecht hit the first homer in the fifth inning to give the home team a 6-4 lead. After Kelowna scored two runs to tie the game, the HarbourCats scored two more to win their inaugural game by a score of 8-6. The next night, Alex De Goti was the star of the game, notching a homer over the left field wall to put the 'Cats ahead 3-2 in the bottom of the eighth inning on their way to a 4-2 victory. On June 7, the home team completed the series sweep with a 7-6 win, largely due to four unearned runs in the second inning, which came off Kelowna errors.

Off the field, Nick Pivetta was selected 136th overall in the Major League Baseball draft by the Washington Nationals, the former Montreal Expos. He would pitch one more game for the HarbourCats before beginning his professional baseball career.

The second series of the season was played against fellow expansion team, the Medford Rogues. Victoria native Connor Russell got the start for the home team and pitched seven innings in a 4-1 loss. However, Nick Pivetta was on the mound for the second game of the series, and he got the victory in a one-sided 11-4 win for the home team. Alex Real had three hits and scored three runs, Brandon Smith

COACH IN CONVERSATION WITH UMPIRE

added two hits, scored two runs, and notched three RBIs, while Chris Lewis put the game out of reach with a three-run, bases-loaded, two-out double that made the score 8-2. After the game, Pivetta announced that he would be joining the Nationals' minor league team in Florida. In one of the most exciting games of the young season, the HarbourCats fell behind 9-1 before an incredible comeback that gave them a 12-11 victory. After scoring six runs to make the score 9-7, the home team had the bases loaded with one out in the bottom of the eighth inning and were threatening to take the lead before a double play put an end to that. In the ninth inning, with Medford now leading 11-8, the HarbourCats again rallied. They loaded the bases, setting the stage for Chris Lewis to drive in two runs to narrow the score to 11-10. Dylan Lavelle, who had arrived in Victoria a few hours before the game, doubled to score two runs and send the fans home happy with a walk-off victory.

Now, it was time for the first road trip of the season. Manager Dennis Rogers noted that he liked the road as it was a time for the players to get to know each other better and to bond as a team. The first road victory came in Kelowna with a 7-2 drubbing of the Falcons. Alex Real was the star of the game, with his two hits, which drove in three runs. After a second road victory with Connor Russell on the mound for seven innings in a 9-1 triumph, reality set in with a 13-6 loss in the final game of the series.

The next series in Bellingham started with a 3-1 loss to the Bells, but the HarbourCats rebounded the next night, riding an eight-inning pitching gem by Bryan

Conant, en route to a 4-2 victory. Mother Nature intervened, and rain cancelled the final game, giving the team some much-needed time off.

Back home, the HarbourCats were the victims of solid pitching by the Bend in a 5-1 loss. Game two of the series featured strong Victoria pitching by Ty Provencher, who went all the way for a 6-1 triumph. It was the first complete game by a HarbourCats pitcher and was unusual, as he was a reliever for his college team. The offence was led by multi-talented opening game starter Rob Nesovic, who hit a three-run homer in the first inning to set the pace. In an afternoon matinee, the home team eked out a 3-2 victory over the visitors, with Bryan Conant silencing the Bend bats in a masterful relief performance. After a five-day break, the team went on the road for six games, putting their 10-4 record on the line.

Four defensive errors cost the team dearly in their first game against Cowlitz in a 4-3 loss. Coach Rogers refused to blame the five days off or the 7 am ferry trip en route to the ballpark, labelling his team's effort as "sloppy." The Black Bears took the second game of the series as well. They scored seven runs in the sixth inning—with two out—to cruise to an easy 9-0 win over the visitors. However, the HarbourCats got their act together and won on Canada Day. It was not easy, as the game was tied

ALEX DE GOTI AT BAT

4-4 after 12 innings, but Alex Real hit a two-run triple in the 13th inning to put the Cats ahead for good. Starter Ty Provecher went nine innings, but the victory went to reliever Joe Navilhon. Then, it was on to Wenatchee. Things did not go well in the first game as the team continued to make errors, and it cost them a 7-2 loss. The only thing different the next night was the score, 8-1. The HarbourCats had now lost four games out of their last five and were not looking good on the field. The Apple Sox completed the series sweep with a 3-2 victory in the final game of the series. Alex De Goti was the offensive star for Victoria, with two hits.

With the road trip over, the HarbourCats faced the Kelowna Falcons in a game at Royal Athletic Park. Arriving back in town about 3:30 pm, they were looking to end their losing streak, but it was not to be. They fell 8-7 to Kelowna, a team they had beaten earlier in the season. However, the team rallied and notched an impressive 11-3 victory over Kelowna, featuring the team's first grand slam by John Schuknecht in the eighth inning that put the game on ice. In a Sunday matinee, the bats were working again as Alex Real smashed a grand slam to lead the team to a 9-5 win. In the opening game of a series against Walla Walla, the sloppiness came back, with the team committing four errors and making several baserunning mistakes in a 6-1 defeat. The trend of poor play continued in the second game against the Sweets in an 11-2 blowout loss. The third game in the series was much the same as the first two. Poor pitching, a lack of hitting, and five more errors led the team to a third straight defeat at the hands of Walla Walla by a score of 16-5.

The next game was in Klamath Falls, about 15 hours travelling time from home. Much to everyone's surprise, the HarbourCats defeated the Klamath Falls Gems, 5-3, with a three-run ninth inning. Victoria's manager, Dennis Rogers, noted that he had the youngest team in the league, and they were just learning how to play virtually every day. He expected play to improve as the season progressed. Good play continued in the second game of the series, with the HarbourCats scoring early and often in a 17-hit, 6-0 shutout for Bryan Conant. Dylan LaVelle had four hits, while Alex Real and Jordan Ellis had three each. In game three of the series, the 'Cats had a 3-0 lead but couldn't hold it and fell to the Gems, 7-4. Failure to score with runners on base was their downfall. The next stop on the road trip was in Medford. It

Much to everyone's surprise, the HarbourCats defeated the Klamath Falls Gems, 5-3, with a three-run ninth inning.

CONNOR RUSSELL SIGNS AUTOGRAPHS FOR YOUNG FAN

was a close game for 6 1/2 innings until the Rogues scored eight runs in the bottom of the seventh for an eventual 15-6 victory. On the good side of the news, pitcher Bryan Conant was named the HarbourCats player of the week. Leaving runners stranded contributed to an 8-0 loss to Medford in the second game of the series. The team fell under .500 for the first time in the season. The Rogues completed a three-game sweep of the HarbourCats with a 3-1 victory. Victoria stranded nine runners on base, unable to bring them home. They also committed three more errors, becoming the worst fielding team in the league.

Back home, the HarbourCats came up with a better effort but still lost to Wenatchee 2-0. Victoria's pitcher, Connor Russell, went eight innings in a losing cause. Unfortunately, he got no scoring support despite the HarbourCats outhitting their opponents. It was the seventh time the home team had lost this season after getting more hits than their opponents. Fortunately, the home team got things figured out in the second game of the series and defeated Wenatchee 3-2. Third baseman Dylan Lavelle had two leadoff doubles and scored two runs for the 'Cats first victory over the AppleSox this season. In the afternoon matinée conclusion of the series, Ty Provencher pitched 8 1/3 innings to lead his team to a 6-5 victory. The HarbourCats scored four runs in the first inning, added singles in the third and fourth, and then held on for the close win.

League play was paused for the All-Star game, held in Victoria. HarbourCats named to the North Division team were Austin Russell, Alex De Goti, Scott Kennedy, Ty Provencher, and Alex Real. Dennis Rogers was named manager of the North Division, and Ed Knaggs of the Wenatchee AppleSox, manager of the South

Division. Festivities began with the home run derby, won by Cody Hough of the Klamath Falls Gems. In the game itself, the attendance of 4,210 easily surpassed the former all-star game attendance record of 2,517 set in 2011 at Corvallis, Oregon. Seventeen Major League Baseball scouts were at the game and at the combine before it, where players demonstrated individual skills. The South Division team outscored their northern counterparts, 7-5, with Kyle Knigge of the Cowlitz Black Bears the individual star with two hits, two RBIs, and a run in three plate appearances. League play resumed after this exciting match.

Back on the road, the HarbourCats visited Kitsap for their first game in Bremerton. Before an announced crowd of 317, they scratched out a 6-5 victory. Timmy Richards led the offensive surge with four hits, while Chris Lewis had three. After surrendering a single run in the second inning, the HarbourCats notched three in the third on their way to the win in the match. They were aided by three BlueJackets' errors. In the second game of the series, the bats were less productive as TJ Murphy threw a three-hitter as his team recorded a 3-0 victory. In the rubber match, Kitsap pitcher, Spenser Watkins, was perfect, facing the minimum 27 batters, striking out 10 HarbourCats, in a 2-0 shutout.

The 'Cats returned home for a series against Corvallis. The first game was played under sunny skies but the 1,292 fans in attendance did not like the final score, a 5-1 Knights victory. Ty Provencher hurled eight innings for the home team, but his teammates could only manage one run in the ninth inning when the game was out of reach. The second game of the series saw better play, but the 'Cats surrendered four runs in the ninth inning, aided by a critical error, and ended the game with the bases loaded when their comeback fell two runs short. The final score of 4-2

The second game of the series saw better play, but the 'Cats surrendered four runs in the ninth inning.

sent the Sunday afternoon home crowd sad. The rubber match saw the Knights narrowly edge the 'Cats, 6-5, in a game that took almost three hours to play. The home team was up 3-1 early, but a four-run seventh inning gave the visitors the win. Again, the HarbourCats outhit their opponents, this time 12-9, but failed to take advantage of their chances. Alex Real, Alex De Goti and Brandon Smith all had two hits in a losing cause. The homestand continued against the Klamath

JOHN SCHUKNECHT AT BAT

Falls Gems, and the HarbourCats bats came alive in an 11-4 win. Logan Lombana went the distance, facing 34 batters and surrendering just four runs. The 'Cats were assisted by a Gems' pitching staff that yielded eight wild pitches and three passed balls that led to five runs. The lowest crowd of the season, 885, watched Klamath Falls' left fielder, Michael Tittle, step in as a pitcher. He threw three innings until he was replaced in the fourth inning when Victoria mounted a challenge and scored twice. Both teams scored three times in the seventh inning, but the Gems outlasted the home team 9-6. Brandon Smith was the scoring leader for the 'Cats with four hits. In the final game of the series, Gems' ace, Nick Sabo, threw eight innings of six-hit ball while his offence had two home runs, including a grand slam by Adam Daymunde. John Schuknecht, with two, and Alex Real, with one, hit homers for Victoria in an 11-6 defeat.

In Walla Walla, the HarbourCats, behind the strong pitching of Ty Provencher, defeated the Sweets 3-1. He went the distance, allowing just five hits and one run while striking out nine. Brett Urabe was 2-2 at the plate and scored a run. The middle game of the series was a nail-biter that was scoreless until the Sweets walked it

DAVID SCHUKNECHT AT BAT

off with a single run in the 10th inning. Victoria failed to score despite three Walla Walla errors. The home team won the series with a 4-3 victory. Dylan Lavelle had two hits for Victoria, while David Schuknecht had the other. The HarbourCats were officially eliminated from playoff contention when they lost 6-4 to Wenatchee in the first game of their series. Despite taking an early 1-0 lead and adding to it in the fourth inning, the 'Cats surrendered four runs in the fifth and two more in the seventh to seal their fate. John Schuknecht and Jordan Ellis had three hits in a losing cause. The middle game of the series did not go Victoria's way either. The 'Cats took an early lead but were unable to hold it and lost 6-2. Alex De Goti and Brandon Smith had two hits each for Victoria. The final game of the road trip was in Bellingham to make up for a rained-out contest earlier in the season. Alex De Goti had two hits and two RBIs, David Schuknecht had two hits and an RBI, while Timmy Richards hit a double in the 3-2 victory. Will Ballowe got the win for Victoria.

The team came home for the final three games of their inaugural season, out of playoff contention but still determined to put on a good show for their loyal home fans. Being short of pitchers, the 'Cats started Daniel Koo, a pitcher for the Abbotsford Cardinals of the BC Premier League and he struggled, surrendering six runs in five innings before he was relieved by his Cardinal teammate, Emilio Foden, who didn't fare much better. Alex Real and John Schuknecht had two hits each in an 8-2 Bells victory. Former Coquitlam Red Alex Calbrick was outstanding for the Bells with four hits and two home runs. The next evening, Bellingham again

> Locals were introduced to the play-by-play announcer for the HarbourCats. Ryan Rouillard, a 19-year-old from Mercer Island, Washington.

prevailed as Victoria took an early lead and could not hold it – a phrase repeated often during the season – losing 4-1. Austin Russell was the offensive star for the home team with two hits; he scored the lone run. The HarbourCats closed out their 2013 season on a winning note as Logan Lombana got the win in relief as the home team outscored Bellingham, 4-3. The difference in the game was a three-run seventh inning highlighted by a Brett Urabe double and a Brandon Smith triple. Alex Real finished with a batting average of .339, seventh in the league and shared the home run lead at six with teammate John Schuknecht. The team finished second in league attendance at 43,003 behind Bend Elks' number of 51,283.

In offseason news, General Manager Holly Jones was named West Coast League executive of the year, the first female to be so recognized. Alex Real was selected as a utility player for the WCL all-star team, while Alex De Goti was named to the second team along with pitcher Bryan Conant. Ty Provencher was given an honourable mention.

Locals were introduced to the play-by-play announcer for the HarbourCats. Ryan Rouillard, a 19-year-old from Mercer Island, Washington, a student at the University of Oregon, was recruited by Oregon alumna Holly Jones and called the games for the 2013 season. He moved on to the Yakima Valley Pippins and eventually worked for the Frisco RoughRiders, a double-A affiliate of the Texas Rangers. He was replaced in Victoria by local product Jordan Smith, well known locally for his call of Victoria Cougars hockey games and UVic basketball games.

3

2014: The Second Season

In October, the team announced that General Manager Holly Jones would be leaving the team to return to her home and family in Oregon. Owner John McLean said he would name a replacement in November. He also added that he had signed three-quarters of the 2014 roster. The announced goal for the upcoming season was to push for a playoff berth. The 2014 schedule was released in November, featuring regional rivalries and several weekend games which were always popular with the fans. The HarbourCats would begin the season on the road with three games in Kelowna and then return for the home opener versus Cowlitz. Jim Swanson was introduced as the new General Manager of the HarbourCats. He brought with him a wealth of experience, including chair of the World Baseball Challenge in Prince George, the MLB analyst for Dan Russell's SportsTalk radio show, sports editor of the *Prince George Citizen*, and a reporter covering the Cougars. There was a local connection to his hiring. HarbourCats sponsors Steve and Joan Wallace knew Jim from their time in the north and told Mr. McLean that Jim should be hired as there was nobody better qualified for the job. Obviously, their persuasion worked. Jim's first task was to attend WCL meetings in Salem, Oregon. As expected, team owner John McLean announced that Dennis Rogers would return as field boss, Bob Miller as co-head coach, and Ben Jackson as assistant coach. The fans would watch games in more comfortable bucket seats, replacing the aluminum benches along the baselines. This upgrade demonstrated the support the team would receive from the City of Victoria, the owner of the baseball park.

In late December, the team announced the signing of three British Columbia

In March, the HarbourCats announced a deal with Sports Traders for naming rights for the ballpark at Royal Athletic Park.

players: Victoria native and former Victoria Mariner Kelly Norris-Jones, who would be a junior at Illinois; Nanaimo's Griffin Andreychuk, who would suit up for the University of Seattle in the fall; and Nick Rutckyj, a Surrey product who had played 10 games for the 2013 version of the HarbourCats. The next players to sign were John Grimsley, son of former major leaguer and two-time World Series champion Jason Grimsley, Brandon Feldman from the Victoria Eagles, outfielders Danny Collier and Carson Schneider from the University of New Mexico, Jacob McAdams from the University of Arizona, and Cameron Cotton from Cal Poly. More players were added to the roster the following week, including Quintin Torres-Costa (University of Hawaii), Will Dennis (Seattle University), Matt Susac (Nevada-Reno), Gabe Clark (Oregon State), and Andrew Calica (UC Santa Barbara). Signings continued in early February with the University of Utah's Bret Helton, UC-Irvine's Cole Kreuter, Pepperdine's Aaron Barnett and Devin Carter, and Oral Roberts' Noah Cummings. In March, the team added ten players to their roster: Bryce Greager from Nevada Reno, Hunter Mercado-Hood from the University of San Diego, Alan Baldwin from the University of Hawaii, Mikey Wright from San Jose State, Wyler Smith from the University of Utah, Michael Gershman from Valley City State, Eric Hegadoren from the College of the Canyons, Alex Rogers of Trinidad State Junior College, Matt Bryan from Treasure Valley Junior College, and Darren Honeysett from Monterey Peninsula Junior College.

The 'Cats announced that a team of players from the BC Premier League's Victoria Mariners and Victoria Eagles would play a pre-season game against the HarbourCats on June 5, giving them experience and offering them a chance to showcase their talent. Another exhibition game would feature the Langley Blaze, who were national senior runners-up in 2013.

In March, the HarbourCats announced a deal with Sports Traders for naming rights for the ballpark at Royal Athletic Park; the deal was for four years with extensions possible. The facility would be known as Sports Traders Diamond at Royal Athletic Park. Off the field, head coach Dennis Rogers stepped away from his duties for family reasons, and his assistant, Bob Miller, took charge. The team advised that Nick Rutckyj would not return to the club as he had tendinitis in his knee.

ERIC HEGADOREN IN ACTION

In April, five more players were signed for the season, rounding out the roster. Sacramento State's Nathan Lukes, Loyola Marymount's Ted Boeke, Kentucky's Thomas Bernal and Andrew Nelson, Orange Coast College's Jacob Hill, and the University of New Mexico's Preston Ryan.

The 'Cats began the season on the road in Kelowna on June 6th. Tim Peabody got the start for the Victoria, and Wyler Smith scored the first run of the season in the HarbourCats' 7-6 victory. Nathan Lukes had four hits for the 'Cats, and Hunter Mercado-Hood had three. Game two was different as Victoria had a 6-1 lead in the fourth inning but surrendered seven runs in the fifth inning to put Kelowna ahead for good. The final score was 9-7. In the series finale, the Falcons upended the HarbourCats 4-1 to win the series.

Next on the agenda was the home opener. Before a crowd of 3,038, Logan Lombana started for the home team and went five innings, allowing two runs. With the game tied 5-5 in the 11th inning, Nathan Lukes hit a two-out double to score Kelly Norris-Jones with the winning run against the Cowlitz Black Bears. Game two was a total reversal as the 'Cats lost 11-4. It was a close game for two innings then Victoria surrendered nine runs in the fourth and fifth innings and the rout was on. However, they turned it around in the final of the series, shutting out the Black Bears 3-0. Mikey Wright got the victory, facing 24 batters in seven

Alex Rogers in action

innings of scoreless ball. Alex De Goti was the star of the series, with four hits including a homer and a double.

Back on the road, the team travelled to Bend. Game one saw Alex Garcia hurl seven stellar innings to lead his team to a 3-0 victory. The next evening, the team extended the win streak to three games with a 4-1 result. Starting pitcher Alex Rogers threw seven scoreless innings before being relieved. Alex De Goti had two hits and two stolen bases to lead his team in offence. In the series finale, the 'Cats blew a five-run lead and dropped a 7-6 decision. After a long trip home, they faced the Bellingham Bells, where pitcher Grant Goodman led his team to a 9-1 win. The next night, Victoria had little offence and lost the second game of the series 7-2. The Bells completed the sweep with a second 7-2 victory. Hunter Mercado-Hood and Griffin Andreychuk had two of Victoria's seven hits, but it was not enough. Adding to the lack of hitting, the 'Cats committed eight errors in the three games. If they wanted to get back on the winning track, they needed to tighten up defensively.

With a rare weekend off, the HarbourCats played a pair of exhibition games against the Langley Blaze. Saturday was billed as Baseball Day in Victoria with a youth skills camp and a game featuring local media and politicians. The 'Cats beat the visitors 5-0. On Sunday, action switched to Duncan, where the Blaze upended the HarbourCats by a score of 10-5.

The regular season resumed on Monday night, but the woes continued for the home team. They dropped a close 4-3 decision to the Bend Elks. Gabe Clark, who

> The Canada Day Game showcased new red caps with skydivers opening the festivities.

had just arrived in town, hit a two-run homer, but it was just not enough offence. The losing skid continued the next evening when the Elks won the match 13-7. Solo home runs by Alex De Goti, Griffin Andreychuk, and Gabe Clark supplied the offence for the home team. Bend swept the series with a 4-1 win before 1,073 fans. The lack of hitting with runners on base cost the team dearly, extending the losing streak to seven. On the good news front, Alex Real had signed a pro contract with the Minnesota Twins.

Back on the road, the team didn't fare much better, dropping a 9-5 decision to the Black Bears. Alex Garcia was the starter and allowed three runs in four innings, but his team didn't give him much support. Sean Watkins had a three-for-four night, and Gabe Clark was two for three, but that was about it for offence. Before the game, the team released Gunner Pullman and Brandon Feldman. The losing streak hit nine with a close 3-2 defeat in game two of the series. Alex Rogers had a good outing but a controversial call in the bottom of the ninth inning allowed the winning run to score. Finally, the HarbourCats won a game in Cowlitz when they outlasted the Black Bears 9-8 in 13 innings. Bob Miller was ejected in the top of the fifth inning.

The home series against the Kitsap BlueJackets featured fireworks on Monday, while the Canada Day Game showcased new red caps with skydivers opening the festivities. In the first game, the HarbourCats edged Kitsap 4-3. With the score tied 1-1 in the sixth inning, Victoria took advantage of wild pitches, an error, and a walk to score two runs to go ahead. After Kitsap tied the score in the seventh, Sean Watkins hit a home run to put the home team ahead for good. Canada Day proved to be a decisive victory for the home team. They scored 13 runs in the first three innings, including seven in the first. Hunter Mercado-Hood went four for four, scored four runs, and drove in six. His big hit in the 19-2 win was a three-run homer. Mikey Wright got the victory in the landslide. The same formula worked in the third game as Victoria had 12 runs before the fourth inning en route to a 17-3 thrashing of the BlueJackets for their fourth consecutive win. Sean Watkins and Wyler Smith had four hits, while Jake Lesinski had three. Don Sullivan threw five innings on his way to the victory. HarbourCats manager Bob Miller began serving a four-game suspension for his ejection in the Cowlitz game. Pitching coach Ben

THE VICTORIA HARBOURCATS HOST THE TORONTO BLUE JAYS YOUTH BASEBALL CAMP, FEATURING FORMER JAYS GREATS ROBERTO ALOMAR, LLOYD MOSEBY, JESSE BARFIELD, DUANE WARD, DEVON WHITE AND OTHERS

Jackson was named to serve as interim manager. The victory was particularly sweet for the home team as former members of the Toronto Blue Jays were in town for a series of youth camps with local players.

Wearing their new red caps, the HarbourCats played their next game in Kitsap. This time, it was great pitching that won the day. Nanaimo's Alex Rogers went seven innings giving up just one run, while Quinton Torres-Costa and Tim Peabody kept the BlueJackets off the scoreboard. Left fielder Wyler Smith made three spectacular catches to negate a Kitsap rally and went two-for-three, including an RBI in the ninth inning to ensure the win 4-1. Still wearing their red caps, the 'Cats won their sixth straight with a 7-3 conquest of the BlueJackets. Wyler Smith went two-for-four at the plate and stole his team-leading 11th base. In the final game of the series, the 'Cats were again victorious as they handed the BlueJackets their 11th straight defeat. Logan Lombana pitched seven innings, giving up a single run in the sixth inning when his team had already scored 12 runs. Will Smith had three hits while Hunter Mercado-Hood, Gabe Clark, Aaron Barnett, and Bryce Greager had two in a game where the team made the most of its baserunners in a convincing 12-1 result.

The road trip continued with three games in Yakima. In the first one, the teams were tied 5-5 after nine innings of play after the 'Cats couldn't hold a 5-1 lead. The game would last until the 15th inning when the home team scored a walk-off victory. Off the field, infielder Cole Kreuter was released as he requested more playing time. He was expected to sign with another team who could give him what he wanted. Game two of the series started well, with the HarbourCats scoring a run in the second inning. Unfortunately, that was all the offence they could provide, and the home team scored eight runs over the next four innings for an easy 8-1 win. Suddenly, the bats had gone silent as they lost their second in a row. The Pippins completed the series sweep with a convincing 12-3 pounding of the 'Cats. They scored early and often and sealed the deal with a five-run seventh inning. The difference in the game was that the home team cashed in on their hits while the visitors stranded far too many runners on base.

Back in Victoria, locals were asked to throw ceremonial first pitches to try to break a record of 4,218 set by the Brevard County Manatees of the Florida State League. The last pitch, thrown by two-time World Series champion Jason Grimsley to his son John, who plays for the HarbourCats, was number 5,253. The game that followed was a good one, too. After Medford had taken a 3-0 lead after seven innings, the HarbourCats found their bats. They scored twice in the eighth to narrow the deficit to one run but surrendered a couple to the visitors in the ninth while scoring only two themselves to fall a run short, 5-4. The issue that had plagued them lately reared its ugly head again as they ended four innings with the bases loaded, including the ninth, leaving 14 runners stranded. The middle game of the

THE HARBOURCATS HELD A FIRST PITCH PROMOTION THAT SAW A RECORD 5,253 FIRST PITCHES THROWN OUT PRIOR TO GAME TIME. DIANA BERRY THROWS HER PITCH.

series was an interesting one with numerous lead changes. The home team notched three runs in the first inning on Gabe Clark's monster of a home run but yielded four runs to Medford to fall behind. Out came the bats and the team scored five runs in their half of the inning to take the lead for good. Nathan Lukes hit a solo shot, and Sean Watkins added a three-run homer. They added a run in the fifth and then held on for a 9-8 decision. Versatile Sean Watkins pitched the ninth inning in relief. The series finale, a Saturday matinée, went to the Medford Rogues, who outlasted Victoria, 4-1. Their starting pitcher, Nathan Kuchta, went 8 1/3 innings, giving up only five hits and was instrumental in the victory.

The road trip continued in Bellingham, where the team lost 2-1 despite Mikey Wright pitching a three-hitter. Hunter Mercado-Hood had the two hits for Victoria and drove in the sole run. After the game, the team announced that pitcher Alex Garcia had left the team for family reasons, and outfielder Devin Carter had left for academic reasons. In the second game of the series, the HarbourCats couldn't overcome a three-run third inning by the Bells in a 3-1 loss when they could only manage one hit, Sean Watkins' home run. The following evening, Alex Rogers and Sean Watkins turned in strong pitching performances, and the 'Cats took advantage of a passed ball and wild pitch to score the two runs in the ninth inning for a hard-fought 5-3 victory.

Back in the friendly confines of Sports Traders Stadium at Royal Athletic Park, the HarbourCats had a solid seven-inning outing by pitcher Quintin Torres-Costa in a decisive 7-1 victory over the Klamath Fall Gems. Nathan Lukes had three hits for the home team, and Aaron Barnett had two. The next game of the series was a decisive 14-8 victory for the home team. Logan Lombana pitched five strong innings, surrendering only one earned run. On the offensive front, the HarbourCats unleashed 14 hits, including two home runs. By the end of the first inning, the score was 4-1 for the 'Cats and a huge seven-run fourth inning followed by a three-run fifth ended the Victoria scoring. Gabe Clark had three home runs to drive in six runs, and Alex De Goti had a two-run homer. Klamath put up six runs in the ninth inning, but it was too little, too late, and the HarbourCats had a three-game winning streak. That came to a crashing end with an extra-innings loss to the Gems. With the game tied 3-3 in the fourth, the 'Cats notched two runs to take the lead. The Gems tied the score in the eighth, and it stayed that way until the 11th inning when the visitors scored six runs to take the lead, and the home team could only score one for a final score of 11-6.

The West Coast League then paused play for the All-Star game in Klamath Falls.

> The Corvallis Knights came to town and defeated the HarbourCats 5-3 in the first game of three.

The event started with a welcome party, followed by a luncheon and home run derby won by the HarbourCats' slugger Gabe Clark. Unfortunately, the rain was so heavy that the game had to be cancelled. That was disappointing for the four Victoria representatives: Gabe Clark, Alex Rogers, Alex De Goti, and Logan Lombana.

Play resumed with the HarbourCats on the road in Cowlitz. Mikey Wright tossed six innings of shutout ball before being relieved by Carson Schneider, who did the same. After the 'Cats scored a single run in the fourth inning on a Black Bears error, Nathan Lukes, who ended the night with three hits, put a ball over the fence for two runs. The team scored single runs in the sixth, eighth, and ninth innings for a 6-0 win. The game scheduled for July 23 was cancelled due to rain, so the teams played a doubleheader, with each game seven innings, the first for the HarbourCats, the next day. In the early game, Alex Fagalde threw 5 2/3 innings en route to a 1-0 shutout. The sole run was scored after a walk and consecutive singles. The late game was tied until the bottom of the seventh inning when the home team pushed home the winning run to win by a score of 4-3.

The Corvallis Knights came to town and defeated the HarbourCats 5-3 in the first game of three. They used good pitching by Jackson Lockwood and timely hitting by Dalton Kelly to win the game. Victoria did get the tying run on first base in the ninth but was unable to bring him home. Looking for a better result in the next game, the 'Cats started Logan Lombana, who threw six innings and gave up five runs. The Knights put the game on ice in the ninth when they plated three runs; Victoria could only score one in their half of the inning, so the rally fell short, and they fell 8-5. The final game of the series was a slugfest as the hometown team outhit the Knights 21-9 and outscored them 19-10. Bryce Greager led the onslaught with four hits, while Griffin Andreychuk, Hunter Mercado-Hood, and Alan Baldwin had three each. It was a great result against a very strong team. After the game, the pitching staff was reduced as Shawn Watkins, Mark Marinch, Quintin Torres-Costa, and Angel Delgado all left the team for various reasons.

The next three games were played on the road in Wenatchee. The team fell 13-4 to the AppleSox and the score could have been worse as the Sox stranded 19 baserunners. HarbourCats pitchers were all ineffective, surrendering 17 walks, and the

THE TEAM CELEBRATES AFTER SCORING

offence was almost nonexistent as well. Game two featured a complete turnaround in play. Starting pitcher Alex Fagalde pitched eight innings to lead his team to a 5-0 victory. The game was scoreless until the seventh inning when the 'Cats scored twice. They would score twice in the eighth and add a single in the ninth for the win. Hunter Mercado-Hood had three hits and Nathan Lukes and Alex De Goti had two each for the HarbourCats. Sloppy defence, unreliable pitching, and a lack of offence combined in the 'Cats 9-2 loss in Wenatchee. Jake Lesinski and Griffin Andreychuk had the only two hits for the HarbourCats, who watched their slim hope of making the league playoffs fade.

With Olympic gold medallist Adam Creek and local hockey stars Jamie and Jordan Benn throwing out the first pitches, the HarbourCats were inspired and defeated Bellingham 4-2. Logan Lombana went seven innings, giving up two hits and two runs. Aaron Barnett had a home run, and Gabe Clark, Nathan Lukes, and Jake Lesinski all had doubles to lead the offence. The second game was a real nail-biter. The HarbourCats scored four runs in the first inning when Jake Lesinski hit a bases-clearing double. Bellingham scored two in the third, the 'Cats answered with one, and the Bells scored twice in the fourth and one in the fifth to tie the score. It would stay that way until the 11th inning. With two outs, Nathan Lukes hit a single, Griffin Andreychuk walked, Hunter Mercado-Hood singled to load the bases, and when Gabe Clark walked, the winning run scored. The HarbourCats guaranteed themselves a series win but would try for the sweep in the next game. Before the game, the club announced that Ryan Keller would be leaving the team as would Wyler Smith and Mikey Wright, who would pitch the first game in the upcoming road trip in Walla Walla. Local pitchers Eric Hegadoren, Drew Davidoff, Dallas Patterson, and Riley Edmonds were added to the roster. The final game of the series went to Bellingham by a score of 4-3. The 'Cats managed only four hits in a listless effort.

The last road trip of 2014 was to Walla Walla where the HarbourCats fell behind early when the Sweets scored six runs in the second inning and added one in the third, aided by walks, before the 'Cats scored two in the third to close the gap. After surrendering two more runs in the fifth, the bats came alive, and they scored five in the eighth. Bryce Greager hit the team's first grand slam, but they were unable to close the gap further and lost the game 9-7. In the second game, the team rode the stellar pitching of starter Alex Fagalde to a 9-1 victory. He pitched seven strong innings before being relieved by Andrew Nelson. Ted Boeke's first home run was one of three hits for the third baseman while Hunter Mercado-Hood had three singles as they led the offence. In the last road game of the season, the HarbourCats won a tight 4-3 game. Alex Rogers started and gave up two runs in the first inning. However, the 'Cats scored three in the fourth when Alex De Goti and Nathan Lukes hit back-to-back doubles followed by back-to-back singles by Aaron Barnett and Alan Baldwin. The Sweets tied the game in the eighth inning, but Hunter Mercado-Hood walked, John Grimsley ran for him, he stole second base and advanced

> In the final home series of the season, the HarbourCats played the Kitsap BlueJackets.

to third on a putout, then scored when Gabe Clark hit a single. Carson Schneider blanked the Sweets in the ninth inning to seal the victory. The team finished with a 13-14 road record.

In the final home series of the season, the HarbourCats played the Kitsap BlueJackets. As might be expected with depleted pitching staffs, the game featured a total of 27 hits. Hunter Mercado-Hood led the offence with four hits. Both teams scored in the first inning and Victoria had four in the second. Kitsap went ahead with six in the third and the 'Cats got one back to narrow the lead to 7-6. The fifth inning featured three runs from Kitsap and a single by Victoria. Three runs in the

In year-end awards, Nathan Lukes and Alex Rogers were named players of the year.

sixth for the home team tied the score 10-10. Kitsap scored once in the seventh, Victoria, two in the eighth, and Kitsap won the game with two in the ninth. Ironically, the run was a home run by former HarbourCat Dylan LaVelle. The game took almost four hours to play. Kitsap Head Coach Ryan Parker was ejected in the top of the 5th inning for arguing with the umpires. Kitsap coaches Kevin Frady and Bryan Kepner were both ejected in the bottom of the 8th inning. The second game did not start well for the home team as they gave up four runs in the first inning and two each in the third and fourth for an 8-0 lead before the 'Cats got on the board with two unearned runs in the fourth. After Kitsap scored a single in the fifth, Victoria scored two runs in the sixth and seventh but that was the end of the offence. Hunter Mercado-Hood led the way with three hits and a stolen base, but his team fell 9-6. The final game of the season was played under sunny skies. After falling behind 6-0, the HarbourCats' bats came alive and they scored four runs in the seventh, largely due to walks and a dropped third strike. Just as if it had been scripted, the home team got a walk-off victory when Hunter Mercado-Hood singled to drive in Alex De Goti from second base for a 7-6 score. Although the team was not successful on the field, with a 12-15 home record and 25-29 overall, they were winners at the gate. 42,563 fans attended the 27 home games for an average of 1,576.

In year-end awards, Nathan Lukes and Alex Rogers were named players of the year.

After the game, head coach Bob Miller announced that he would not be returning to the team for next season as he needed to devote full time to his position as head coach of California's Cuesta College. He noted that Victoria was a "first-class operation," and the team had good chemistry, although they made too many mistakes. On the positive side of the season, Hunter Mercado-Hood finished second in batting average with .385 and second in RBIs with 46 and Gabe Clark's eight home runs tied for second in the league. As well, the word was out around the NCAA that Victoria was a great place to play with knowledgeable fans; this would help with recruiting for the 2015 season.

In August 2014, team GM Jim Swanson announced that Graig Merritt, a scout for seven years with the Tampa Bay Rays, would be the new head coach. He had previous experience in the BC Premier League, and his scouting work for the Tampa Bay Rays made him familiar with the talent in the BC and US Pacific Northwest. Shortly afterwards, Alec Adame was named pitching coach. He and Merritt had played together at Chico State when the school won the NCAA Division II championship in 1999. They both became MLB scouts with Adame working for the San Diego Padres, Tampa Bay Rays, and St. Louis Cardinals, based in southern California. Together, they could assess talent on the Pacific coast.

Recruiting was already underway for the 2015 season. First to sign were Alex Rogers, Griffin Andreychuk, and Alex Fagalde.

At the same time, recruiting was already underway for the 2015 season. First to sign were Alex Rogers, Griffin Andreychuk, and Alex Fagalde. Next were Gabe Clark and newcomer Michael Gretler, both from the Oregon State Beavers. From the Washington Huskies came Henry Baker and Zach Bonneau, and from the University of New Mexico, Preston Ryan and Carson Schneider. Josh Mitchell from the University of Pittsburgh also signed. In late September, the 'Cats added returnee Mikey Wright, along with Dane Fujinaka and PJ Floyd from Sacramento State. December signings included Evan Cassolato and A J Alcantara from UC-Irvine and Carl Stajduhar from the University of New Mexico.

In the midst of building a team for 2015, it was announced that John McLean had lost control of the team in a civil lawsuit to Matthew Stoudt, a former partner. He had minority partners but was the team's spokesman. Because of the change in ownership, the HarbourCats required league approval to operate. WCL president Dennis Koho and Stoudt were in Victoria in late December for meetings, and approval was expected by the end of the year.

4

2015: Under New Ownership

Early in January, Brad Norris-Jones, who had been handling marketing for the team was named assistant general manager. The 2015 schedule was released and would start on June 6th with the Kelowna Falcons in town. The team set a goal of winning 35 games out of the 54 scheduled and to make the playoffs.

On January 21, the HarbourCats teamed with the Greater Victoria Baseball Association, Fairmont Empress Hotel, and 103.1 Jack FM/Ocean 98.5 to bring the Seattle Mariners Winter Caravan to town. Local fans were able to meet Mariners' play-by-play announcer, Dave Simms, pitcher James Paxton, Charlie Furbush, former pitcher and Victoria native Steve Sinclair, and the Mariner Moose mascot.

February's signings included Ryan Wilson and Chase Lambert of Pepperdine, Matt Blais of UC-Davis, Sean Davis and Jackson Thoreson of St. Mary's College, Cam Santos of Chico State, and Ryan Anderson of UC-Davis. March signings included the University of San Diego's Seve Romo, Kacy Smith, and Kevin Collard, Cal Poly San Luis Obispo's Austin Dondanville, Nick Meyer, and Ben Polshuk, and LA Mission Junior College's Mareno Rankin. It was also announced that Evan Cassolato would not be joining the team due to another commitment and Ryan Anderson would not be playing as he was injured. At the end of March, Scott Davis and Jake Pries from UCLA and Kevin Amezquita from East Los Angeles College signed contracts.

The biggest news was not on the field, but off. On April 20, 2015, the team announced that four BC residents had become the new owners of the team, subject to league approval. Victoria's John Wilson of Wilson's Transportation and Jim Swanson,

General Manager of the club, were joined by Ken Swanson and Rich Harder from the lower mainland. As expected, the ownership was approved by the league. Local ownership was considered critical to the continued success of the franchise. All four owners brought different skills to the group and worked together to make the HarbourCats a household name in Victoria.

Before the season opener, the Vic High R&B band recorded a video on a bus with the group singing Take Me Out to the Ball Game. It was used to promote the use of BC Transit to get to games. The band performed the song live at the opener, and the video was played during the seventh-inning stretch for the remainder of the season.

4,627 fans packed the stands for the opening game of the season against the Kelowna Falcons. Festivities started with skydivers, singer Mike Demers on the promenade, and Victoria Mayor Lisa Helps throwing out the first pitch. Alex Rogers took the mound for the home team and went 6½ innings of five-hit, scoreless ball. His twin brother, Brady, played at second base and recorded one hit. Chris Fougner was the offensive star of the game with three hits while Jackson Thoreson had a double and a triple and Kyle Francis had two singles in a 9-2 victory. The fireworks on the field were followed by a fireworks display enjoyed by young and old alike. Returnee Mikey Wright was the pitcher for game two. He went three innings, giving up two runs on two hits with five walks and two strikeouts before being relieved by Josh Walker. PJ Floyd had two hits for the 'Cats in a losing cause as they dropped the game 5-2. In a Sunday matinee, the Falcons pounded out seventeen hits and overwhelmed the HarbourCats 8-3. The home bats went quiet, and their pitching was not effective.

The next series was against Kitsap. Before the game came the good news that Nathan Lukes, who had starred for the team in 2014, had been selected in the seventh round of the MLB draft by the Cleveland Indians. Four runs in the first inning with two out set the pace for the game. Kevin Collard, Dane Fujinaka, and Brady Rogers had two hits and PJ Floyd drove in three runs. Dominic Topoozian got the win with seven scoreless innings on the way to a 7-2 triumph. Game two

The good news came that Nathan Lukes, who had starred for the team in 2014, had been selected in the seventh round of the MLB draft by the Cleveland Indians.

ALEX ROGERS IN ACTION

was a much closer contest. The HarbourCats had a three-run lead after two innings but couldn't hold it and the visitors won with a single run in the 10th for a 5-4 result. Kevin Collard was the hitting star with three. In the series closer, a Thursday afternoon matinée, he hit the team's first home run of the season and added a double and a single, driving in two runs. Alex Rogers was on the mound for the 'Cats and yielded just four hits, one run, and two walks, and recorded four strikeouts in his six innings of work. This was the first year that schoolchildren were invited to the park for a special day. Their enthusiastic support drove the team to a 4-2 victory.

In the first road trip of the season, the HarbourCats travelled to Bend, Oregon for a three-game series. The opening game was one they would like to forget as they committed seven errors and gave up 25 hits in a one-sided 24-5 loss. The good news was that Gabe Clark and Alex De Goti would be joining the team on the road trip and should add some much-needed offence. Dane Fujinaka left the team for personal reasons. In the middle game of the trip, the team played better but still fell to the Elks, 5-1. Brady Rogers had two of the team's four hits to lead the offence. The Bend Elks completed the series sweep with a 3-2 victory. The 'Cats managed to win the final game of the series as Sean O'Toole pitched five innings

The team announced that more players would be arriving as they finished off their academics, were getting over injuries, or were playing in the NCAA College World Series.

before being relieved by Alex Rogers and Josh Mitchell. Jackson Thoreson had two hits and Gabe Clark got his first home run of the season to lead the team to a close 4-3 win. The trip continued in Cowlitz where the Black Bears outscored the visitors 3-2. Victoria scored first in the fifth inning when Nick Meyer reached first base on an error and was advanced when Chris Fougner hit a single and Zach Bonneau reached base on a fielder's choice. Unfortunately, they could not hold that lead as they surrendered three runs in the bottom of the inning. A single run in the seventh was all they could produce as Cowlitz held on for the victory. Game two produced the same result; the team was coming close to victory but coming up one run short. Cowlitz again scored three runs in an inning – the fourth this time – and held on despite a late Victoria rally. Kevin Collard again led the offence with two hits and a stolen base, while Alex De Goti had a double. After the game, the team announced that more players would be arriving as they finished off their academics, were getting over injuries, or were playing in the NCAA College World Series. The series concluded with a complete turnaround as the 'Cats scored early and often in a convincing 17-6 result. They pounded out 17 hits, including Nick Meyer's four-hit performance, and Kevin Collard's three hits, including a home run. The 'Cats scored five runs in the first inning to get started, then added four in the second, five in the third, one in the fourth, and two in the fifth. They were helped by five walks and four Cowlitz errors. Alex Rogers pitched five innings of three-hit ball and got the "W."

The two teams travelled to Victoria for a three-game series. The visiting Black Bears outlasted the HarbourCats 11-8 in a game that took over four hours to play. The lead changed hands during the game, and it was tied 8-8 after regulation play. In the top of the 10th, Cowlitz scored three runs and then held on as the home team loaded the bases but could not bring the runners home. Newly arrived player Michael Gretler hit a two-run homer in the second inning, but the visitors scored three runs in the fourth and fifth inning to put their team ahead. A four-run sixth inning featured singles by PJ Floyd, Alex De Goti, and Austin Guibor and a double by Jackson Thoreson. Scoring was aided by two walks and a passed ball, but the team surrendered a run to Cowlitz in the seventh and couldn't add any more runs.

Newcomer Jake Pries made his debut as an outfielder for the HarbourCats. His grandfather, Don Pries, was both a player and manager for the Victoria Tyees in the early 1950s when they played at Royal Athletic Park. The family has fond memories of Victoria, as it was here that Jake's grandfather married Patricia Mason. In what was becoming an all too familiar scenario, the HarbourCats gave up too many runs in the early innings in the second game of the series and were never able to catch up. With the score 11-3, they plated five runs in the eighth inning, but it was too little, too late. Jake Pries hit his first homer of the season and Michael Gretler hit a single for the only hits of the inning, but the scoring was aided by two errors, four wild pitches, and a balk. It took until the third game of the series for the HarbourCats to taste success. Down 1-0, they tied the score in the fourth inning after Michael Gretler walked, stole a base, advanced to third on a putout, and scored on AJ Alcantara's single. In the seventh inning, the 'Cats scored three runs with two outs and added two in the eighth for a 6-1 victory. Dominic Topoozian threw 7 1/3 innings, giving up only one run on six hits, and was credited with the win. In a player move, Brady Rogers asked for his release for academic matters and pitcher Henry Omana would join the team on the next road trip.

Back on the road in Kitsap, the HarbourCats won a 5-4 decision over the BlueJackets. After scoring the first run, the team surrendered three in consecutive innings, but came back with three in the fifth inning and a single in the seventh to secure the victory. Alex De Goti led the hit parade with two. The second game was a 6-2 decision for the BlueJackets. Victoria got down early, hampered by their lack

Victoria got down early, hampered by their lack of hits, their inability to score with runners in scoring position.

of hits, their inability to score with runners in scoring position, and their tendency to commit errors. It was the same story in the final game of the series, as the 'Cats were down 4-0 before they scored two runs in the seventh inning on one hit, aided by walks and wild pitches. However, Kitsap scored three in the bottom of the inning to put the game out of hand and the two runs Victoria got in the eighth were not enough for the comeback. No player had more than one hit as the bats went silent in a 7-4 loss.

The first game of the home series against Wenatchee AppleSox went to the

The first game of the home series against Wenatchee AppleSox went to the visitors, 11-8. This game was like a pair of heavyweight fighters exchanging blows.

visitors, 11-8. This game was like a pair of heavyweight fighters exchanging blows. The visitors scored first, but the home team countered with two runs in the second inning to take the lead. After surrendering four in the top of the third inning, the HarbourCats scored six in their half of the inning to lead, 8–4. However, the AppleSox scored two in the fifth and one in the eighth to tie the game and then won it with three unanswered runs in the ninth inning. Jackson Thoreson had a double while Alex De Goti and AJ Alcantara had triples in a losing cause. Game two was a pitcher's battle as Dominic Topoozian and Hunter Wells went head-to-head for six innings. The sole run of the game was scored by the visitors in the second inning on a home run by Evan Douglas. The 'Cats were unable to score off their four hits. Revenge was sweet in the final game of the series. Victoria scored five runs in the first inning, added more along the way and then watched the AppleSox tie the score 10-10 in the ninth inning. It took eleven innings to decide this contest, which was almost four hours long. Jake Pries walked, advanced to second on a Jackson Thoreson single, advanced to third on a PJ Floyd single, and scored the winning run when Chris Fougner was walked.

With a break in league play, the team played a Canada Day exhibition series against the defending Senior A champion Langley Blaze. After a 2-1 loss on fireworks night, the 'Cats rebounded and took the second game, 12-11. However, the game was not as easy as it might have seemed. After taking a 10-0 lead, the home team gave up nine runs in the fifth inning and two more that allowed the visitors to take the lead, before walking it off with two runs in the bottom of the ninth.

The long drive to arrive in Corvallis was followed by a ball game that took over five hours to play. The HarbourCats were up 3-2 in the third inning after Kevin Collard's home run scored Chase Lambert and Austin Guibor, who had singled ahead of him. However, the Knights scored once in the fourth inning and the game became a pitcher's duel until the 17th inning when the home team got the run they needed due to some sloppy HarbourCats play and won the game, 4-3. On Independence Day, the 'Cats took an early lead and were up 2-1 when the home team plated three in the eighth en route to a 4-2 win. The series finale was in much the same vein. The visitors scored first but fell behind and could never recover in a second consecutive 4-2 loss. AJ Alcantara had three hits, including a double, and Kevin Collard notched his fourth home run in a losing cause.

Back at home, the team played against a backdrop of red haze caused by wildfires in the interior, rebounded and hammered the Kitsap BlueJackets 10-0. AJ Alcantara had three hits, including a two-run homer, while Michael Gretler, Jake Pries, and Ben Polshuk had two hits apiece. Austin Dondanville pitched six strong innings and Josh Walker finished the game; they allowed only three walks while striking out seven. The score in the middle game of the series was closer. Kitsap took a 1-0 lead in the third inning, but Victoria got that one back in the fifth when Scott Jarvis singled and eventually scored on a fielder's choice. The winning run in the 2-1 victory came in the seventh when Austin Guibor lined a single to score Chris Fougner from third base. Chase Lambert had two hits while Kevin Collard continued his good hitting, driving in both runs. Jonathan Buckley started for Victoria while Shawn Kennedy II got the win in relief with Josh Mitchell gaining the save. In the series finale, the HarbourCats completed the sweep with a convincing 8-2 decision. Jake Pries set the stage with a two-run homer in the first inning and

AUSTIN DONDANVILLE IN ACTION

the team added two runs in each of the sixth, seventh, and eighth innings. Griffin Andreychuk had three hits to lead the offence while Matt Blais got the victory for his 5 2/3 innings of one-hit baseball. After the game, the team released outfielder Kevin Amezquita and pitcher/fielder Kyle Francis.

On the road again, Mother Nature intervened, and the first game in Klamath Falls, Oregon, was rained out. The teams played a doubleheader the next day with two seven-inning games. In the first one, the HarbourCats gave up four runs in the second inning but recovered to narrow the lead with one in the third as Austin Guibor scored with two out after three straight singles. The six-run fourth inning proved to be the turning point of the match as the 'Cats sent ten men to the plate. Michael Gretler, Scott Jarvis, Torin Goldstein, and Griffin Andreychuk hit four straight singles, and Austin Guibor and Kevin Collard had doubles. One run was scored on an error as was the last run of the game, in the sixth. Dominic Topoozian got the victory, and Shawn Kennedy II got the save in the 8-5 decision. In the second game of the doubleheader, the HarbourCats scored early and often in an 8-2 victory. Chris Fougner was the hitting star of the game as he went four for four and drove in four runs. Henry Omana got the win and Sean O'Toole, the save. Victoria completed the series sweep with a convincing 7-1 score. Austin Dondanville was on the mound and worked five innings for the decision. Michael Gretler and Mareno Rankin had three hits and Griffin Andreychuk hit a homer to lead the offence.

In Medford, the 'Cats got off to a good start with two runs in the first inning on Austin Guibor's home run and added singles in the third and fourth with two

Josh Mitchell in action

Griffin Andreychuk in action

> Josh Mitchell threw six innings of one-hit ball and Austin Dondanville and Henry Omana shut out the Rogues for three innings in relief.

more in the fifth en route to a 6-4 win. They won their eighth game in a row with an 8-2 decision in the middle game of the series. With that win, they climbed above .500 for the season. They started well with four runs in the second inning, adding more in later innings. Chris Fougner's single followed by Chase Lambert's two-run double set the tone for the game. AJ Alcantara had three hits before being rested and replaced by Ben Polshuk. Matt Blais was on the mound for six innings and gave up only two runs; Tei Vanderford pitched the rest of the game, surrendering just one hit. The team set a new win record with their ninth straight when they defeated the Rogues by a score of 5-1. Josh Mitchell threw six innings of one-hit ball and Austin Dondanville and Henry Omana shut out the Rogues for three innings in relief. With the game tied 1-1 in the fourth, the 'Cats struck for four runs in the seventh inning. After PJ Floyd doubled, the Medford shortstop made a critical error that opened the doors for the offence. Griffin Andreychuk and Ben Polshuk had two hits in the game.

Next on the agenda was a home date with the Bellingham Bells, the top team in the division. The first game lasted over four hours and the visitors emerged with an 8-7 victory. A home rally in the bottom of the ninth fell one run short. Scott Jarvis had two hits in a losing cause. In the second game, the HarbourCats got off to a good start with a 4-0 lead after four innings but could not hold off the powerful Bells who notched three in the fifth and two more in the sixth to take 5-4 lead. Victoria tied the game in the seventh, but Bellingham came back with a single run in the eighth to win the game 6-5. Chris Fougner led the offence with two hits. Game three did not go well for the home team, either. It was a close 3-2 game until the Bells scored two runs in the eighth and one in the ninth to win 6-2. It was the not the result the team wanted as it put them further in the hunt for a playoff spot. They would have to play better after the all-star game if they wanted to have a successful season.

The HarbourCats had only one representative in the WCL All-star game played in Bellingham. Pitcher Dominic Topoozian said it was an honour for him to be at the game as he felt there were others who could have been selected as well. He pitched one scoreless inning with a strikeout. The South team beat the North team 3-0.

Then it was back to regular season play. The HarbourCats travelled to Bellingham

PJ Floyd in action

hoping to find a way to beat their nemesis. The game was a seesaw affair with several lead changes but, once again, the team fell short. They actually led 2-1 in the fourth inning when Ben Polshuk hit a home run that also scored AJ Alcantara, who had singled. However, the Bells notched two in the fifth and sixth and all the 'Cats could manage was singles in the sixth and ninth. Alcantara ended the game with three hits. The team signed pitcher Eric Hegadoren, who pitched 1/3 of an inning allowing two walks, three stolen bases, a hit batsman, and recording one strikeout. There was nowhere to go but up for him and the team. Finally, in the middle game of the series, the HarbourCats figured out how to beat Bellingham. Austin Dondanville threw 6 2/3 strong innings of one-run ball, striking out two and allowing two walks. Alex De Goti had two hits, drove in a run, and scored two runs to lead the offence. He also had a stolen base. It was the team's first victory over the Bells and the 'Cats hoped it was not the last. Unfortunately, the bats went silent in the series finale as the Bells posted a 2-0 shutout.

Friday, July 24, 2015 was an historic day as it marked the first rained-out game at Royal Athletic Park in the three years of play. The following day, Victoria and Walla Walla played a doubleheader. In the first game, they were down 3-0 until the fifth inning when the bats came alive and produced four runs on an Austin Guibor grand slam. After surrendering two runs in the sixth and one in the seventh, the team came back to win on a strange play. It all started as normal with Kevin Collard hitting a double. After AJ Alcantara was hit by a pitch and Reno Rankin ran for him, Austin Guibor walked to load the bases. Ben Polshuk was hit by a pitch, driving in one run and a second run resulted from a sacrifice fly by Jackson Thoreson. With the score now tied, the Walla Walla pitcher was trying to intentionally walk PJ Floyd, but the pitch went wild, and Austin Guibor scored the winning run from third base in the 7-6 decision. The second game was more conventional. Ben Polshuk led off the second inning with a triple and eventually scored on a sacrifice fly. In the fourth inning, he had a single, stole a base, and scored on a Michael Gretler single. After Walla Walla scored in the fifth, the 'Cats got that one back and held on for a 3-2 decision. The final game of the series was rained out.

After a day off, play resumed with the opponents the Cowlitz Black Bears. This game was what the doctor ordered to make everyone feel good. After surrendering one run in the top of the first inning on a homer on the second pitch of the game, Victoria stormed back with four in the first to take the lead, three on a Jackson Thoreson homer and the final run off a Ben Polshuk single and PJ Floyd double. After that, they scored two in the second, two in the third, one in the fourth, and three in both the sixth and seventh innings. Dominic Topoozian got the win with seven innings of work. Griffin Andreychuk was the hitting star with four. The team announced that pitchers Jonathan Buckley, Josh Mitchell, and Alex Rogers were now gone so they had added Brett Irvine, Jason Willow, and Nick Seginowich of the Victoria Mariners. Calvin Christiansen of Glendale College and Shawn Anderson of Burnaby Collegiate were due soon. Game two went to Cowlitz as they scored one in the third, three in the fourth and an insurance run in the ninth to top the 'Cats by a score of 5-3. Austin Dondanville went six innings in the loss while the offence was led by two hits from Ben Polshuk, Nick Meyer, and Alex De Goti. In the final game of the series, which took over three hours to play, the HarbourCats got back on track and scored an 8-3 victory. AJ Alcantara hit a grand slam in the fourth inning to lead the offence. Victoria pounded out 12 hits including doubles by Kevin Collard and Alex De Goti. Matt Blais got the win with 6 1/3 innings of work.

After a day off, play resumed with the opponents the Cowlitz Black Bears. This game was what the doctor ordered to make everyone feel good.

A trip to Wenatchee produced a winner in the first game as the HarbourCats came away with a 10-5 victory. Starter Henry Omana gave up four runs, but Tei Vanderford surrendered none and Sean O'Toole, only one. On the offensive side, Stan Jarvis led the hit parade with three while Griffin Andreychuk, Alex Guibor, AJ Alcantara, Ben Polshuk, and PJ Floyd had two each. The teams combined for 27 hits. In game two, the HarbourCats bounced back from a 4-1 deficit with five runs in the third inning en route to an 8-6 victory. Griffin Andreychuk continued his batting prowess with three more hits, while Kevin Collard added two, including a triple. Josh Walker got the start for Victoria and tossed five innings, giving up five runs and striking out six. The team kept their playoff hopes alive with a decisive 21-10 pounding of Wenatchee. Dominic Topoozian started for the visitors and went six innings with two earned runs and five strikeouts. Mikey Wright, Jason Willow, Brett Irvine, and Sean O'Toole were used in relief. Kevin Collard was one single short of the cycle, while Austin Guibor, Jake Pries, and Michael Gretler had doubles.

Back home, 4,307 fans turned out to cheer on their team to an 11-5 victory over the visiting Yakima Valley Pippins. The game was tied 3-3 in the sixth inning when the home team notched three runs and added five in the eighth. Alex De Goti went three for five, including a double, while Austin Guibor added a double and a single. Austin Dondanville got the victory with seven strong innings, including six strikeouts. The race toward a playoff berth continued as the HarbourCats upended the Pippins 10-3. It was a close match until the fifth inning when the home team exploded for four runs to take a 7-2 lead. Kevin Collard continued his hitting exploits with a homer, a double, and a single, and the team took advantage of mistakes by their opponents – hit batsmen and walks. Matt Blais got the win with eight innings of stellar pitching. Just when things were going well, the team hit a roadblock. Despite the inspiration of Alex De Goti being the first player named to the Wall of Honour, the team was flat. Yakima put up four runs in the fifth inning to blow the game open and the home team never survived. A late rally came up a bit short. Zach Bonneau was a triple away from going for the cycle in a losing cause. The loss all but eliminated the 'Cats from the wild card playoff position.

The final series of the year was in Bellingham. The HarbourCats kept their faint playoff hopes alive with a 9-2 victory in the Washington city. Dominic Topoozian was brilliant over seven innings, yielding just five hits. Kevin Collard again led the offence with a home run, a double, and a single while Griffin Andreychuk, AJ Alcantara, ad Michael Gretler had two hits each. The HarbourCats were officially

> The final series of the year was in Bellingham. The HarbourCats kept their faint playoff hopes alive with a 9-2 victory in the Washington city.

eliminated from post season play in the second to last game of the season when they dropped a close 4-3 decision to the Bells. Griffin Andreychuk's fifth home run pushed Victoria's league-leading total to 36. A ninth inning rally fell one run short. On the last day of regular season play, the HarbourCats upended the Bells by a score of 6-4 to gain a bit of revenge. Alex De Goti finished his Victoria career with a three-for-five day and Ben Polshuk and PJ Floyd had two hits each. If it were any consolation, the team finished above .500 for the first time ever and again led the league in attendance with an average of 1,910 fans per game. After the game it was announced that the entire coaching staff would return for the 2016 season. Griffin Andreychuk was named Player of the Year.

The league announced all-star team selections and four HarbourCats were named to the second team: Griffin Andreychuk, Kevin Collard, AJ Alcantara, and Dominic Topoozian.

In off field happenings, a section of a mural of Marilyn Monroe which usually graced the storefront of Floyd's Diner, was found near Athletic Park. It was returned to its rightful place to the delight of all patrons.

Off-season signings began with Matt Smith of Sacramento State, followed closely by the return of AJ Alcantara (UC Irvine) and PJ Floyd (Sacramento State) along with newcomer James Outman (Sacramento State). Next to sign were Austin Dondanville and Nick Meyer (both Sacramento State), Tom Rykker (University of San Diego) and Colin Ashworth (Orange Coast College). Late September signings included Nyles Nygaard (University of Washington), Nick Woitysiak (Paradise Valley College), James Kannenberg (University of San Francisco), Ryan Anderson (UC-Davis), and Brayden Resch (North Dakota State). Michael Gretler would return for another season and four new players would come from Fresno State: Joe Prior, Scott Silva, Jake Stone, and Mark Reece.

The HarbourCats held a Hot Stove event in November with Rogers Sportsnet analyst and former Toronto Blue Jay Gregg Zaun as the star speaker. It was well attended and added to the baseball buzz in the off-season. To further increase baseball awareness, the HarbourCats would be hosting the 2017 Baseball Canada Senior championship in late August 2017. This event brings together the best men's amateur teams from across the nation. Teams include ex-pros who play because they still love the game in addition to young stars on their way up the baseball ladder.

In league news, it was announced that the Klamath Fall Gems would move to Gresham, Oregon and the Medford Rogues had dropped out of the league. New divisions were created with Victoria, Kelowna, Bellingham, Wenatchee, and Walla Walla in the North and Yakima Valley, Kitsap, Cowlitz, Corvallis, Bend, and Gresham in the South. The playoff format was changed to build more interest. The divisional winners of the first half would play the divisional winners of the second half in the playoff semi-final. If one team won both halves of the season, the team in that division with the next-best overall record would get the second playoff spot. Ironically, if this system had been in place in the 2015 season, Victoria would have made the playoffs for the first time.

Victoria was scheduled to open the 2016 season in Walla Walla on June 3rd, and the home opener would be June 7th against Wenatchee. The HarbourCats launched a "Drive for 5000 Campaign" in an attempt to break the league single-game record attendance set during last season's home opener. There would be a special guest at that game, Krazy George, who was best known for his drum beating and cheerleading at BC Lions home games who is credited with starting the wave that is now seen everywhere in the sporting world.

VICTORIA HARBOURCATS 2015 TEAM PHOTO

5

2016: The Record-breaking Season

The first signing of the new year was Josh Burgmann from Nanaimo who would play his college ball for the University of Washington. Also joining the team for the upcoming season were Will McAffer (South Dakota State), Casey Costello (Orange Coast College), and Chayce Kaaua and Dakota Dean (University of Hawaii). Nine players were signed in early February: Calvin Faucher and Chris Vargas (both UC-Irvine), Blake Hannah, Ryan Steindorf, and Brad Pluschkell (UC-Davis), Skyler Henderson (Vernon College), Brendan Hornung (University of Hawaii), and Mason Hilty and Zach Cordova (Dixie State University). Josh Mitchell (University of Pittsburgh) would be returning for another season, joining newcomers Holden Lyons (Oklahoma City University), and Christian Jarnagin and Brandon Lane (both from Everett Community College). In late April, the team announced that Alex Rogers and Michael Gretler would not be back for another season but that Cam Schneider (Cal Poly), Greg Casper (South Dakota State), Matt Mosca (Mesa Community College), Jack Wolger (UC Berkeley), and Matt Lautz (UC Santa Barbara) would be joining the team. In late May, 10-day contracts were signed by Ethan Skujia (UBC), Justin Bundy, Will Dawson, and Cole Sullivan (all Northeast Texas Community College), Jordan Ackerman (Bluefield College), and Jamie Cooper (Occidental University). These players would help to fill the gaps in the lineup until signed players arrived after their NCAA seasons were complete and they did have the chance to gain a regular position. Justin Brown (University of Portland) was given a regular contract. The team also announced that Tom Rykker, Chris Vargas, and Mason Hilty would be unable to play this summer.

Off the field, the HarbourCats made changes to their personnel. Jim Swanson moved from vice president and general manager to managing partner, Brad Norris-Jones moved to general manager, and Brittany French became the assistant general manager. Richard Michaels joined the executive team as director of community relations and corporate partnerships, Jonathan Hodgson as baseball operations and communications advisor, Martin Newham as marketing consultant, and Sean Petriw as director of print properties. John Pollard was added as marketing director.

In West Coast League business, Donnie Marbut, former head coach of the Washington State Cougars, was named the new president, taking over from WCL vice president and the first general manager of the HarbourCats, who had handled the job on a temporary basis. Port Angeles was named a new franchise in the league, owned by Matt Acker, who also owned the Kitsap Blue Jackets. They would start play in the 2017 season and would create a natural rivalry for Victoria.

The HarbourCats announced their coaching staff for 2016. Graig Merrit would return as head coach with Joe Meggs and Andrew Wilson back as assistants. While Jerry Pena and Alec Adame would be unable to return for personal and professional reasons, Joe Fabre and Kelly Norris-Jones were added to the coaching team.

To warm up for the season, the HarbourCats played exhibition games against the Victoria Eagles Alumni and the Victoria Selects, a group of former pro players coached by Charlie Strandlund. Then, it was on to Walla Walla for the first series of the season. The team struck out thirteen times and could only manufacture one run when Cody Snider singled, stole second, and was driven home by a Hayden Jaco double. James Kannenberg threw six innings, surrendering two runs on four hits, and Colin Ashworth pitched two scoreless innings. Despite the 2-1 loss, coach Graig Merritt was pleased with the effort. In the second game, the 'Cats gave up two runs in the first inning, then scored one in the second when Matt Smith reached first on an error, gained second on an overthrow, stole third base, and then scored on a Dakota Dean single. They added two runs in the third to take a 3-2 lead but couldn't hold that score, surrendering two runs in the fourth and four in the seventh to the Sweets, who came away with an 8-3 decision. Cody Snider had

The headliner for the home opener against the Wenatchee AppleSox was Krazy George, well known for his cheerleading at the BC Lions home game and officially credited with creating The Wave.

KRAZY GEORGE ON THE FIELD; SOUVENIR BOBBLEHEAD – KRAZY GEORGE. HELEN EDWARDS PHOTOS

a hit and a walk, while Matt Smith had a hit and drove in one run, and Dakota Dean had two hits and one RBI. The final game of the series was a 7-4 victory for the home team. They scored early and often, building up a 7-0 lead before the HarbourCats threatened in the ninth inning, but their four runs came short of a full comeback. Justin Bundy had two hits in a losing cause.

The headliner for the home opener against the Wenatchee AppleSox was Krazy George, well known for his cheerleading at the BC Lions home game and officially credited with creating The Wave, found in most current sporting venues. He beat his drum and entertained the fans while the team was entertaining them on the field. A crowd of 4,544 watched their team demolish the AppleSox in an 11-1 game. Dalton Erb was masterful in his start, retiring 20 consecutive batters before allowing a walk in the seventh inning. He struck out 13 and gave up just one hit. Nick Woitysiak came in to pitch the ninth inning and gave up a single run. The 'Cats scored twice in the third inning on Cody Snider's home run with Justin Brown on base and then added five in the fourth, three in the fifth, and one in the eighth. Snider finished the game with three hits, while Matt Smith had two. Game two was another home victory, this time by a 12-4 score. Aided by two errors, they scored six runs in the third inning to set the pace. After a Riley Guntrip walk, Justin Brown doubled. Wyatt Young's double brought them home, and he scored on a Cody Snider single. The fourth and fifth runs were scored on errors. Colin Ashworth got the victory with seven innings of five-hit baseball, striking out six. Game three was a different scenario. Wenatchee scored in the first two innings to build up a 3-0 lead, but the 'Cats got one in the second on a Matt Warkentin home run, then notched two in the fourth when Dakota Dean's double plated Jarron Silva and Joe Prior. After the AppleSox tied the score in the sixth, the home team got two more to take the lead and added an insurance run in the eighth. Dakota Dean had three hits, while Jarron Silva, PJ Floyd, and Wyatt Young added two each. James Kannenberg started and pitched five innings before being relieved by Ethan Skuija, who got the win, and Holden Lyons, who earned the save. The 6-4 decision gave the home team the series sweep and evened their season record at 3-3.

In Kelowna, the game scheduled to be played was rained out and shifted to June 12th as part of a doubleheader. The series opened strong for Victoria as they scored an 8-5 decision over the Falcons. The key to success was a three-run fifth inning to put the 'Cats ahead for good. PJ Floyd and Jake Prior had two hits for the winners, while Hayden Jaco contributed a double. Casey Costello went six innings for the win, and Greg Casper finished in relief. In the second half of the doubleheader, Holden Lyons got the win in relief of Josh Mitchell. The third game was postponed to a later date.

In MLB draft news, pitcher Dalton Erb was selected 894th overall and would sign with the San Diego Padres; as a result, he left the team. Former player Alex De Goti was drafted 457th by the Houston Astros, and Josh Burgmann, who had signed with the HarbourCats but not played, was selected by the St. Louis Cardinals in the 30th round.

In MLB draft news, pitcher Dalton Erb was selected 894th overall and would sign with the San Diego Padres; as a result, he left the team.

Four new players from the University of California-Davis arrived in town on June 12. Ryan Steindorf, Blake Hannah, Ryan Anderson, and Brad Pluschkell would make their debuts against the Gresham Grey Wolves. Will McAffer threw 5 1/3 innings to lead the team to a 2-0 shutout. Griffin Andreychuk and AJ Alcantara had three hits for the winners, with both recording a double. Ben Polshuk, Austin Dondanville, and Tommy Jew joined the team just before the second game of the series, and all three contributed to a 9-5 victory. Dondanville went four innings, giving up one run and striking out seven, Polshuk had three hits, including a home

The victory pushed the winning streak to eight. Next, the Cowlitz Black Bears came to town and the hit parade continued.

run, and Jew played well at shortstop. The third game of the series became a tribute to an Oaklands Elementary kindergarten teacher who was retiring after 35 years of teaching. Almost the entire school population turned out to support him, as well as former students and colleagues. On the playing field, the HarbourCats swept the GreyWolves with a close 3-2 decision. Ryan Steindorf got the win in relief of James Kannenberg. Griffin Andreychuk continued his hot hitting with three more hits and added a stolen base. Matt Smith and Brad Pluschkell had two hits apiece. The victory pushed the winning streak to eight. Next, the Cowlitz Black Bears came to town and the hit parade continued. Griffin Andreychuk added three more hits, including a double and a home run, while Jake Silva had three, and Brad Pluschkell and Cameron Cannon had two each. Josh Mitchell went seven innings before being relieved by Skyler Henderson. The 11-1 result pushed the win streak to nine, equalling the best streaks in the 2014 and 2015 seasons. The next game was a bit closer, but still a victory, 6-4. In this match, Cowlitz scored three times in the first inning, so the 'Cats had to come from behind. They scored twice in the first and fourth innings to take a lead, only to see their opponents tie the game in the fifth on a bases-loaded walk. The winning runs came in the eighth when a Cameron Cannon double drove in Matt Lautz, and he then crossed the plate after a Jake Stone single. Riley Guntrip and Cody Snider had hit back-to-back homers in the fourth inning. Jack Wolger got the start and was relieved by Casey Costello, Austin Dondanville, and Holden Lyons, who secured the victory. The win streak was pushed to eleven as the HarbourCats shut out the Black Bears on Father's Day, 5-0. 2,584 fans watched the home team score three runs in the first inning on a Griffin Andreychuk walk, an Austin Guibor single, Jake Stone walk, and a Joe Prior single. They were also aided by two errors at crucial times. The 'Cats added three more runs in the seventh inning and rode the pitching arm of Will McAffer for six innings as he struck out 10 batters while allowing only two hits. Ryan Steindorf and Greg Casper combined for the last three innings. In league news, Will McAffer was named Pitcher of the Week.

With a few days off in the schedule, the HarbourCats played the Victoria Selects in an exhibition game. Then, the Kitsap BlueJackets came to town. Austin

Dondanville had a no-hitter until the seventh inning when he gave up two runs on three hits. PJ Floyd had a good night at the plate with two hits and two stolen bases. Victoria went up early in the match and was up 5-0 before Kitsap got on the board. The final run by the home team came in the seventh, and they had to hold on as their opponents notched three in the ninth to make it closer than it needed to be. Nevertheless, the 6-5 squeaker pushed the streak to twelve, including 10-0 at home. Will McAffer was on the mound for the middle game in the series and led his team to a 5-1 victory, logging six innings of two-hit ball and striking out eight. After Kitsap scored in the second to take a temporary lead, AJ Alcantara, who had walked, then stolen a base, scored on a Matt Lautz single to tie the score. The 'Cats added one run in the fourth and put the game out of reach with three in the eighth. The game result was a combination of timely hitting and great pitching. Fans could bring their four-legged friends to the ballpark for Bark in the Park on a sunny Sunday afternoon. This game was very close, with Kitsap scoring four runs in the fourth inning to take a 4-2 lead. Fortunately, for the home team, they notched two runs in their half of the fourth to tie the score. After Kitsap again went ahead by one run, the 'Cats tied it in the seventh, so the game went to extra innings. Fans were exhilarated when their team scored a walk-off victory when Brad Pluschkell scored on a Ben Polshuk single and a Kitsap fielding error.

On the road in Wenatchee, the HarbourCats defeated the home team 7-4 to extend their winning streak to 15, eclipsing the 2011 record set by the AppleSox. Wenatchee took a two-run lead in the third, but the visitors scored three in the fourth and added one in the sixth. Wenatchee tied the game in the seventh but a big three runs in the eighth secured the victory for the HarbourCats. Ben Polshuk and Jake Prior hit homers to lead the offence while Austin Dondanville secured the win in relief of James Kannenberg and Colin Ashworth. Holden Lyons cleaned up in the ninth inning. Sweet sixteen came in a 9-4 triumph over the AppleSox. The HarbourCats got off to a good start with a run in the first and three in the second. After Wenatchee narrowed the lead with three in the third, the 'Cats added two in the fourth, surrendered one in the seventh and put the game away with a three-run eighth inning. Jake Stone hit a three-run homer, Jarron Silva added a triple,

> After travelling through the night to catch the early Coho ferry, the HarbourCats played the Kelowna Falcons and upended them, 9-1.

THE TEAM CELEBRATES A VICTORY ON JUNE 30, 2016 VS. KELOWNA. HELEN EDWARDS PHOTO

and Joe Prior and Cody Snider had doubles to lead the offence. Jack Wolger went six innings for the win, while Blake Hannah and Cameron Schneider finished the game. Next up was a close 7-6 decision over the AppleSox. AJ Alcantara had two hits, including a homer, while Matt Lautz, Brad Pluschkell, and Tommy Jew had two hits each. Down 2-0 early, the team scored three times in the second, aided by a Wenatchee error. With the game tied 5-5 in the seventh, the 'Cats offence struck for two runs and limited their opponents to one. It was not a good outing for the pitchers of either team, but Josh Mitchell got the win for Victoria.

After travelling through the night to catch the early Coho ferry, the HarbourCats played the Kelowna Falcons and upended them, 9-1. Joe Prior had three hits, while Cody Snider had a triple, and Ben Polshuk hit a homer to drive in two runs in the fourth inning to start the scoring. Six runs in the seventh inning sealed the deal. Will McAffer got the win with Carson Schneider handling the final four innings. An all-time WCL record crowd of 5,133 fans watched the fireworks on the field, followed by the pre-Canada Day fireworks show. The HarbourCats got their nineteenth straight victory with a 7-0 defeat of Kelowna in the first of two games on Canada Day. Austin Dondanville pitched the complete seven innings, giving up only one hit and striking out five. Ben Polschuk's grand slam was the key blast in the game, coming in the fifth inning to put the game out of reach. The second game of the doubleheader was a rescheduling of a rained-out game in Kelowna; Victoria was the visiting team and got an early lead, fell behind, then left the tying run on base. The streak was over, but now there was a different goal – to win 40 games. On the positive side, the team clinched the first-half title and would thus be in the playoffs for the first time. In the final game of the series, the team rebounded and beat Kelowna by a score of 10-4. The bats came alive, and they scored one in the first via Cody Snider's two-out single, gave up two in the third, then notched four of their own in the third, scoring with two out after a Tommy Jew walk, a Ben Polshuk walk, a Joe Prior walk, and a Cody Snider triple; he then scored on an error by the right fielder. The HarbourCats plated another five in the sixth to seal the victory. Rather than a ceremonial first pitch, the fans celebrated Graig Merritt's birthday by singing Happy Birthday. Ben Polshuk was named the West Coast League player of the week after going four-for-14, with three home runs, 10 runs batted in, six runs scored, and nine walks for a .577 on-base percentage.

On the road again, the 'Cats upended the Cowlitz Black Bears 9-3. Cowlitz scored three in the first inning but then Cameron Schneider shut them down in the remainder of his five innings of work, striking out nine. Jack Wolger hurled three shutout innings with two strikeouts, and Skyler Henderson closed in the ninth with one strikeout. After scoring single runs in the third and fifth innings, Victoria plated nine in the sixth. Ben Polshuk had two hits, as did Jake Stone and Tommy Jew. After the second game was rained out, the teams played a doubleheader the following day. The first half of the twin bill was a Victoria victory by a 5-0 score. Austin Dondanville went the distance, allowing only three hits. Jake Stone had three hits, including a double and a triple, while Austin Guibor had a double as well. In the late-finishing second game, Josh Mitchell shut out the Black Bears with five innings of two-hit baseball, and Holden Lyons finished the game. The 'Cats' only runs were scored in the fourth inning when Tommy Jew's triple

After a long overnight bus trip and an early ferry ride, the HarbourCats faced the Bend Elks.

plated Ryan Anderson who had walked and Riley Guntrip, who had reached on a fielder's choice.

After a long overnight bus trip and an early ferry ride, the HarbourCats faced the Bend Elks. Scoring two runs in the first inning when Griffin Andreychuk scored on a Joe Prior home run, they added one in the eighth for a 3-1 decision. Will McAffer faced 12 batters, Blake Hannah, 16, and Greg Casper, the final seven. The middle game of the series was not one of their best efforts as Bend scored five runs in the first inning and added 10 more to defeat Victoria 15-8 for the first official home loss of the season. Jack Wolger lasted only 1 2/3 innings before being

Game one was a rare loss for the 'Cats. Up 6-2 after two innings, they were unable to hold the lead and were defeated 9-8.

replaced by Kyle Mora. Colin Ashworth threw the last three frames. Matt Lautz had three hits, AJ Alcantara had a double and a home run, and Matt Smith and Cameron Cannon had two hits each. Local fans enjoyed the final game of the set when the HarbourCats scored in the 11th inning on a bases-loaded Cameron Cannon single for a 6-5 decision. PJ Floyd had a home run and a single and Joe Prior had two singles to lead the offence.

After that game, the North and South all-star teams were named. Six HarbourCats were named to play in the game in Cowlitz. Pitchers Will McAffer, Austin Dondanville, and Josh Mitchell would join second baseman Griffin Andreychuk and outfielders Ben Polshuk and Jarron Silva.

In the meantime, the HarbourCats travelled to Gresham for a three-game series. Game one was a rare loss for the 'Cats. Up 6-2 after two innings, they were unable to hold the lead and were defeated 9-8. The teams had 26 hits between them, including Tommy Jew's early two-run homer. Dakota Dean had three hits while Matt Lautz, Ryan Anderson, Matt Smith, Tommy Jew and Cameron Cannon had two each in a losing cause. The second game was a decisive 12-4 victory that took over three hours to play. The GreyWolves took a 2-0 lead in the second inning but could only manage two more in the sixth, while the 'Cats had one in the third and a big five in the fourth, adding one in the seventh, three in the eighth, and one in the ninth. Joe Prior had three hits, including a double, while PJ Floyd hit a triple that drove in two runs. According to manager Merritt, the team had felt the loss of pitchers, including James Kannenberg, who had been injured and Casey Costello, who left to take summer classes. However, he felt the remaining staff would pick up the slack. In the final game of the series, Victoria had an early three-run lead but couldn't hold it and lost 9-6. Joe Prior had a home run and a single to lead the offence. Then, it was on to Bend, Oregon, for another three games. In game one, the Elks took a 2-0 lead in the first inning, but the visitors got single runs in the fifth and sixth innings and five in the seventh to win the game 7-3. Josh Mitchell pitched a complete game, giving up three runs on nine hits and striking out seven. The HarbourCats loaded the bases in the seventh inning, scored the first run when Austin Guibor was hit by a pitch, a second one when Dakota Dean got a single, two more when Tommy Jew reached first base on an error, and the final run on a fielder's choice. They left 12 men on base. In the second game, the Elks got some revenge as they defeated Victoria 4-2. Blake Hannah started for the 'Cats and went five innings, allowing two runs on three hits; Holden Lyons was tagged with the loss for his three innings of work. AJ Alcantara and Ben Polshuk had two hits for the HarbourCats. In the final game of the series, the HarbourCats got back on track and upended the Elks by a score of 7-3. They pounded out 12 hits, including

Facing Bellingham pitchers throwing 98, 93, and 91 miles per hour, the HarbourCats lost the game 5-3.

doubles by Dakota Dean, Tommy Jew, and Riley Guntrip, while Joe Silva had a triple. Carson Schneider threw the first six innings, allowing just one run on six hits and Greg Casper and Austin Dondanville came in as relievers. Joe Prior was named Player of the Week for going 11-for-20 with a double, homer, five runs batted in, and four runs scored. The team added pitcher Indigo Diaz from North Vancouver and re-signed Ethan Skuija from the UBC Thunderbirds.

In the all-star game, the South team beat the North team by a score of 4-0. Ben Polshuk finished third in the home run derby, Austin Dondanville and Josh Mitchell pitched one inning each, and Ben Polshuk and Jarron Silva played in the outfield. Griffin Andreychuk did not play due to an ailment and Will McAffer did not pitch. Then, it was back to regular play.

Facing Bellingham pitchers throwing 98, 93, and 91 miles per hour, the HarbourCats lost the game 5-3. The Bells went ahead with a run in the fourth and added three in the fifth before the home team got on the board. Austin Guibor and Riley Guntrip had two hits, and PJ Floyd had a double, but the bats were quite quiet. Game two started out well for the 'Cats as they held a 3-0 lead but couldn't hold it as the Bells notched three in the eighth to tie the game. In the 10th inning, the visitors scored five runs to win the game 8-3. Will McAffer was strong on the mound, striking out nine, but left when the score was 3-2. The final game of the series was a better game. Victoria scored early with three in the first inning, added one each in the third and fourth, and finished with two in the sixth. AJ Alcantara had four hits to lead his team to a 7-5 victory. Cam Schneider worked seven innings, giving up one run, and was credited with the win. It wasn't easy as the Bells fought back, loading the bases twice in the ninth inning, but the relief pitchers

AJ ALCANTARA IN ACTION

minimized the damage to only three runs. Griffin Andreychuk was unable to play as he had dental surgery; he would miss the next series as well.

The next series was in Corvallis. In game one, Victoria took a two-run lead in the first and added three more, but Corvallis fought back to tie the game after regulation time. In the twelfth inning, Ben Polshuk was hit by a pitch, Brad Pluschkell hit a single, and both scored on an Austin Guibor triple. Colin Ashworth held the home team off the board as the 'Cats defeated the Knights 7-5. The middle game in the series went to the Knights, who had 17 hits and outscored the HarbourCats 9-2. Dakota Dean had three hits to account for one-third of the team's hits. In the rubber match, Blake Hannah hurled eight innings of shutout ball, and Cam Schneider cleaned up as Victoria shut out the Knights 5-0. Ryan Anderson had three hits, including a double and a homer. Tommy Jew and Jake Stone also hit home runs.

Back at home against Walla Walla, Will McAffer threw 6 1/3 scoreless innings, walking two and striking out four for a 3-0 victory. Riley Guntrip had two hits and scored two runs and Tommy Jew had two hits, driving in two runs. Game two was one-sided as the HarbourCats upended the Sweets by a score of 13-2. As a result of the 18 hits, all fans won a coupon for a free chicken burger from Beacon Drive-In. Ryan Anderson drove in five runs while Ben Polshuk added a three-run home run. Cam Schneider went six innings for the victory, and Ethan Skuija handled the final three innings. Between the sixth and seventh innings, Daniel Sanchez proposed to Kortney Hannah, the sister of pitcher Blake Hannah. She said yes! The 'Cats swept the series with a close 3-2 result in game three. Josh Mitchell went seven innings, giving up two runs on four hits and striking out ten, while Austin Dondanville closed it out with four strikeouts. Jake Stone had three hits, including a double, and drove in two runs while Brad Pluschkell had two hits.

The next games were in Bellingham. Game one was a Bells victory by a score of 5-2. Victoria took an early lead after Austin Guibor doubled and scored on an error, but Bellingham tied the score and then went ahead in the third inning. PJ Floyd had two hits for the team. Victoria loaded the bases in the eighth inning but were unable to score. In the middle game, the teams exchanged runs and the game was tied in the eighth when the Bells walked it off with a two-out, single in the bottom of the ninth. Brad Pluschkell had two hits for the 'Cats who also stole three bases but came up one run short, 4-3. The final game of the series went to the HarbourCats, 9-2. Blake Hannah threw six innings of two-run ball while Holden Lyons, Josh Mitchell, and Ethan Skuija finished the game in relief. Ryan Anderson

With that victory, Victoria clinched the overall title for 2016.

had three hits while Austin Guibor, Brad Pluschkell, and Riley Guntrip had two apiece. In the last series of the season, in Kitsap, Victoria defeated the BlueJackets, 7-2, in the first game. Austin Dondanville went eight innings allowing two runs on eight hits, while striking out six. Cameron Schneider pitched the final inning in relief. Ben Polshuk had three hits and drove in one run, while AJ Alcantara had two hits and drove in two runs, and PJ Floyd had a hit and drove in two runs. With that victory, Victoria clinched the overall title for 2016. In the middle game, Will McAffer went six innings of shutout ball, and Indigo Diaz and Kyle Mora finished in relief as Victoria outscored the BlueJackets 7-0. Austin Guibor hit a triple that drove in two runs and scored a run; PJ Floyd had two hits, including a double and drove in two runs. The final game was a 4-1 decision for the visitors. Josh Mitchell threw six scoreless innings, striking out six while Greg Casper three one scoreless inning with three strikeouts, and Holden Lyons finished the game yielding one run on three hits, striking out two. Ben Polshuk, Ryan Anderson, Tommy Jew, and Joe Silva all hit doubles for the 'Cats. It was the last game that Victoria would ever play in Kitsap, as the franchise would be moving to Port Angeles in the next season.

Yakima Valley Pippins spoiled the opener of the last homestand when they upended the HarbourCats 10-7. PJ Floyd and Brad Pluschkell had four hits for Victoria to lead the offence. Tying the record for the most victories in a season,

On the last day of the regular season, the HarbourCats won their 40th game with a convincing 11-4 decision over the Pippins.

39 set by the 2011 Wenatchee AppleSox, would have to wait for another day. The HarbourCats won their 39th game with a 6-2 victory. A three-run sixth inning put the game away when a Ryan Anderson double was followed by a PJ Floyd triple and a Tommy Jew homer. Blake Hannah went six innings for the victory. On the last day of the regular season, the HarbourCats won their 40th game with a convincing 11-4 decision over the Pippins. They scored four runs in the first inning as base hits from Griffin Andreychuk, Ben Polshuk, Ryan Anderson, and Tommy Jews combined with an error to get them started. Another four runs in the sixth inning put the game on ice. Brad Pluschkell had three hits, including a homer, while Griffin Andreychuk and Ben Polshuk had two each. Kyle Mora worked five innings before being relieved by Indigo Diaz, Matt Lautz, and Colin Ashworth.

The next goal was to win the first playoff series in team history, but that was not to be. Falling behind in game one in Bellingham, the 'Cats tied the game in the third inning. The game continued like that until the seventh inning when the Bells scored the winning run. Riley Guntrip had a double, but generally, the bats were quiet in the 3-2 loss. Back home, the HarbourCats didn't fare any better. They obviously ran out of steam and dropped a 12-1 decision to the Bells. It was a disappointing finish to a very successful season, but the loyal fans stayed to the end of the game to salute their team. On a positive note, the HarbourCats became the first team in the WCL to break the 60,000-attendance mark, with 60,466 fans passing through the gates.

In local honours, AJ Alcantara was named Player of the Year and Austin Dondanville and Josh Mitchell, Pitchers of the Year.

Two junior national team members from Abbotsford were signed.

Six HarbourCats were named to the year-end all-WCL team. Head coach Graig Merritt was named WCL coach of the year and managing partner Jim Swanson, WCL executive of the year. Five players were named to the first team: Brad Pluschkell, AJ Alcantara, Josh Mitchell, Austin Dondanville, and Will McAffer, while PJ Floyd was named to the second team as a utility player.

After the season, the club announced that Graig Merritt was not offered a contract extension and would not be returning next season. The new coach was Brian McRae, who had played outfield in the major leagues from 1990 to 1999 for the Kansas City Royals, Chicago Cubs, New York Mets, Colorado Rockies, and Toronto Blue Jays. The son of former all-star Hal McRae, he had been managed by his father when he played for the Royals. He worked for five years for MLB.com radio and had appeared on Baseball Tonight for ESPN. As the general manager of the Kansas City Sluggers Youth Academy, he worked with players aged eight to 17.

Signings for the 2017 season included Josh Mitchell, returning for his third season, and Blake Hannah and Colin Ashworth, returning for their second season with the team. Two junior national team members from Abbotsford were signed. Carter Loewen would play with the University of Hawaii Rainbows and Tanner Rempel at Colorado Mesa University. Two other Rainbows signings were Ethan Lopez and Kekai Rios. Coming back for a second season were Matt Lautz and Casey Costello. Harrison Bragg and Reed Smith from Mississippi State University would play for the 'Cats in the summer, as would Bryce Bonner and Harry Shipley from Purdue and Ryan Ricci from George Mason University. Late November signings were Will LaRue, Riley Pletcher, and Matt Kent from Xavier University.

In league news, the move of the Kitsap BlueJackets to Port Angeles where they would be named the Lefties, was confirmed in early September. The West Coast League would remain at 11 teams for the 2017 season.

6

2017: Would This Be the Year?

The HarbourCats added their first international player in February 2017 when Po-Hao Huang of Fu Jen Catholic University in Taiwan signed on the dotted line. He had played in North America in the summer of 2016 for the Elmira Pilots of the Perfect Game Collegiate League. Wyatt Young (Pepperdine) would return for 2017, and Washington State Cougars AJ Block and James Mullins would be new players. February signings included Jack Owen (Auburn University), Sam Crocker (Florida Tech), Jacob Castillo (Mt. San Antonio College), and Hunter Vansau (Mississippi State). In early May, the team signed Chavez Fernandez from the Bahamas who played at Polk State College, Ryan Hooper (UC-Davis), DJ Porter (Cal Baptist), and Shane McGuire (San Diego).

On May 16, 2017, the HarbourCats made history when they signed Claire Eccles, the West Coast League's first female player.

On May 16, 2017, the HarbourCats made history when they signed Claire Eccles, the West Coast League's first female player. A student at the University of British Columbia, she had played for Canada at the Women's Baseball World Cup in South Korea the previous September and helped her team to a silver medal. She was primarily a pitcher but could also play in the outfield. Older Victoria fans would remember the days of the Victoria Seals when Eri Yoshida, the Knuckleball

SEASON OPENER IN PORT ANGELES

Princess, pitched for the Chico Outlaws in a Golden League game. Brad Norris-Jones was on vacation in Hawaii when he watched a baseball game with a young girl absolutely crushing the ball. At that point, he wondered if a female could play in the West Coast League. With the support of the General Manager and coach, he had a conference call with three girls from Team Canada. One had used up her college eligibility, so she was not able to play, but the last girl to speak said she had played with boys all her life and she had a knuckleball. The news of her signing was trending on ESPN, *Sports Illustrated*, *Washington Post*, and the *Los Angeles Times*. It turned out to be a good move for the HarbourCats as Claire proved that females could play at the college level against males and served as an inspiration for the next generation of players.

The 'Cats season opened across the Strait of Juan de Fuca in Port Angeles as that city welcomed the Lefties to the league. A crowd of 3,017 watched the visiting team win by an 11-2 score. AJ Block got the start for Victoria and worked three innings, giving up one run on two hits while striking out 8. Adam McKillican also worked three innings and was given the "W." On the offensive side of the ball, Po-Hao Huang – known by his "English name" of Bernie, reached base four times with a single, a double and two walks. Harry Shipley and Ethan Lopez also had doubles. Victoria scored early and often with four runs in the first inning, two in the second, and one in the third before the Lefties got their two in the third. A sole run in the sixth and three in the ninth completed the offence for the HarbourCats.

After that special one-game showcase of the new franchise, the team travelled to Yakima Valley to play the Pippins in their home opener. The visitors got off to a good start with two runs in the first inning, one in the second, and two in the fourth. Colin Ashworth got the start but left in the fourth inning after surrendering six runs (five earned) on eight hits and was relieved by Ryan Ricci. Ethan Fox, who had been signed as a 10-day player, drove in three runs as a designated hitter and then came in to pitch in the fifth inning and worked two scoreless frames. Kevin Collard had three hits, including a triple, while Harry Shipley, Noah Prewett, and Justin Orton had two each. The 'Cats won the game with two runs in the seventh inning, securing the 7-6 victory and going 2-0 in the new season. In the next game, the team suffered their first loss as the Pippins rode a seven-run sixth inning to an 11-4 decision. Victoria had built up a 4-2 lead at that point but could never recover. Noah Prewett had a double and a triple to lead the offence in the early innings, but then the bats went cold. The 'Cats got back on the winning ways in the final game of the series when they outscored the Pippins 6-2. Ethan Skuija got the start and went 3 2/3 innings, giving up only one run on three hits; however, he ran into trouble as he surrendered six walks. Noah Prewett came in for 2 1/3 innings

Noah Prewett had a double and a triple to lead the offence in the early innings, but then the bats went cold.

and limited the Pippins to one run on four hits while Adam McKillican finished the game, allowing only three hits. Victoria scored one run in the first inning and added three in the third to take a 4-0 lead. The teams then scored two runs each over the last five innings. The 'Cats helped their pitchers by completing four double plays to defuse difficult situations.

Now, it was time for the home opener against the Wenatchee AppleSox. Before the game, a Zamboni dragged the base paths, and skydivers delivered the game ball, which Victoria Mayor Lisa Helps threw for the ceremonial first pitch. Ethan Fox started the game but ran into trouble and gave up five runs (four earned) on six hits in his four innings of work. After surrendering three runs in the fourth, the home team notched two in their half of the inning to make it close, but a four-run fifth inning put the game out of reach, and the result was a 9-4 loss. Justin Orton had three hits, while Kekai Rios and Ethan Lopez had two. Coach McRae noted that his team had chances to get back into the game but didn't capitalize on their opportunities. Game two had a better result for the home team. AJ Block worked six innings, allowing two runs on five hits and striking out five while Taylor Prokopis

Coach McRae noted that his team had chances to get back into the game but didn't capitalize on their opportunities.

and Travis Kuhn finished the game in relief. Wenatchee scored first with a single run in the first, but Victoria came back with two in the second when Riley Zayicek homered to drive in Kevin Collard, who had reached base on an error. They added two in the third and two more in the sixth to put the game away, 6-2. The wheels fell off in the third game as the visitors shut out the home team 9-0. Colin Ashworth got the start and was relieved by Adam McKillican. Claire Eccles saw her first action and gave up two runs on one hit when the game was out of reach. Po-Hao Huang had three hits to lead the offence.

The HarbourCats then played in Wenatchee's home opener. It was a close affair and was tied until the AppleSox walked it off with a single after two walks put a runner in scoring position. Harry Shipley, Noah Prewett, and Jake Garella had two hits in a losing cause. Isaac Mullins worked five innings, giving up four runs on five hits. Luke Boyd had two innings of one-hit ball, and Greg Casper worked the eighth and ninth innings and gave up the winning run in a 5-4 score. The AppleSox made it three in a row over the HarbourCats with a close 7-6 victory in game two of the series. Down early, the 'Cats got single runs in the fourth, fifth, and sixth innings to get close. They notched three runs in the eighth thanks to three errors, but that was as close as they got. Harry Shipley had three hits, including a triple, to lead the offence. In game three, the 'Cats rode a second-inning grand slam by Jake Garella to a 5-3 victory. Bryce Bonner went three-for-four at the plate. Ethan Fox got the start and worked four innings while Luke Boyd threw 2 2/3, AJ Block threw 1/3, and Travis Kuhn tossed the last two innings.

Back home, the HarbourCats played a two-game series against the Lefties. AJ Block started the first game for the home team and worked five innings of one-hit ball. Taylor Prokopis and Travis Kuhn worked two innings each in relief. Cole

ANDREW VAUGHN IN ACTION

Weiss had a great night at the plate, going three-for-five, while Kevin Collard and Bryce Bonner had two hits apiece in a 4-1 victory. The second game was another Victoria win as Jake Garella led the team with two hits, and Harry Shipley had a triple in the 7-3 decision. The game was close until the 'Cats notched three in the seventh and two in the eighth to secure the win. Andrew Vaughn joined the team after a great season at Cal-Berkley, where he hit .349, had a slugging percentage of .555, recording 76 hits, 50 runs batted in, and 121 total bases. His time with the HarbourCats would be limited as he had been invited to the US collegiate nation team tryout camp. He saw his first action in this series.

On the road, the 'Cats dropped a close decision to the Walla Walla Sweets, 2-1. Andrew Vaughn, Harry Shipley, and Po-Hao Huang hit doubles, but Victoria left seven runners stranded. Isaac Mullins was the starter and went six innings, giving up two runs on six hits. After the second game was rained out, it was replaced by

On the road, the 'Cats dropped a close decision to the Walla Walla Sweets, 2-1.

a doubleheader the following day. The HarbourCats again lost 2-1 with all the scoring coming in the third and fourth innings of the seven-inning game. DJ Porter had three hits for Victoria, and Luke Boyd worked four innings before being relieved by Greg Casper and Indigo Diaz. The Sweets completed the series sweep with a 6-5 victory in the second half of the doubleheader. They took an early lead with a run in the first when Kevin Collard's double scored Po-Hao Huang, who

DJ PORTER IN ACTION

had doubled, and three in the second when Tucker Johnson walked, advanced on a passed ball, and scored on an Ethan Lopez double. After he stole a base, Jake Garella walked as did Andrew Vaughn, setting the stage for Po-Hao Huang to single, driving them both home. However, the team couldn't hold the lead, surrendering two runs in the fifth and four in the sixth while only adding one in the seventh. They would be glad to get home.

Adam McKillican threw a masterful 6 2/3 innings of one-hit ball to lead the HarbourCats past the Lefties, 6-1, in a school day field trip event. He gave up a two-out double in the first inning before setting down 17 consecutive batters. Davis Wendzel had a triple, and Kevin Collard, DJ Porter, and Tucker Johnson had doubles. The score could have been much higher as the 'Cats stranded 11 runners. With the victory, Victoria moved to 4-0 against its cross-strait rival.

Claire Eccles got her first start in an exhibition game against the Kitsap BlueJackets, now playing in a Seattle senior league. With 2,373 fans in the stands, she tossed three innings, giving up two runs on three hits. The HarbourCats scored five runs in the second inning on four hits, including Andrew Vaughn's first double, which drove in two. After the visitors notched two in the third, the 'Cats' offence produced two in the third, one in the fourth, and three in the fifth to win the seven-inning game handily, 11-2.

The Corvallis Knights came to town and took an early lead but fell 4-2 to the 'Cats. AJ Block started the game and worked six innings. He was one of six pitchers for the home team; Jake Taggert got the win in relief. Riley Zayicek tied the score when he hit a towering home run in the fourth inning to score Kevin Collard, who had singled. The 'Cats added two more in the eighth when Po-Hao Huang drove in a run and then scored when Davis Wendzel got a single. It was a hard-fought battle over a formidable opponent, one of the powerhouse teams of the WCL. The second game was a rude awakening to the realities of baseball. The game was close for four innings with the Knights holding a 4-3 lead, but they put the game out of reach with three in the fifth and five in the sixth to win 12-4. Davis Wendzel was the hitting star with three hits and a run batted in. Game three was like game two, with the Knights blasting the 'Cats by a score of 14-4. It was a tough outing for pitchers Luke Boyd and Liam Steigerwald, while Taylor Prokopis and Radd Thomas shut the door a bit too late, and Claire Eccles pitched a meaningless ninth inning, giving up two hits and one run. For the second game in a row, Davis Wendzel was the offensive star, going two-for-four with a two-run homer in the second inning that narrowed the gap to 6-3. Seven runs in the fifth inning proved to be the downfall as the team fell to 9-10 on the season. It didn't get any better when the Walla Walla Sweets came to town. Starter Jack Owen went five innings of two-run ball, but the bullpen had a bad day, surrendering eight runs. Victoria didn't score until the seventh inning with two runs on a Jake Garella homer and a Kevin

The next night, Victoria got home runs from Tucker Johnson, Kevin Collard, Ryan Zayicek, and Noah Prewett to defeat the Sweets 6-1.

Collard double that scored DJ Porter, who had reached on a fielder's choice. Ethan Lopez had two hits in a losing cause as the 'Cats dropped a 6-4 decision. The next night, Victoria got home runs from Tucker Johnson, Kevin Collard, Ryan Zayicek, and Noah Prewett to defeat the Sweets 6-1. Hunter Vansau made a fantastic catch in the outfield in deep centre field in the third inning with a runner on base that would have made it a much closer game. Adam McKillican threw seven innings of scoreless ball to secure the victory. The final game of the series went to Walla Walla, who outscored the 'Cats 7-6. Trailing 6-1 in the seventh, the team got two runs and then added three in the eighth to tie the score. The visitors won the game with a sole run in the ninth, and the 'Cats went out in order. Harrison Bragg and Nick Moroney homered for the home team.

In Corvallis, the Knights broke open a 1-1 tie with three runs in the sixth inning en route to a 9-1 thrashing of the 'Cats. AJ Block got the start and went five innings, allowing three runs; Taylor Prokopis gave up three runs in the sixth, and Radd Thomas went two innings, surrendering five runs on four hits. The sole Victoria run came in the sixth inning when Po-Hao Huang singled, and Sam Cachola came in to pinch run, advanced to second on a Jake Garella walk, stole third, and scored on a sacrifice fly by Nick Moroney. In the second game of the series, Luke Boyd pitched a strong seven innings, and Travis Kuhn finished the game for a 5-0 shutout of the Knights. The 'Cats got two runs in the first inning on a Hunter Vansau double and a Kevin Collard sacrifice fly and added single runs in the second, third, and eighth innings. Harrison Bragg, Jake Garella, and Tanner Rempel also hit doubles to lead the offence. The third game was a second victory for the 'Cats. Jack Owen hurled seven innings of two hit ball with eight strikeouts, Noah Prewett allowed one run in an inning of work, and Indigo Diaz pitched a scoreless ninth inning en route to a 4-0 shut out of Corvallis. Davis Wendzel and Andrew Shaps got doubles in the 11-hit barrage.

In one of the wildest games of the year, 1,003 home fans watched the HarbourCats come all the way back from an 8-2 deficit to win 12-11 over the Cowlitz

In one of the wildest games of the year, 1,003 home fans watched the HarbourCats come all the way back from an 8-2 deficit to win 12-11.

Black Bears. In the seventh inning, Riley Zayicek launched a three-run homer to narrow the lead to 8-5. Tanner Rempel hit a dinger to make it 10-6 in the eighth inning, and the offence came alive in the ninth. With the score now 11-6 for the Black Bears, Riley Zayicek singled and then scored on a Hunter Vansau home run. Harrison Bragg singled and then scored on a Kevin Collard homer to bring the count to 11-10. After Ethan Lopez was hit by a pitch, Andrew Shaps walked, and both advanced on a wild pitch. Po-Hao Huang then was hit by a wild pitch and Ethan Lopez scrambled home to tie the score. Andrew Shaps scored the winning run on a Noah Prewett single. Claire Eccles got her first win of the season in relief as she gave up a run in the ninth but then got the final Cowlitz batter to hit into a double play. Game two featured pre-July 1st fireworks display after the game,

CLAIRE ECCLES IN ACTION

which was attended by 3,484 fans. They were treated to a come-from-behind 'Cats victory, 6-5. The team started off well with three runs in the first. Harry Shipley walked, advanced to second on a Noah Prewett single and scored on a fielder's choice. Harrison Bragg then blasted a home run that plated Noah Prewett. They added single runs in the third, seventh, and eighth innings and sent the fans home happy. The HarbourCats swept the Black Bears on Canada Day with a close 2-1 decision. Cowlitz got on the board first with a run in the third but was shut down the rest of the way. Adam McKillican got the start and worked 6 1/3 innings, allowing the sole run. Blake Hannah, Indigo Diaz, and Travis Kuhn pitched in relief. Hunter Vansau was the offensive star of the game with two hits. His double in the fifth inning scored Nick Moroney, while Harry Shipley drove in the other run with a sacrifice fly. The team's fifth consecutive victory brought their record to 15-13.

The 'Cats lost two of their key players due to injury. AJ Block and Davis Wendzel were unable to continue the season and left the team. In Kelowna, the bats came alive as the HarbourCats had 19 hits and thrashed the Falcons 14-1. Taylor Prokopis worked five innings and gave up one run on three hits, while Noah Prewett and Radd Thomas finished the job with scoreless innings. Victoria scored early and often and was helped by three Kelowna errors. Hunter Vansau led the hit parade with three, including a home run, Tucker Johnson had three hits, and Riley Zayicek and Harrison Bragg had doubles. The coach made several substitutions late in the game when the score was no longer in doubt. Game two took over three hours to play as the teams combined for 15 runs on 21 hits. Kelowna had a 2-0 lead before Victoria scored one in the third and three in the fourth. The Falcons plated three of their own in the fifth to take the lead only to see the 'Cats score a single run in the

ADAM MCKILLICAN IN ACTION

sixth. Tied 5-5 after regulation play, the game was won in the 11th inning when the HarbourCats plated an amazing five runs. Riley Zayicek and Hunter Vansau both drove in two runs with triples to lead the offensive barrage. Andrew Shaps and Bryce Bonner had three hits each. Travis Kuhn got the victory in relief while Jack Taggert threw a clean 11th inning to secure the save. Victoria swept the series with a 12-2 pounding of the Falcons. Cole Weiss had three hits, including a homer, and drove in four runs while Tucker Johnson had three hits and scored two runs, and Hunter Vansau had a home run. The 'Cats outscored their opponents 36-8 in the three-game set. Victoria pitcher Jack Owen was named WCL player of the week.

In the first game of a homestand against the Bend Elks, the 'Cats' bats went cold, and they lost 11-2. Isaac Mullins got the start and went six innings, surrendering 11 hits and six runs, only three of which were earned as his teammates committed three errors in the field. Ironically, Victoria had an early two-run lead after Harry Shipley's single in the second, scored Bryce Bonner and Ethan Lopez but that was the extent of the offence. The middle game of the series went to the home team as the 'Cats had 15 hits and scored 11 runs to defeat the Elks 11-5. Down 2-0, they notched three in the fifth as Hunter Vansau singled home Tanner Rempel and Cole Weiss; he later scored on a Tucker Johnson single. Four more runs in the seventh and eighth put the game on ice. Adam McKillican started and worked six innings and was relieved by Indigo Diaz and Blake Hannah. Hunter Vansau finished the game with five hits, while Tucker Johnson had three. The Elks finally won a game with a 6-1 decision. The only offence for the home team came in the fifth inning when Jake Garella doubled and then scored on Nick Moroney's single. Liam Steigerwald started for the 'Cats and gave up three runs on six hits.

The league announced the all-star game selections. Adam McKillican, Indigo Diaz, and Jack Owen were the pitchers selected, while Hunter Vansau was the sole position player. Vansau, who was hitting .426 on the season with four home runs, was also named WCL player of the week.

For the next homestand, the team flashed back to an early era and honoured the Victoria Mussels. Wearing baby blue uniforms, they struck for six runs in the first inning as Andrew Shaps and Bryce Bonner blasted three-run home runs. However, that was the end of the offence. Taylor Prokopis got the start, surrendering six runs on seven hits, Jack Taggart gave up one run on two hits, Matt Kent pitched one inning and gave up two runs on four hits; and Radd Thomas pitched the last two innings, surrendering three runs on two hits. It was not a pitcher's battle by any stretch of the imagination, as the 'Cats lost 12-6. In game two, the teams combined for 23 runs on 26 hits, and both teams committed four errors. In all, nine pitchers were used, and only Indigo Diaz, Andrew Shaps, and Travis Kuhn did well, all in relief. Claire Eccles got the start for the HarbourCats and went two innings and gave up four runs (two earned) on six hits. The versatile Andrew Shaps started as the designated hitter, going three-for-four and scoring three runs, then came in to pitch. He called it "a crazy night." Shawn McGuire also had three hits and scored three runs in the 'Cats' 13-10 victory. The series concluded with a Yakima win, 6-3. The HarbourCats' bats went silent, although Andrew Shaps continued his prowess with three hits, including a triple, while Hunter Vansau added a home run. Jack Owen got the start and surrendered four runs on six hits while striking out seven. Indigo Diaz gave up two hits, Wyatt Boone had a scoreless inning, and Jack Taggart worked the ninth, surrendering two runs on four hits.

In all, nine pitchers were used, and only Indigo Diaz, Andrew Shaps, and Travis Kuhn did well, all in relief.

With a break in the regular season, the HarbourCats played two exhibition

In the first game, the 'Cats scored early and held on for a 4-3 victory. Game two was tied at 17-17 after regulation play and was called a draw.

games against the Burnaby Bulldogs, BC senior men's champions. In the first game, the 'Cats scored early and held on for a 4-3 victory. Game two was tied at 17-17 after regulation play and was called a draw.

Next on the agenda was the All-Star game in Yakima Valley. Prior to that game, Hunter Vansau finished second in the home run derby. Travis Kuhn was added to the Victoria contingent. In the game itself, the South team defeated the North team by a score of 5-2.

The 'Cats then travelled to Bellingham to face the Bells. Andrew Shaps continued his torrid hitting with three hits while Harrison Bragg got the team on the board with a two-run homer in the fourth inning and added a single. DJ Porter also hit a homer to propel the HarbourCats to a 5-2 victory. Jack Owen got the start and worked six innings, allowing just three hits and striking out eight. Noah Prewett, James Bradwell, and Travis Kuhn all pitched one inning in relief. The next night, Victoria was again the victor, in a 9-7 decision. Five runs in the first inning set the pace for the 'Cats, and they survived a Bells' rally with five of their own in the third and one in the fourth to take the lead. Cole Weiss scored the go-ahead run on a wild pitch in the sixth, and Shane McGuire had a pitch-hit homer in the ninth to add an insurance run. Newcomer Kyle Stubbins got the win in relief of Taylor Prokopis who struggled in the early innings. The final game went to the home team as the Bells put up four runs in the first inning and continued to score, building up a 7-0 lead before Victoria got on the board with four runs in the sixth when Shane McGuire got a single, Noah Prewett walked, both advanced on a wild pitch, and McGuire scored on a putout. Cole Weiss walked, and then Po-Hao Huang homered to drive in three runs. Sam Cachola drove in two runs. The comeback fell short when the 'Cats could only score three in the seventh. Adam McKillican got the start and gave up seven runs in five innings.

In Victoria, the Falcons came from behind to trip up the 'Cats, 6-5 in extra innings. Shane McGuire finished the game with four hits, including a homer, while Kevin Collard had three hits, including a double. Jack Owen threw seven innings of shutout ball, but his bullpen let him down. Wearing their powder blue throwback Victoria Mussels' jerseys, the HarbourCats started slowly with a single run in the third when Hunter Vansau hit a double that scored Harry Shipley, who had doubled to start the frame. They added another one in the fifth and then struck for five in the sixth on five hits to extend the lead. One more run in the seventh on Harrison Bragg's homer and four in the eighth ensured the victory. In that inning, Po-Hao Huang and Shane McGuire hit two-run singles. Adam McKillican returned to form and hurled 6 1/3 innings, giving up three runs on four hits and striking out six. There was an awkward incident after the game when a streaker wearing only socks jumped over the fence and ran across the field. He scaled the opposite fence and disappeared from sight. Kelowna took the final game of the series, 9-7. Despite logging 14 hits in the game, the HarbourCats failed to hold a lead and lost when the Falcons scored three times in the ninth inning and held the home team off the scoresheet. Hunter Vansau had three hits for the 'Cats, and Noah Prewett and Harry Shipley had two each. Travis Kuhn suffered the loss in the ninth inning. After the game, Claire Eccles left the team due to her national team commitments.

On the road in Cowlitz, Victoria scored five runs over the first three innings and outlasted the Black Bears 6-3. Wyatt Boone got the start and worked six innings of three-run ball with four strikeouts, and Garrison Ritter finished in relief. Shane McGuire was the offensive star of the game going four-for-four at the plate and Harry Shipley, Hunter Vansau, and Andrew Shaps added doubles. Noah Prewett added a solo home run in the eighth for the icing on the cake. Game two was a

Shane McGuire was the offensive star of the game going four-for-four at the plate and Harry Shipley, Hunter Vansau, and Andrew Shaps added doubles.

'Cats victory as well, as they scored twice in the first inning and added five in the fourth to secure the 9-2 win. Blake Hannah pitched seven innings, giving up one run on three hits; Garinder Sarana worked one inning with one run on one hit; Mikey Musselwhite hurled one inning with one hit, a walk and two strikeouts; and Radd Thomas finished the game with one hit and two strikeouts. Harry Shipley had two hits, including a triple, Kevin Collard had two hits, Hunter Vansau and Noah Prewett had doubles, and Po-Hao Huang had a triple as the 'Cats had 13 hits. In game three, the Black Bears outhit the HarbourCats 11-10 and outscored them 11-6. Victoria had a two-run lead when Cowlitz tied the score and the teams exchanged single runs until the eighth when the Black Bears counted four to seal their victory. Matt Kent went six innings and gave up seven runs on seven hits. On the offensive side, Harry Shipley and Hunter Vansau hit homers, and Harrison Bragg had a double.

Back home, the Bellingham Bells came to town and defeated the 'Cats 11-9. It was Nick Pivetta bobblehead night at Royal Athletic Park to recognize the former HarbourCat who threw the first pitch in team history and was then playing for the Philadelphia Phillies. However, the pitching was not stellar in this effort as the team surrendered 19 hits while only getting 10 themselves. Shane McGuire, who had been named WCL Player of the Week, had a hit, drove in two runs, and scored two. Hunter Vansau and Andrew Shaps had two hits in a losing cause. Jack Owen left the team as he was shut down by his NCAA team, the Auburn Tigers. Game two went to the HarbourCats as they had 15 hits in a 10-4 decision. After the Bells scored early, the 'Cats came back with two in the third inning on home runs by Kevin Collard and Hunter Vansau. They added three in the fourth on three hits, two walks, two stolen bases, and an error. The Bells fought back with two in the sixth, but the 'Cats got that back and then added three in the seventh. Taylor Prokopis worked 5 2/3 innings and gave up three runs on seven hits while striking

That victory put the team back in the playoff hunt with three games to go in the season.

out five. Kevin Collard finished the evening with three hits, and Andrew Shaps and Tucker Johnson had two. That victory put the team back in the playoff hunt with three games to go in the season. Bellingham gained some ground in the playoff race with a 6-2 victory in the final game of the series. Victoria took a 1-0 lead into the fifth inning but surrendered two runs to the Bells in the fifth and four more in the ninth. The 'Cats used seven pitchers, emphasizing the loss of key personnel. Shane McGuire had two hits, including a home run.

The last two games of the season were where they had started it, in Port Angeles. They won the first game 6-4 after coming from behind. The Lefties took a 2-0 lead with single runs in the first two innings, then Victoria scored four in the third to take a lead. Port Angeles tied the game in the third, but that was the end of their scoring. The 'Cats scored single runs in the fourth and eighth innings to secure the victory. Kevin Collard led the offence with three hits, including a double, while Hunter Vansau, Andrew Shaps, Harrison Bragg, and DJ Porter had two each. The team used six pitchers, with Taylor Prokopis getting the win in relief. The final game of the season was a strange one with 33 runs on 38 hits and had the Lefties outlasting the 'Cats 17-16. Victoria used 10 pitchers, and the Lefties used five. Hunter Vansau, Shane McGuire, Harrison Bragg, and Johnson had three hits to lead the offence.

Shane McGuire was named Player of the Year, and Adam McKillican was the Pitcher of the Year.

The HarbourCats opened the playoffs in Victoria against Kelowna. It was a close game at 2-2 until the 'Cats scored a run in the fourth to take the lead. They added three in the sixth and two in the seventh for an 8-2 victory. Hunter Vansau, Andrew Shaps, and Harrison Bragg had two hits each to lead the offensive side. Ethan Fox got the victory in relief. Game two shifted to Kelowna, where smoke from wildfires made the sky an eery red. The 'Cats scored three runs in the second inning and never relinquished that lead in a convincing 11-5 victory. Blake Hannah went six innings, allowing two runs on four hits for the win. Po-Hao Huang had a three-run homer and had five runs batted in to lead the offence. With the series won, the 'Cats had to wait for the result of the South Division championship, locked at 1-1 between Corvallis and Yakima Valley.

With Corvallis defeating Yakima Valley, the final was set. Game one was played in Victoria, where Corvallis scored a run in the second inning only to see Victoria tie it up. Action shifted to the sixth inning where Corvallis got one run and the 'Cats replied with two to take the lead. The Knights scored single runs in the next three innings to take a 4-3 lead, setting the stage for the hit heard around the world (or at least in the Capital Regional District). Justin Orton walked to start the

HARBOURCATS DEFEAT CORVALLIS IN GAME ONE OF THE CHAMPIONSHIP FINAL

Po-Hao Huang (Bernie) and Andrew Shaps celebrate

ninth inning. He advanced to second on an Andrew Shaps single and scored on a wild pitch to tie the score. Then it happened – Andrew Shaps scored on a Po-Hao Huang double, and the crowd went wild, yelling, "Bernie!" Game one was ours by a 5-4 margin. Action then shifted to Corvallis, where the Knights shut down the HarbourCats in a 6-0 decision. Victoria managed only two hits. Now, the whole season was down to one game. The 'Cats took a one-run lead in the first inning when Shane McGuire, who had singled, advanced on an error, advanced to third when Tucker Johnson was hit by a pitch and scored on a wild pitch. The Knights scored single runs in the next four innings and then limited the Victoria come back to one run to win the championship game 4-2. Blake Hannah went six innings, and Ethan Fox finished the game. Po-Hao Huang was the offensive star with two hits, while Andrew Shaps and Jack Orton had two each. It was a sad finish to the season, but it was the farthest the HarbourCats had gone in the playoffs and boded well for the future.

Several loyal fans met the bus when the team returned from the road trip and applauded the tremendous effort.

In year-end awards, Jack Owen was named the WCL pitcher of the year for his minuscule 1.01 ERA and selected for the first all-star team. Shane McGuire, Hunter Vansau, Adam McKillican, and Travis Kuhn were named to the second team, while Harrison Bragg, Harry Shipley, Andrew Shaps, and AJ Block were given honourable mentions.

Now, it was time to focus on the 2018 season. Hunter Vansau was signed to return, as were Tanner Rempel and Ethan Fox. Local product Jason Willow was also signed. In November, the club announced the signing of brothers Jaxxon and Jeddediah Fagg, along with their teammate from Georgia Southern University, Lawson Humphries. Trevin Reynolds from Colorado-Mesa was also signed. Claire Eccles would return for another season, as would Ethan Lopez. Carter Loewen from the University of Hawaii committed to Victoria, as did Jack Smith (Washington State). Kekai Rios (University of Hawaii) would return as well.

Royal Athletic Park was the main venue for the 2017 Canadian baseball championship in August 2017. The Victoria Mavericks were the host team with their lineup featuring former LA Dodgers prospect Kyle Orr and Blue Jays draft pick Bobby Scott. Players at this level are doing it for the love of the game, and it shows in their play. The home run derby featured balls being hit into the water at Ogden Point. Nova Scotia's Jake Sanford of Cole Harbour won the contest. The championships began with early games at Royal Athletic Park and Lambrick Field, with the final games on Sunday. The Burnaby Bulldogs, representing BC, won the title

That victory put the team back in the playoff hunt with three games to go in the season.

with a 5-3 victory over New Brunswick. Plans were already in the works to host the 2018 championship.

Brian McRae, who was entering the second year of his contract, announced his coaching staff for 2018. New was Todd Haney, who had played parts of five seasons with the Montreal Expos, Chicago Cubs, and New York Mets; he would be an assistant coach. The returning coaches were Jason Leone and Troy Birtwistle. 2017 pitching coach Mike Spears would not return, and his place would be taken by Ian Sanderson, who was the pitching coach for the Lower Columbia College Red Devils.

The West Coast League announced that the Portland Pickles would join play for the 2018 season, moving from the Great West League. The Pickles ownership group, Rose City Baseball, also purchased the Gresham GreyWolves baseball club who had played the last two seasons in the WCL and would now compete as an independent summer collegiate team at Mt. Hood Community College in 2018.

7

2018: Close But No Cigar

Early in January, the club announced more players for the upcoming season. Ty Haselman (UCLA), the son of former Montreal Expos catcher Bill Haselman, and Tanner Haney (University of Texas), son of HarbourCats assistant coach Todd Haney, were signed. Also playing this summer would be Cole Roederer (UCLA), Rowdey Jordan (Mississippi State), Connor Nantkes (Washington State), and Cade Brown and Nate Walker (University of San Diego). February additions to the roster were Michael Stovman (Indian Hills Community College), Michael Malinchak and Aharon Modlin (Pepperdine), Caleb Ricketts (University of San Diego), Harrison Spohn and Nick Plaia (Cal Baptist), Tyler Hilton (Mesa Community College), Alec Griggs (Baylor), and Gunnar Friend (NAIA Avila). Two players from Cuba were signed to play in the summer: Alejandro Ortego Lopez and Adriel Quesada Peña (Unión de Reyes).

John Wilson decided to sponsor the home ballpark for the next five years. It became known as Wilson's Group Stadium at Royal Athletic Park. New this season would be a retired, vintage double-decker bus retrofitted to hold groups of 30-40 for home games. This would prove to be a popular viewing point for games. Another viewing area was added to the right field line. Pivetta's Pen honoured the first starter in team history who was then pitching with the Philadelphia Phillies.

John Wilson decided to sponsor the home ballpark for the next five years. It became known as Wilson's Group Stadium at Royal Athletic Park.

THE UPPER DECK PARTY BUS

The HarbourCats played two exhibition games against the Port Angeles Lefties, losing both by scores of 8-6 and 9-7. Then it was on to the regular season. As was normal in summer ball, many of the key players were still involved with the NCAA tournament and would join the team after their college games were over. Ethan Fox was given the start of the home opener as he had last season. In front of 3,372 fans, he pitched 3 2/3 innings and gave up two runs on four hits. Wenatchee pitchers shut out the home team until the eighth inning, when they scored their only run of the game. After two walks, Brodan Bydeweg had a single and Nate Pecota scored on a single by Chang-Chih Yen for a final score of 2-1. The second game was a reversal of the first one. The 'Cats scored early to take a 4-0 lead after two innings and added single runs in later innings. Garett Goodall got the start and went five innings, allowing one run on five hits and striking out six. On the offensive side, Nate Pecota, Jeddediah Fagg, and Jack Smith had two hits for the home team. An attendance of 5,240 watched the exciting 7-1 victory and then enjoyed a fireworks display. In the final game of the series, an afternoon matinée, Wenatchee overwhelmed the 'Cats and won by a score of 14-2, aided by four errors.

The next team to visit Victoria was the Yakima Valley Pippins. In the opening game of the series, Samuel Brunning worked four innings, then was relieved by Garrison Ritter, who recorded the "W." The 'Cats scored a run in the second inning to take the early lead when Jeddediah Fagg doubled, Dustin Miller walked, Hayden

In the opening game of the series, Samuel Brunning worked four innings, then was relieved by Garrison Ritter, who recorded the "W."

Jaco was hit by a pitch, and a double steal scored the run from third base. Five runs came home in the second inning to end the scoring, but it was enough for a 6-3 victory. Trey Bigford had a single, scored a run, and drove in a run, while Jeddediah Fagg had a double and scored two runs. Game two was a close one. Victoria scored three runs in the second inning, then added one in the fourth and two in the sixth to build up a 6-1 lead. However, Yakima mounted a late attack and scored four runs in the ninth inning to make the final score, 6-5. Hayden Jaco had a double and a home run, while Jack Smith had two singles. The 'Cats played small ball to success with three stolen bases (Jeddediah Fagg, Nathan Flores, and Hayden Jaco). The third game featured opening night starter Ethan Fox, who worked 3 1/3 innings and surrendered three runs on four hits as Yakima defeated Victoria 5-2. Nick Plaia led the offensive attack with a double and two singles, driving in one run, and Adam Imwalle added a triple.

With some time off, the 'Cats played an exhibition series against the Coquitlam Angels with former Toronto Blue Jays player Kelly Gruber as the honorary coach. Fans were able to meet the former all-star third baseman and get photos taken with him. The first game went to the home team, 4-1. Game two featured a Claire

With some time off, the 'Cats played an exhibition series against the Coquitlam Angels with former Toronto Blue Jays player Kelly Gruber as the honorary coach.

Eccles bobblehead to recognize her efforts as the first female player in the West Coast League. She had recently rejoined the team after playing softball for the UBC Thunderbirds. The 'Cats won that game to sweep the series. After surrendering a single run in the second inning, they came back with four in the fourth to take the lead. Harrison Spohn singled to start things off, advanced to third on a Jeddediah Fagg double and scored on a Dustin Miller single. Silas Grinstead singled, advancing Miller to second, then both Fagg and Miller scored on a Caleb Ricketts single. Finally, Grinstead got home on a wild pitch. Victoria added a single run in the sixth and two in the seventh en route to a 7-4 decision.

Now it was time for a road trip, beginning in Kelowna. In the opening game, the 'Cats came from behind to take the match 13-7. After Victoria opened the scoring with a single run in the third, the Falcons replied with four. The 'Cats got those runs back in the fourth, then Kelowna got one back in the fifth. The teams traded two-run innings in the seventh and eighth, and the game went to extra innings. The 'Cats won the game with six runs in the 10th inning. The highlight of the game was a grand slam in the fourth inning by Nate Pecota, who ended the night with three hits, six runs batted in, and four runs scored. Cade Brown, Harrison Spohn, and Nick Plaia added doubles. Gunnar Friend secured the win as he pitched the ninth and 10th innings and gave up only one hit while striking out three. The second game went to the Falcons by a score of 7-1 as their starter, Jared Akin, worked eight innings, allowing only one run on seven hits while walking two and striking out five. The sole highlight for Victoria was an eighth-inning homer by Trey Bigford for their only run of the game. The 'Cats bounced back to take the rubber match 4-3. They scored two in the second and one in the fifth to take a 3-0 lead, but the Falcons responded with two in the fifth and one in the sixth to tie the score. The winning run came on a Jeddediah Fagg homer in the eighth inning, and the game ended with the potential game-tying run for Kelowna left on third base. Garrett Goodall got the start and worked 5 2/3 innings before being relieved by Nathan Walker, Tyler Yoshihara, and Po-Jui Huang.

Next on the agenda was a series against Port Angeles. The Lefties scored early and often in a 10-4 defeat of the 'Cats. The only Victoria player to get more than one hit was Nicky Gibbs, who had two. Nick Plaia had a home run in a losing cause. The middle game was a lot closer, and when it was all over, the HarbourCats secured a 6-5 victory largely due to a big five-run sixth inning. It began when Mat-

The middle game was a lot closer, and when it was all over, the HarbourCats secured a 6-5 victory largely due to a big five-run sixth inning.

thew Clayton walked and was driven home by a Jack Smith triple. He then came home on a Dustin Demeter put-out. Hayden Jaco walked, advanced on a Harrison Spohn double and scored on a wild pitch while Spohn scored on an error. Trey Bigford, who had advanced to first on the error, eventually scored on a second Lefties error. Carter Loewen, who worked the sixth inning, was credited with the win. The series concluded with a Father's Day matinée in which the Lefties prevailed 8-7. Playing before a crowd of 3,021, the Lefties took an early lead and never trailed.

NICK PLAIA IN ACTION

Michael Malinchak had two hits, including a double, and Cade Brown had two singles. Nick Plaia had a double as a pinch-hitter. The teams played errorless ball.

On the road in Bend, the HarbourCats shut out the Elks by a score of 6-0 behind the five innings of three-hit pitching by Tyler Thomas. Jeddediah Fagg had a double, while Harrison Spohn had a triple and drove in four runs. The next evening, the 'Cats again prevailed, but it was a much closer game. The fifth inning proved to be the deciding factor in the game. With the bases loaded, Caleb Rickett hit a single, Nick Plaia hit a double, and Dustin Miller singled. Starter Justin Solt worked five innings and gave up two runs on five hits with two strikeouts. The series concluded with a close 7-6 loss to the Elks. Despite four doubles by Nick Plaia, Harrison Spohn, Dustin Demeter, and Dustin Miller, the 'Cats failed to capitalize with runners on base and stranded eight. Jeddediah Fagg homered to tie the score in the ninth inning, but the Elks pushed ahead the winning run in the 10th.

Then, it was home for three games against Bellingham. In the opening game, Victoria scored three in the first inning. Jason Willow reached first base on an error and came home on a Jeddediah Fagg double. Jack Smith then hit a home run to plate two runs. The 'Cats scored a run in the third when Jeddediah Fagg homered and, after the Bells had tied the score in the fifth inning, took the lead in the fifth on a Jason Willow homer and got what would prove to be the winning run when Nick Plaia drove in Michael Malinchak who had earlier singled. The final score of 6-5 for the 'Cats snapped the Bells' eight-game winning streak. In the next game, the Bellingham bats came alive and pounded fifteen hits in a 10-2 thumping of Victoria. Harrison Spohn was the star of the game for the home team, going three-for-four and stealing a base. In the series-ending matinée, the Bells prevailed 4-3 in a hard-fought match. After Bellingham scored singles runs in three innings to take the lead, the 'Cats tied the score in the fifth, taking advantage of a huge error by the Bells. After Dustin Demeter walked, Adam Imwalle singled, and Cade Brown walked, Jason Willow hit a single, and the three base runners scored on an error by the right fielder. However, the Bells got a single run in the eighth to win the game and send the 1,931 fans home unhappy on Dog in the Park Day.

On the road in Walla Walla, the HarbourCats came from behind to defeat the

On the road in Walla Walla, the HarbourCats came from behind to defeat the Sweets in extra innings.

Sweets in extra innings. Down 3-0 after the first inning, they scored a run in the third when Jason Willow, who had advanced to first base on an error and moved to second on a Jack Smith single, scored on a Nicky Gibbs single. Dustin Demeter led off the fourth inning to narrow the lead and also scored in the sixth on an error to narrow the lead to 4-3. The Sweets plated two in the sixth, but Victoria got those back in the seventh and added one in the ninth to tie the game. With the game in extra innings, Michael Malinchak singled, moved to third on a Jason Willow single and scored on a sacrifice fly by Jack Smith. Tyler Yoshihara was credited with the win after working four hitless innings, giving up one walk and striking out four. The Sweets got their revenge in the middle game when they upended the 'Cats by a score of 6-1. The sole run came early as Jeddediah Fagg singled, advanced to third base on an error, and scored on a Michael Malinchak sacrifice fly. Starter Justin Solt gave up only three hits, but one was a three-run homer in the fourth that pretty well put the game on ice. In game three, a huge seven-run third inning propelled the Walla Walla Sweets past the visiting Victoria HarbourCats by a score of 9-7. The 'Cats offence came from Cade Brown's double and home run and doubles by

Reaffirming Canadian citizenship with
Gerry Pash and Harvey the HarbourCat

Jeddediah Fagg and Tanner Haney. Starter Owen Sharts was pulled after nine runs, only two of which were earned as the defence committed four errors over the course of the game. The loss put the team's season record at 10-11.

An all-Canadian matchup centered around Canada Day. Fresh off six straight victories, the Kelowna Falcons extended that streak to seven with an 8-4 victory over the HarbourCats. Four runs in the second inning gave the visitors the lead. Nicky Gibbs belted a two-run homer to narrow the lead in the fifth inning, but Kelowna got two in the sixth to extend their lead. The remainder of the home scoring came in the seventh. Dustin Demeter and Nick Plaia both finished two-for-four on the night. A crowd of 3,135 witnessed fireworks on the field in the second game as the 'Cats upended the Falcons 18-7. Garrett Goodall got the start and worked five innings, giving up only one run on six hits while walking one and striking out six. Ryan Rutherford, Jacob Potter, Po-Jui Huang, and Tyler Yoshihara finished the game in relief. Dustin Demeter had a monster night for the 'Cats with four hits, including a double and a homer, driving in eight runs. Nick Plaia went three-for-four with a double, triple, and a homer and three walks; he also scored four runs. Others to hit doubles were Cade Brown, Michael Malinchak, Dustin Miller, and Tanner Haney, while additional homers came from Dustin Demeter and Dustin

One of the features of the Canada Day festivities was a ceremony before the game in which citizens could reaffirm their citizenship

Miller. After the game, the fans were entertained by a spectacular fireworks show to celebrate Canada Day. One of the features of the Canada Day festivities was a ceremony before the game in which citizens could reaffirm their citizenship by taking the oath that new Canadians swear when they become Canadians. Kelowna spoiled the show by upending the HarbourCats 6-3. Blake Wagenseller hit his first home run of the season to lead off the game and stole a base. Despite scoring single runs in the next three innings, the 'Cats were unable to hold the lead as they surrendered one in the fourth, two in the fifth, two in the eighth, and one in the ninth.

In Bellingham, the 'Cats halted the Bells' win streak at four games with a close

After the game, the fans were treated to a fabulous fireworks show.

4-3 victory. Ethan Fox got the start and worked five innings of scoreless baseball, but his team couldn't get him any run support behind him. Bellingham got two runs in the seventh, but the 'Cats came back with two in the ninth to tie the game. In the 11th inning, Victoria scored twice, and the Bells could only manage one. Tyler Yoshihara got the win in relief. Dustin Demeter had two hits to lead the offence. The next game went to Victoria 4-2. They scored a run in the fifth on an error by the pitcher. After the Bells tied the score in their half of the inning, the 'Cats notched three runs in the 10th when Ethan Fox hit a double, advanced on a Harrison Spohn single, and both scored on a Caleb Ricketts home run. They then held on as the Bells got one run in their half of the inning and left the tying runs on base. Joe Casey and Ryan Ober, who helped lead the Oregon State Beavers to the 2018 NCAA College World Series title the prior week, were in the lineup and played their first game as HarbourCats. On Independence Day, the 'Cats spoiled the party with a 3-2 decision. Mason Shaw worked five innings of scoreless baseball, allowing only four hits and striking out one. Silas Grinstead led the offence with a pair of hits. After the game, the fans were treated to a fabulous fireworks show.

To keep in top playing form during some time off, the team played exhibition games against the Highline Bears of Seattle. The HarbourCats won both games to sweep the short series. In the first game, they won a close 5-4 contest as Joe Casey, Dustin Miller, and AJ Lewis hit doubles and Michael Malinchak homered. Team defence was stellar as the Bears had 10 hits but failed to bring them home. The second game was a one-sided contest as the 'Cats unleashed ten hits and scored 13 runs en route to a 13-1 decision. The coach made several substitutions as the score mounted so that 18 players had at least one at-bat. AJ Lewis and Blake Wagenseller had home runs, and Trey Bigford hit a double.

After travelling to Oregon, the HarbourCats played the Corvallis Knights. After taking a 2-0 lead in the first inning, they gave up five to the Knights and never really recovered, dropping a 9-8 decision. A rally in the sixth, seventh, and eighth innings fall just short. Michael Malinchak had three hits, including a double, drove in two runs, and scored one. Dustin Demeter also had three hits, driving in two runs. Game two was a close 2-1 victory for the Knights. The sole Victoria run came in the third inning and narrowed the lead to 2-1, but the 'Cats couldn't get any closer. Corvallis completed the series sweep with a convincing 10-2 drubbing of the HarbourCats. Scoring early and often, the home team built up a 10-0 lead before the 'Cats got on the board with a couple of runs in the ninth inning. Caleb Ricketts had two hits for Victoria in a losing cause, driving in the runs with a single.

Back home, the 'Cats entertained the Bend Elks and defeated them in a dramatic 5-4 come-from-behind game. Bend got on the board first with a single run in the first but the 'Cats plated two in the fourth to take a lead and added one more in the sixth. The Elks came back to tie the game and send it to extra innings. In the top of the 10th, they scored once but a two-run single by Jeddediah Fagg drove in two runs for the margin of victory. It was one of his three hits on the night as he returned to his early-season form. The 'Cats beat the Elks 6-3 in the second game. They built up a 5-0 lead before the Elks got on the board and coasted to the win. Mason Shaw worked five shutout innings and Justin Solt and Ping-Chun Ho finished the game. Jeddediah Fagg returned to his early season form and banged out three hits, while Hunter Vansau had two hits, including a homer. The final game went to the Elks by an 8-6 score. The lead changed hands often in this game, but

The 'Cats went into Cowlitz and narrowly defeated the Black Bears 4-3. Ethan Fox got the start and left after five innings with the game tied 3-3.

a four-run seventh inning sealed the deal for Bend. The 'Cats used seven pitchers, including starter Gunner Friend. Rowdey Jordan, Dustin Demeter, Matthew Clayton, and Ryan Ober all had doubles to lead the offence.

The 'Cats went into Cowlitz and narrowly defeated the Black Bears 4-3. Ethan

Fox got the start and left after five innings with the game tied 3-3. The winning run came in the seventh inning when Nick Plaia doubled and scored on an error. The middle game of the series was another one-run decision. The 'Cats scored a run in each of the fourth and fifth innings, then allowed the Black Bears to tie the score. They won it in the 10th inning when Joe Casey singled, advanced to second on a Blake Wagenseller single, and then scored on a Dustin Miller single. Hunter Vansau added to his home run total with a solo blast in the fourth inning. Cowlitz won the final game of the series with a close 6-5 decision. The 'Cats scored three runs in the second inning when Nick Plaia doubled, Matthew Clayton singled, AJ Lewis singled, driving home Plaia, Cade Brown doubled to score Clayton, Tanner Haney singled, and Brown scored on a fielder's choice. They added two more in the fifth when Tanner Haney reached first base on an error and was brought home by a Dustin Demeter homer. Unfortunately, the team couldn't hold the lead and let the Black Bears tie the score, sending the game to extra innings. Cowlitz scored the winning run in the 13th inning, a disappointing end to the match.

It was then time for the All-star break, and the game was played in Port Angeles. Jeddediah Fagg, Garrett Goodall, and Tyler Yoshihara were chosen to represent the Victoria HarbourCats. Fagg had one walk and one strikeout, while Goodall threw one inning with one run on two hits and one shutout. Yoshihara went one inning and surrendered three runs on two hits with one walk. The North Team defeated the South Team by a score of 10-6.

Regular season play resumed with the Corvallis Knights in town. The opening game of the series was a narrow come-from-behind win for the Knights, 3-2. The 'Cats took an early lead with a run in the third inning on a Nick Plaia homer; Corvallis tied it in the sixth and notched two in the ninth to take a lead. A ninth-inning comeback for Victoria fell one run short. Dustin Demeter hit a homer to narrow the lead, and the game ended with the tying run sitting on third base. The next evening, the 'Cats had a more productive game and defeated the Knights, 11-5. Corvallis scored in the first inning, but the HarbourCats got that back when Nick Plaia singled, stole second base, and scored on a Hunter Vansau single. They added two in the fifth, two in the seventh, and three in the eighth. Mason Shaw went 5 2/3 innings for the win, allowing four runs (two earned) on six hits, one walk, and eight strikeouts. Ryan Ober had four hits, including a home run, and drove in four runs. Cade Brown and Hayden Jaco hit doubles, and Nick Plaia, AJ Lewis, and Jaco had stolen bases. The HarbourCats won the final game with a 15-6 decision with 5,165 fans in attendance. With this victory, they snapped a losing streak against the Knights that had reached six games, dating back to the playoffs the prior season.

Before the game, head coach Brian McRae and assistant coach Todd Haney conducted a free MLB Players Alumni Association clinic for Island youth baseball players.

Trailing 4-1 in the fourth inning, they plated six runs in the fourth and added eight more over the last four innings. Jeddediah Fagg, Harrison Spohn, Nicky Gibbs, Ryan Ober, and Tanner Haney all had home runs for the 'Cats. Hunter Vansau had three hits and scored two runs, while Caleb Ricketts scored one run and had three hits. Landon Anderson worked six innings, allowing four runs on six hits.

Before the game, head coach Brian McRae and assistant coach Todd Haney conducted a free MLB Players Alumni Association clinic for Island youth baseball players. They were joined by James Lofton and Shawn Chacon. The following week, McRae would be joined by former Blue Jays players Roberto Alomar, Lloyd Moseby, Jesse Barfield, Ricky Romero and J.P. Arencibia in the Toronto Blue Jays Academy Honda Super Camp. This not only helped young island players but also increased awareness of the HarbourCats organization.

The next series was a cross-strait affair with the Port Angeles Lefties. In game one, the home team came from behind to defeat the 'Cats 9-6. The Victoria offence was led by Jeddediah Fagg, who went three-for-four at the plate, scoring two runs and driving in two. Rowdey Jordan hit a home run in a losing cause. In the second game, the HarbourCats took an early lead but surrendered six runs in the seventh inning and fell 8-6. Michael Malinchak had two hits and drove in two runs, while Hunter Vansau hit another homer to lead the offence. In the final game of the series, the 'Cats fell behind early and could never recover in a 9-7 loss. Rowdey Jordan, Ryan Ober, Matt Clayton, Blake Wagenseller, and Dustin Miller all had doubles to lead the offence. A ninth-inning comeback fell a bit short.

Seeking to achieve some success on the field, the HarbourCats entertained the Walla Walla Sweets. Game one was a satisfying 10-3 win for the home team. Gunnar Friend worked five innings of scoreless ball, allowing four hits, one walk, and striking out three. Hunter Vansau hit his fourth home run of the season to extend his career franchise record to 12, two better than the mark set by Kevin Collard, and added a double and a single. Other home runs were hit by Dustin Demeter and Jeddediah Fagg. Interestingly, the HarbourCats were missing six players and two assistant coaches who had been suspended after a dugout-emptying fight in

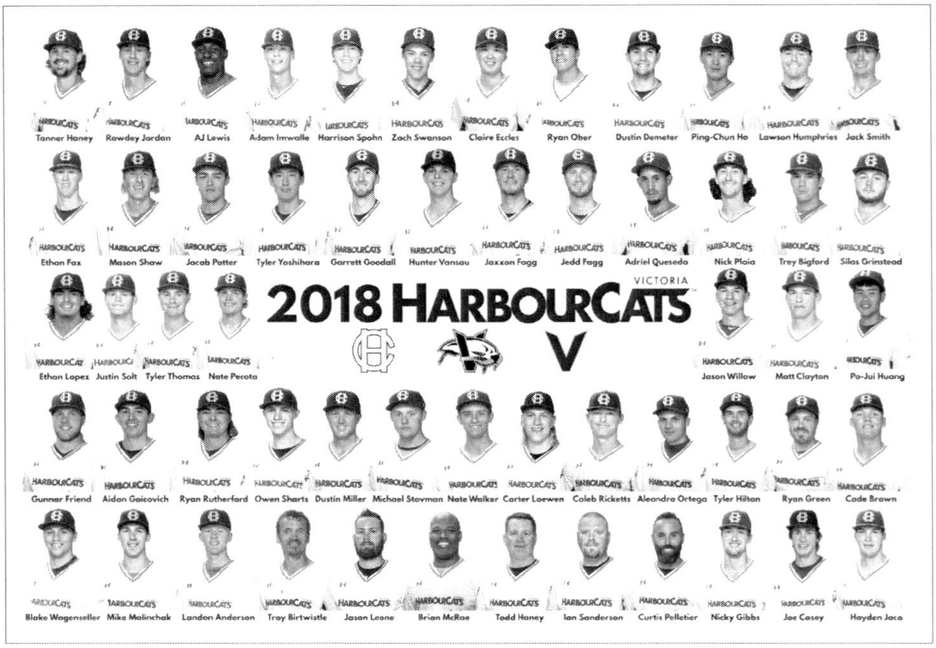

VICTORIA HARBOURCATS 2018 TEAM PHOTO

Port Angeles. The next night, the game was closer, but it was a hometown victory. The 'Cats used five pitchers—Mason Shaw, Mikey Musselwhite, Hayden Jaco, Justin Solt, and Aidan Goicovich—to secure the 4-3 win. A home run by Harrison Spohn in the seventh inning broke the tie and was the margin of victory. Matt Clayton went two-for-three at the plate and drove in two runs to lead the offence. The HarbourCats secured the series sweep with a 6-4 decision in game three. They scored two runs in the first two innings and added two more in the seventh for the victory. Rowdey Jordan was the hitting star of the match, with three hits, including a two-run homer in the seventh inning. Landon Anderson had a strong game on the mound, working six innings of shutout ball with only three hits and two walks allowed while striking out three.

With the weekend free, the 'Cats played a series of exhibition games. First on the agenda was the Nanaimo senior men's team followed by two games against the Mavericks League all-stars who would be playing in the provincial championships. In one of the most interesting games of the season, the HarbourCats entertained Universidad de ciencias de la culutra Fisica y el deporte de Mantanzas, translated as the University of Physical Sciences and Sports Culture of Mantanzas, in the town of Unión de Reyes. The young players had been playing games this summer against Vancouver Island baseball teams and were aged 16-19. Alejandro Ortego Lopez, from the Cuban squad pitched for the HarbourCats in a game against a mid-island senior team in Nanaimo that had to be called with the score 7-7 after six innings as Serauxman Stadium lacked night lighting. Adriel Quesada Peña pitched for the 'Cats in 5-4 win over the Victoria Mavericks. After that game, fans attended a concert by the band Chilliwack. The final game of the weekend featured the Cuban team playing the HarbourCats. The young visitors played with passion for baseball and showed why they are so well received at home in defeating the Victoria team, 8-4. The HarbourCats players were impressed with their work ethic and how excited they got over almost every play. Fans were left amazed at some of the defensive plays the young Cubans made. There is a reason why they do so well in the Matanzas provincial championships.

Regular play resumed with the HarbourCats on the road in Yakima Valley. They started off well in the first game with nine runs in the first three innings but let their opponents back into the game, and with the score tied 9-9, Yakima walked it off in the ninth inning on three singles. Nick Plaia was the offensive star for the 'Cats with three hits, including a double, scoring three runs and driving in one. Hunter Vansau also had three hits, including a double, scoring two runs and batting in one. Hayden Jaco had a double and Ryan Ober added a triple. Game two was tied in the fifth inning when the Pippins scored twice in the seventh inning to take the lead. The game was won in the ninth inning with the 'Cats sent nine men to the plate and scored six runs to win the game, 8-4. With the bases loaded after singles by

With the bases loaded after singles by Michael Malinchak and Rowdey Jordan and Harrison Spohn hit by a pitch, Nick Plaia hit a sacrifice fly to score the first run.

Michael Malinchak and Rowdey Jordan and Harrison Spohn hit by a pitch, Nick Plaia hit a sacrifice fly to score the first run. Dustin Miller drove in two runs with a double, then scored on a Jeddediah Fagg double. He crossed the plate on a Ryan Ober single who notched the final run on a balk. Aidan Goiscovich got the win in relief of Gunnar Friend. The final game of the series went to the HarbourCats in a come-from-behind 6-5 decision. Trailing 3-1 after five innings, they scored three in the sixth to take the lead, then watched as the Pippins got two runs in the eighth to take the lead. Two runs in the top of the ninth gave the 'Cats the lead for good. Jeddediah and Jaxxon Fagg had two hits each to lead the offence, while Trey Bigford got the win in relief with 1 2/3 innings of one-hit ball.

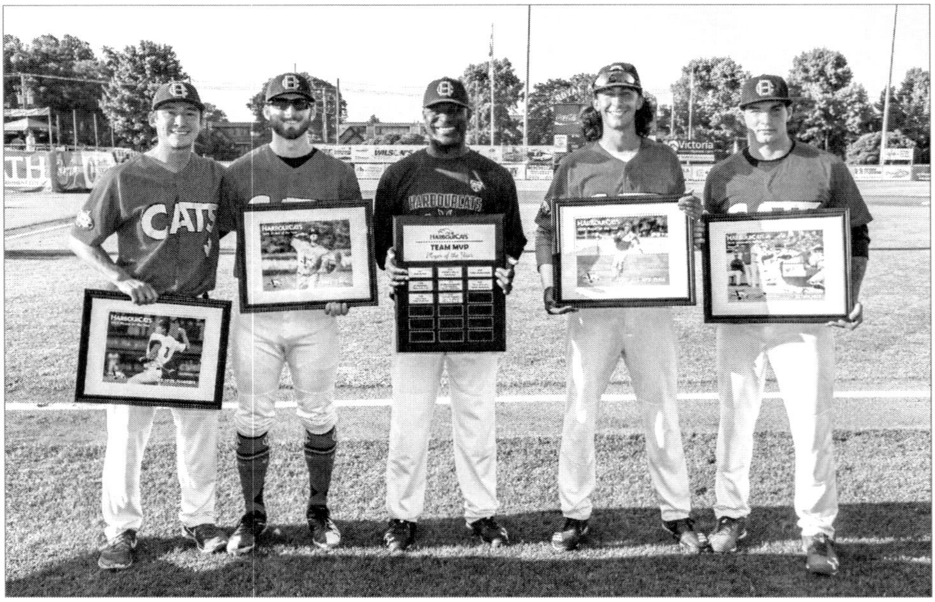

WINNERS OF YEAR-END HONOURS

Hopes for a playoff berth got stalled in Wenatchee when the 'Cats fell 7-3 to the AppleSox. Wenatchee scored all their seven runs in the third inning on starter Mason Shaw, and the team just couldn't recover. Jaxxon Fagg had a pair of hits and drove in one run, while Jeddediah Fagg and Tanner Haney had doubles. With the game tied 1-1 after five innings of game two, the AppleSox counted four runs en route to a 5-2 victory. Caleb Ricketts and Michael Malinchak had two hits each for the losing team. The home team swept the series with an 11-4 decision over the HarbourCats. Down 6-2 in the fifth inning, the 'Cats could only manage two in the eighth, which made the score closer, but when the AppleSox plated five in the eighth, the game was essentially over. Victoria's limited offence was led by doubles from Dustin Miller, Jeddediah Fagg, Nicky Gibbs, and Trey Bigford.

Managing partner Jim Swanson received a surprise when some of the team's sponsors recognized his 50th birthday with a full-colour ad in the *Times Colonist*.

Hoping to keep their slim playoff hope alive, the HarbourCats played their final homestand against the Portland Pickles. Gunnar Friend got the start and worked six innings of three-hit ball with no runs scored and three strikeouts. Lawson Humphries worked two innings, giving up two runs on three hits, and Tyler Yoshihara pitched the ninth inning and held the Pickles off the board to preserve a 4-2 victory. Rowdey Jordan went two-for-three at the plate, including a triple, while Hunter Vansau had another home run to increase his franchise record. Wearing their throwback baby blue Victoria Mussels jerseys, the 'Cats offence came to life as they crushed the Pickles 13-6 in a game that took almost three hours to play. Three runs in the first frame and four in the second put the team ahead 7-3, and they never looked back. Jaxxon Fagg's three-run homer set the pace for the game in the first inning, and Hunter Vansau's grand slam in the second put the game on ice. Mason Shaw got the start and worked 2 1/3 innings before he was relieved by Adriel Quesada who completed 3 2/3 innings with two runs on four hits and got the win. It all came down to the final game of the season with 3,076 fans in attendance. The dream came to a crashing end when the Pickles demolished the HarbourCats by a score of 10-3. The team only managed three hits off Portland pitching.

Before the game, Nick Plaia, who stole a club record 19 bases in the season, was named HarbourCats MVP, and Hunter Vansau had his jersey retired and added to the HarbourCats Wall of Honour. He had set the franchise record of 14 home runs over two seasons. The HarbourCats again topped the league in regular season attendance with 62,599 fans through the 2018 season. Garrett Goodall and Tyler Yoshihara were named Pitchers of the Year, and Hayden Jaco won the initial Community Service Award.

Nick Plaia, who stole a club record 19 bases in the season, was named HarbourCats MVP, and Hunter Vansau had his jersey retired and added to the HarbourCats Wall of Honour.

In late August, Victoria again hosted the Canadian senior men's baseball championships, with games at Lambrick Park and Royal Athletic Park. Eight former HarbourCats played on the Victoria Mavericks: Alex Rogers, Brady Rogers, Austin Russell, Connor Russell, Dylan Thorp, Charlie Strandlund, Eric Hegadoren, and Brodan Bydeweg. The team representing British Columbia defeated the Victoria team 4-2 in the final.

In September, the WCL announced that it had added a twelfth franchise: the Ridgefield Raptors, which would begin play in the 2019 season. The league would now feature a balanced divisional alignment with two six-team divisions representing the North and South. The new season would start on June 4, 2019, with the HarbourCats on the road in Wenatchee.

8

2019: Little Did We Know It Would Be Our Last For a Couple of Years

In early January, fan favourite Alex De Goti, also known as "Mr. HarbourCat," returned to Victoria to help coach McRae with a youth clinic at the Pacific Institute for Sports Education. He reflected on his time here and noted that "It's a great city with great fans." He was preparing for another season in the Houston Astros farm season at Round Rock, Texas, to play with the Triple-A team. On the business side of baseball, General Manager Brad Norris-Jones announced that he was leaving the HarbourCats after six seasons to join Pacific FC as the new executive vice president of operations.

In other news, the ownership group of the Victoria HarbourCats informed the West Coast League of its intent to add a team in Nanaimo that would play out of Serauxman Stadium. The idea had the support of WCL Commissioner Rob Neyer and Nanaimo Mayor Leonard Krog. The group planned to work with the City of

In May, the HarbourCats signed a deal with Duncan-based Red Arrow Brewery that made that company the official beer supplier of the franchise.

Nanaimo to upgrade the historic venue, adding lights and other amenities to bring it up to WCL standards. They would use the very successful Victoria franchise as a model.

In May, the HarbourCats signed a deal with Duncan-based Red Arrow Brewery that made that company the official beer supplier of the franchise. With the

HARVEY THE HARBOURCAT RIDES THE ZIPLINE

deal, HarbourCats Ballpark Blonde, Piggy Pale Ale, and Kustom Kolsch would be featured at all home games and would also be available in liquor outlets across Vancouver Island and on tap in a selected number of bars and restaurants.

After Brian McRae was unable to fulfil his role as head coach for the 2019 season, assistant coach Todd Haney was promoted to the position. As the director of player development for the NCAA Division 1 Texas State University Bobcats in San Marcos, he would use his knowledge of local players to bring them to the HarbourCats for summer baseball.

Building on the success of the game last season with the Unión de Reyes team from Cuba, the HarbourCats decided to act as a baseball ambassador. The Port Angeles Lefties would be coming to Victoria on June 2 to play the Cuban team at Royal Athletic Park. Due to politics, they would never be able to do this in their home country, and it was too good an opportunity for them to turn down. In the evening, the Victoria team would play the Cubans. They would also play them later in the month. For some reason, the score of the game against Port Angeles was never recorded, but the first game against the HarbourCats was a 10-2 victory for the visitors. A game on June 10 resulted in a 5-2 decision for the Cubans.

In May, the HarbourCats announced signings for the 2018 season. Back for another season was Garrett Goodall from Nanaimo. Joining him on the team would be Cade Smith (University of Hawaii) and Joe Butler (Illinois State). A new addition to the ballpark would be a zipline with about 200 fans being able to use it at every game. The zipline was installed in extra space beyond the outfield fence. Two telephone poles were set up in the park by Telus to anchor the line, and staff from WildPlay Element Parks, TRB Construction, and Chinook Scaffolding all worked to bring the line to reality. Fans who wished to ride the zipline were encouraged to purchase tickets for $12.50 at the team office before the games. Any unsold tickets would be sold at the games for $15.00. Of course, fans had to have a game ticket to ride.

In Major League Baseball news, former HarbourCat Andrew Vaughn was selected third overall in the first round of the 2019 draft by the Chicago White Sox. He had played seven games for the 'Cats before playing for the USA Baseball College team.

Cade Smith was selected as the starter for the season opener, continuing the tradition of giving BC players this honour as Victoria opened the 2019 season in Wenatchee against the AppleSox. With the HarbourCats leading 2-1 in the fourth inning, they surrendered two runs to the home team, exchanged two runs in the seventh, and gave up two in the eighth for a final score of 7-4. Smith went six innings, allowing four runs on three hits, before being relieved by Ryan Watson, who finished the game with four runs on five hits. The two runs scored by the 'Cats in the seventh inning were unearned because of an error. The teams committed five errors, demonstrating early-season rust. Griffin Paxton led the offence with a hit and a run batted in, while Nick Adams, Frankie Niemann, and Parker Bramlett had the other hits for Victoria. Todd Haney got his first win as head coach as the

Todd Haney got his first win as head coach as the team bounced back in game two with an 8-3 victory. They scored four runs in the first inning.

team bounced back in game two with an 8-3 victory. They scored four runs in the first inning. Parker Bramlett led off and reached first on an error, stole second, advanced to third on a passed ball, and scored on a Matt Clayton single. The teams exchanged runs in the third inning, but the 'Cats outscored the AppleSox 3-2 over the last three innings for the victory. Matt Clayton and Tanner Haney had two hits for Victoria, and Aaron Celestino worked six innings, giving up one run on four hits with five strikeouts. The HarbourCats won the series with an 8-5 defeat of the AppleSox in the third game. They scored five runs in the second inning and added three more runs in later innings to secure the win. Frankie Niemann had five hits, including a double to lead the offensive surge while Griffin Paxton and Nick Adams contributed triples.

SKYDIVERS ENTERTAIN THE CROWD AND DELIVER THE GAME BALL

The home opener began with sky divers and a military flyover. The players wore new Victoria Police Department-themed third jerseys. Playing against Corvallis, a WCL powerhouse, the HarbourCats took a one-run lead in the fifth inning when Tanner Haney hit a lead-off home run but the Knights counted one in the sixth and won the game 2-1 with a single run in the eighth. Nick Plaia struck out with the bases loaded in the bottom half of the ninth inning to end any comeback. Dillon Larson got the start and worked five innings of scoreless baseball before being

The home opener began with sky divers and a military flyover. The players wore new Victoria Police Department-themed third jerseys.

relieved by Grayson Jones, Ryan Watson, and Luka Green. The second game could best be described as a learning experience as the Knights upended the 'Cats 12-7 in a game that took over three hours to complete. They scored early and often and had a 10-0 lead before Victoria got on the board. A five-run sixth inning made the score closer, but that was the end of the offence. Frankie Niemann again led the offence with three hits, including a double, and drove in two runs. Nate Pecota and Griffin Paxton also had doubles in a losing cause. Australian Josh Gessner got the start and was rocked early for seven runs. Game three was Alex De Goti bobblehead day. Perhaps that inspired the team as they upended the Knights by a score of 4-1. Nate Pecota led off with a double, advanced to third on a fielder's choice, and scored on an error by the second baseman. Frankie Niemann, who had reached base on a fielder's choice, scored when Emilio Nogales hit a double. The 'Cats added single runs in the third and fourth innings, while Cade Smith worked four innings, giving up one run on four hits. Calvin Turchin hurled four scoreless innings, and Matt Amrhein handled the ninth inning. After the game, Victoria pitcher Josh Gressner left the team as he had turned pro with the Philadelphia Phillies and would head to play Single-A ball.

Next on the agenda was a three-city road trip. After a ferry trip and a long bus ride, the team arrived in Yakima Valley for a two-game series against the Pippins. The 'Cats took an early one-run lead but gave up three to fall behind. Aaron Celestino got the start and worked five innings with four runs on eight hits and three

Next on the agenda was a three-city road trip. After a ferry trip and a long bus ride, the team arrived in Yakima Valley for a two-game series.

strikeouts. Frankie Niemann and Emilio Nogales had doubles for Victoria in a 4-2 defeat. The HarbourCats took the second game of the series by a score of 5-3. They won the game with four runs with two out in the eighth inning to erase a 3-1 deficit. Matt Clayton walked, Tyler Pettit hit a single, Frankie Niemann drove in Clayton with a single, Harrison Spohn made it to first base on a dropped third strike, and Pettit scored on the play. After Spohn advanced to second on a wild pitch, Parker Bramlett hit a single and Niemann and Spohn scored after stolen bases. Dillon Larson made the start and worked 3 2/3 innings and surrendered two runs on four hits, Joseph Brandon gave up one run on five hits in 3 1/3 innings of work, and Luka Green and Matt Amrhein held the Pippin scoreless over the last two innings.

In Kelowna, the HarbourCats scored early and often in a 15-5 drubbing of the Falcons. Tyson Hays went five-for-five at the plate in his HarbourCat debut, including a triple and two homers, drove in seven runs, and scored three. Nick Plaia and Nick Adams also homered for the 'Cats. Ryan Watson got the start, working six innings giving up one run on four hits, walking four and striking out six. Game two was one-sided as well. The HarbourCats broke the game open in the fourth inning when they scored five times on only three hits. While Parker Bramlett and Tyler Pettit hit singles, and Emilio Nogales had a double, the scoring was assisted by two walks and two errors. Jack Hyde was on the mound for the 'Cats. He worked six innings, allowing one run on four hits while striking out seven. Branson Wilson, Jaiden Beck, and Derek Salata all pitched one inning in relief in the 12-1 decision. Kelowna narrowly edged the HarbourCats in the final game of the series, 4-3. With the game tied 3-3 after regular time, it went to extra innings, where the Falcons scored for the walk-off victory.

Back home at Wilson's Group Stadium at Royal Athletic Park, the HarbourCats welcomed the Bend Elks and defeated them 5-3 in the opening game of the series. After the visitors took the lead in the second inning and added one more in the fourth, the Victoria offence went to work. Griffin Paxton started the inning off with a single, advanced to second on a Chase Wehsener single, reached third on an error, and scored on a Tyson Hays sacrifice fly. Wehsener then crossed the plate on a Tanner Rempel single. Parker Bramlett, Nick Pecota, Jason Willow, and Tyson Hays all had stolen bases. Before the game, Claire Eccles, the first and only female player in the West Coast League, had her number retired and placed in the Ring of Honour. She was recognized for the impact she had on girls in sports and hoped that others would follow her example. In the second game, the 'Cats jumped off to a 6-0 lead in the first inning and never looked back. Newcomer Chase Wehsener continued with his hot bat, going three-for-four at the plate, including a double, while Frankie Niemann was four-for-five and drove in four runs. Ty Schindel, Nick Plaia, and Tyler Paro all had triples in the decisive 17-7 victory. Playing in front of hundreds of screaming school children, the 'Cats swept the series with another one-sided decision, this time by a 17-5 score. After taking a 2-1 lead in the second inning, the home team put the game away with seven runs in the fourth inning and repeated that feat in the sixth. Jason Willow had three hits, including a home run, drove in three runs and scored twice, while Frankie Niemann had three hits, including a double and a home run, drove in four runs, and scored three. Chase Meidroth had a double and a triple, Tanner Haney had a double, Matt Turner added a home run, as did Kyle Harper as the HarbourCats pounded out 19 hits. Dillon Larson worked the first three innings, giving up four runs on five hits. Luka Green had two innings of work and allowed only one hit and struck out three, while Derek Salata and Jaiden Beck worked the last four innings.

In Yakima, the HarbourCats continued their winning ways over the Pippins. Starting with five runs in the first inning when they sent ten men to the plate, they cruised to victory. Parker Bramlett started the hit parade with a double, while Chase Wehsener, Frankie Niemann, Griffin Paxton, Nick Adams, Nate Pecota, and

Trevor Paro all hit singles. They added two in the third, four in the sixth, and two in the seventh on their way to a 13-4 decision. The team then moved on to Portland, where they narrowly lost to the Pickles, 6-5. They started well with a 4-0 lead after four innings but surrendered four runs to the Pickles in the eighth inning and could not mount a comeback. Kyle Harper had two hits, including a home run, drove in two runs, and scored two, while Jason Willow, Tyson Hays, and Harrison Spohn had doubles. Game two was also a close decision. With the 'Cats up 2-0, the home team scored three runs in the eighth to take the lead and the 3-2 victory. Their offence was led by Nate Pecota's double and Kyle Harper's triple. The final game of the series went to Victoria in another close decision, 7-5. There were several lead changes in the game, and it wasn't until the ninth inning that the 'Cats took the lead. Jason Willow had three hits, including a double and a home run, drove in two runs, and scored two, while Chase Wehsener, with a double and a homer, drove in three runs and scored twice. The team's fortune had surely turned around once those two talented players arrived in town.

Wearing their red Canada-themed jerseys in advance of July 1 celebrations, the HarbourCats defeated the visiting Wenatchee AppleSox by a score of 14-5. They started early with four runs in the first inning when Nate Pecota's single scored Chase Wehsener and Nick Plaia, and there could have been more runs as the bases were left loaded. After Wenatchee scored three to make it close, the 'Cats replied

Wearing their red Canada-themed jerseys in advance of July 1 celebrations, the HarbourCats defeated the visiting Wenatchee AppleSox by a score of 14-5.

with four more in the fourth that including a two-run triple by Griffin Paxton that scored Chase Wehsener and Jason Willow. They notched two more in the fifth, and four more in the seventh with the big hit a grand slam homer by pitch hitter Nick Adams. Nick Plaia had a three-hit night, driving in three runs and scoring two. After the game, it was announced that Chase Wehsener had been named WCL Player of the Week for going 12-for-28 with two homers. The middle game of the series was much closer and was not decided until the 10th inning. Victoria took a three-run lead in the first inning as Parker Bramlett and Jason Willow, who had singled, were driven home by Frankie Niemann and Chase Wehsener was brought home by a Griffin Paxton groundout. Wenatchee scored three in the fourth and one in the fifth to take the lead, but the HarbourCats tied the game in the bottom of the ninth inning when Parker Bramlett, who had advanced to first base after being hit by a pitch, advanced on an error by the pitcher and scored on an error by the first baseman. That set the stage for the 10th inning, where Tyler Pettit singled and was driven home by a Matt Turner double. Matt Amrhein got the win in relief. The game featured a give-away of a free funeral, a promotion that garnered worldwide

Game three was a slugfest for both teams as they blasted out 29 between them; the game took four hours and twenty minutes to play.

press. The winner, who was 33, said he didn't plan on using his winnings soon. Game three was a slugfest for both teams as they blasted out 29 between them; the game took four hours and twenty minutes to play. Wenatchee got on the board early with a six-run first inning that chased starter DJ Peters. The HarbourCats responded with three in the second, leaving the bases loaded. After the AppleSox extended their lead with two in the third, the home team notched six big runs in the fourth, added one in the fifth, and two in the sixth to take an 11-8 lead. However, college baseball being the game it is, that lead was erased with four runs for the Sox in the eighth. In the 11th, the 'Cats walked it off when Jason Willow, who had reached first on a single and advanced to third on a Tyson Hays single, scored the winning run on a wild pitch, sending the crowd of 1,568 home happy.

Next to come to town were the Kelowna Falcons. The 'Cats scored twice in the second inning and never looked back in defeating the Falcons 5-2. Parker Bramlett, Griffin Paxton, and Emilio Nogales all had two-hit nights for the home team while Harrison Spohn hit a double. Jack Hyde started the game and worked five innings of two-hit, one-run ball, with one walk and four strikeouts, while Hunter Hennigh and Connor Barison came in in relief. In the second game, Victoria came from behind to take a 10-5 decision. Down 3-0 after the first inning, they capitalized on a five-run sixth inning to take the lead for good, adding a single run in the seventh and two in the eighth for insurance. Jason Willow had a triple and a homer while Parker Bramlett and Nick Plaia recorded doubles. The crowed of 4,533 enjoyed spectacular fireworks show after the game. In an all-Canadian matchup on Canada Day, the HarbourCats defeated the Falcons in a close game. Victoria took a 2-0 lead after five with single runs in the fourth and fifth innings, but Kelowna scored in the seventh and eighth to tie the score. The 'Cats got one back in the eighth but gave up the tying run to the Falcons in the ninth inning. That set the stage for a dramatic 10th inning. Kelowna took the lead with one run, and then with two out, Chase Wehsener scored Griffin Paxton, who had walked, and Nate Pecota, who had reached base on a fielder's choice, with his walk-off double. It was the seventh consecutive victory for the HarbourCats and moved them into first place in the North Division standings. After the game, Parker Bramlett was named the WCL's Player of the Week for his eight-for-eighteen week with seven walks and seven runs scored.

The team warmed up for the crucial series against the Bellingham Bells with an exhibition game against the Seattle City Selects. They won the game 6-3 as Chase Meidroth, Harrison Spohn, and Matt Clayton all hit doubles to lead the offence. Zach Swanson worked five innings, giving up two runs on three hits while striking out three. The Bellingham team put an end to the HarbourCats win streak with a decisive 12-2 decision. They scored early and often, including a seven-run fourth inning, which put the game out of reach. Victoria didn't score until the seventh inning and that was far too little, too late. The only significant hit was Emilio Nogales' double. In the second game of the series, the 'Cats bats went silent, and they were shut out, 8-0, logging only four hits. The Bellingham victory moved that team to within one game of the HarbourCats in the standings with one game to go – and they held the tiebreaker. Finally, the 'Cats got their game in order and defeated the Bells by a score of 8-1 to capture the first-half North Division crown and the playoff berth that went with it. Jack Neely threw the first four innings, allowing one run on no hits with three walks and four strikeouts, and Aaron Celestino worked five in relief with one hit, one walk, and four strikeouts. Jason Willow and Harrison Spohn hit homers, and Tyson Hays had a double to lead the offence.

The second half of the season began with a home series against the Ridgefield Raptors. The visitors won that match, 4-3, because of a three-run seventh inning.

The second half of the season began with a home series against the Ridgefield Raptors.

A HarbourCat ninth-inning rally fell one run short. Tyson Hays hit a homer, and Chase Meidroth had a double, while Tanner Haney had two hits and drove in a run. Game two also went the Raptors' way in an 8-5 decision that took almost four-

and-a-half hours to complete. The HarbourCats built up a 4-2 lead but gave up three runs in the ninth inning while only responding with one to tie the score after regulation play. The teams continued scoreless until the fourteenth inning when the Raptors scored three to take the lead, and the home team could not match them. Emilio Nogales had three hits for the 'Cats, while Jason Willow, Tyson Hays, and Nick Plaia had two each. The series concluded with a close 3-2 victory for the HarbourCats. Down 1-0 after the top of the first inning, they scored twice in their half of the inning to take the lead. The teams exchanged runs in the eighth, but that was the end of the scoring. Kyle Harper led the offence with a double and a home run while four pitchers worked to gain the victory. Dakota Hawkins worked five innings, with one run on four hits and five strikeouts, Hunter Hennigh worked two innings with one hit and three strikeouts, Luka Green had one inning with one run on one hit, and Matt Amrhein pitched the ninth inning for the save. Aaron Celestino was named the WCL Pitcher of the Week for his ten scoreless innings and 14 strikeouts in two games.

The HarbourCats then travelled to Ridgefield for a single game. Down early, they rallied with two runs in the third, sixth, and eighth and one in the ninth for an 8-2 decision. Calvin Turchin got the start for the 'Cats and worked six innings, allowing two runs on five hits with two strikeouts. Branson Wilson finished the game on the mound. Frankie Niemann led the offence with two hits while Nick Adams, Jason Willow, Chase Meidroth, and Tanner Haney contributed doubles.

Then it was on to Bend for a normal three-game series. In the opener, Victoria built up a 4-0 lead before the Elks got on the board, added four in the sixth, two in the seventh, and two in the ninth for a 12-3 victory. Chase Meidroth had four hits in the game, including a double and scored a run while Nick Plaia had a double and a home run to drive in two runs and Nate Pecota had two hits and scored twice. They followed this game with an equally impressive 13-4 decision. It was a close game with Bend leading 3-1 when the HarbourCats offence exploded for nine runs in the sixth inning to blow the game open. They sent fourteen men to the plate and capitalized on two Elks errors. Chase Wehsener reached base on an error and came home on Frankie Nieman's triple for the first run. He scored when

It was a close game with Bend leading 3-1 when the HarbourCats offence exploded for nine runs in the sixth inning to blow the game open.

Griffin Paxton advanced to first on an error. Tyler Pettit walked and then he and Paxton scored on a Chase Meidroth double. After stealing a base, Meidroth scored on a Ty Schindel single. Parker Bramlett was hit by a pitch, Nick Plaia walked, and with the bases loaded, Chase Wehsener drove home two runs with a single. After a Frankie Niemann walk, Kyle Harper hit a double to bring home Plaia and Wehsener. Three runs in the ninth inning were the icing on the cake. Although Victoria committed three errors, Bend had seven and that contributed to their downfall. The HarbourCats swept the series with a close 7-5 victory. Leading 2-0 in the sixth inning, they surrendered five to the Elks and had to come back for the victory with

Although Victoria committed three errors, Bend had seven and that contributed to their downfall.

one in the seventh and four in the eighth. Dakota Hawkins worked the first 5 1/3 innings and surrendered four runs (two earned) on five hits with two walks and two strikeouts, while Connor Barison had 2 1/3 innings of work with one run on two hits, two walks, and one strikeout to gain the win, and Matt Amrhein picked up the save with 1 1/3 innings of scoreless relief with two strikeouts.

Next on the road trip was a visit to Walla Walla. The first game went to the Sweets who outscored the 'Cats, 6-3. Nick Plaia and Harrison Spohn had doubles while Tyson Hays and Kyle Harper homered in a losing cause. In game two, the HarbourCats scored in the first inning with two out when Griffin Paxton walked, advanced to second on a Tyson Hays walk, and scored on Emilio Nogales' single. After the Sweets got that run back in the second, the 'Cats put up six in the fourth to end the scoring and ensure the victory. Emilio Nogales had two hits, including a home run, driving in two runs, Nick Adams added two of his own, with a homer, driving in one run, and Harrison Spohn had a double and a home run. Calvin Turchin went six innings for the 'Cats allowing one run on seven hits with one walk and three strikeouts and Connor Barison handled the last three. In the longest game of the season – five hours and 44 minutes – the HarbourCats outscored the Sweets 4-3 in nineteen innings for the longest in WCL history behind the 20-inning contest between Kitsap and Corvallis in 2009. Down 3-1, the 'Cats put up two in the ninth to tie after which the teams battled for what seemed like hours. The winning run was scored on a bases-loaded sacrifice fly by Chase Meidroth while Derek Salata, who entered the game in the 16th inning recorded his fourth shutout inning to preserve the victory. Nick Plaia's two-run homer had tied the score in the ninth inning. After the long game, the team made their way home and got a day off to prepare for the next home series.

Karen Doerksen, wife of the late Humboldt Broncos bus driver Glen Doerksen, and her family were the special guests at the first two Victoria-Yakima Valley games. Glen Doerksen was among the 16 people killed when the Saskatchewan Junior Hockey League Broncos team bus was hit by a semi-truck in April of 2018. John Wilson, one of the HarbourCats' owners and head of a family business, noted, "This is our way, as the HarbourCats, to show our love for one family that has been deeply impacted."

The HarbourCats scored early and put the game out of reach with six runs in both the sixth and seventh innings in a dynamic 17-2 victory. The bats came alive with eighteen hits including doubles by Jason Willow, Ty Schindel, and Emilio Nogales and a homer from Nate Pecota. Kyle Harper went four-for-five at the plate and drove in four runs while scoring two. Aaron Celestino went six innings on the mound shutting out the Pippins on nine hits while striking out eight. The middle game of the series was a 9-1 victory for the home team. Holding a slim one-run lead, the 'Cats scored four in the sixth to take the lead. Chase Meidroth had three hits on the evening, including a homer, and Parker Bramlett added a homer of his own. Dakota Hawkins got the start and went six innings, allowing three hits and no runs. He credited his teammates who made three double plays behind him and a diving catch in the outfield. The second game was a complete opposite of game one. After the 'Cats scored in the first inning to take an early lead, the Pippins came back with 12 runs including a seven-run sixth inning. Chase Wehsener and Kyle Sherick had home runs in the 12-4 loss.

The All-Star game was played in Bend and featured six HarbourCats who made a huge impact in the North Division's impressive 14-1 decision. The big difference in the game was a nine-run second inning in which the North sent 14 men to the plate. Parker Bramlett finished the game with four hits, driving in one run, and scoring one. Jason Willow had a double that drove in three runs, and he scored one run. Frankie Niemann had one hit, two walks, and scored a run. Nick Plaia

The All-Star game was played in Bend and featured six HarbourCats who made a huge impact in the North Division's impressive 14-1 decision.

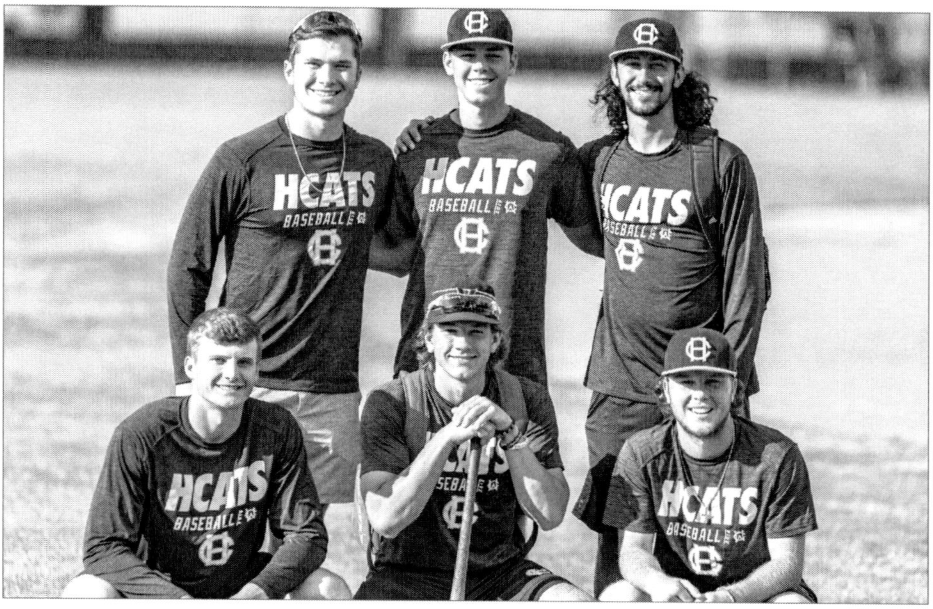

HarbourCats representative at the All Star game

reached base twice, once on a walk and the other on an infield error. Tyson Hays went two-for-two in his limited time in the game. Jack Hyde started for the North and allowed one hit in his one inning of work. It was a satisfying trip for the group, who would then join their teammates in Ridgefield for a short two-game series.

The first game in that series featured several lead changes and scoring in multiple innings. When it was all over, the Raptors had a 7-6 victory. Nate Pecota, Griffin Paxton, and Harrison Spohn each had two hits and drove in one run, while Kyle Sherick added a homer. The HarbourCats bounced back in the second game of the series and emerged with a 7-3 win. Chase Meidroth contributed three hits, including a home run, drove in three runs, and scored one. Parker Bramlett also had three hits, and he scored one run. Ty Schindel had two hits, including a homer and scored one run. Nate Pecota had a double and a single, scored one run and drove in one. Frankie Niemann had a double and scored one run.

With a day off from league play, the 'Cats hosted the Burnaby Bulldogs. The visitors put on a hitting display, recording 15, en route to an 11-4 drubbing of the HarbourCats who managed only seven hits. Nick Adams' double was the highlight of the home offence.

Back in regular season games, the Cowlitz Black Bears came to town. After surrendering one run to the visitors in the first inning, the 'Cats scored in four of the next six innings before a late ninth-inning rally by the Bears fell short. A crowd of 2,239 witnessed a 12-3 thumping. Nick Plaia had a home run in his two hits, drove in four and scored three. Nate Pecota's two hits included a double; he scored one run and drove in two. Frankie Niemann contributed a double. Parker Bramlett set a new franchise record with his 20th stolen base. The team took full advantage of their offensive opportunities, leaving only three runners stranded and walking eight times. Calvin Turchin was on the mound and worked five innings, allowing one run on five hits, one walk, and striking out seven. The next game was totally different as it was close and went to extra innings. After Cowlitz scored one run in the first inning, the 'Cats notched four in the third to take the lead. Singles by Kyle Sherick, Nick Plaia, and Harrison Spohn and a double by Griffin Paxton spurred the offence. Hitters also reached base on an error and a walk and were advanced on a wild pitch and a stolen base. The Bears came back with three in the sixth to tie the score. Chase Meidroth's single in the 10th inning scored Kyle Sherick, who had earlier singled to give the 'Cats a 5-4 decision. The HarbourCats completed the series sweep with a 7-3 victory in the third game. Dakota Hawkins worked the first six innings and gave up two runs on four hits with one walk and two strikeouts, and Derek Salata finished the game with one run on one hit, one walk, and two strikeouts. Chase Meidroth and Griffin Paxton had two hits, and Matt Clayton blasted a home run. Nate Pecota, who would be leaving the team after the next road series because of school commitments, had a home run and a double, driving in one run and scoring two. Jason Willow would also be leaving immediately. They were only the first to leave as school starts much earlier in the southern US than in Canada. Coach Todd Haney noted that this is a real issue for the league as the season is far too long, and many teams are no longer competitive in the late games.

The HarbourCats' four-game winning streak came to a crashing halt in Bellingham as the Bells got to pitcher Mitch Lines early and had a 5-1 lead after two innings. They added five more before the 'Cats offence got on the board with five in the sixth. Parker Bramlett and Harrison Spohn had doubles. In the middle game, the HarbourCats offence came alive, and they had a five-run before the Bells could score. Branson Wilson pitched a complete game, a rarity in summer college ball, allowing only one run on four hits and one walk while striking out six. Harrison Spohn led the offence with a single, home run, and a stolen base. Tyson Hays had a double and Chase Meidroth and Griffin Paxton had stolen bases in the 5-1 victory. The rubber match went to Victoria, but it took extra innings to settle the close encounter. The Bells scored four runs in the first inning but the 'Cats got one back in the second as Tanner Haney's single drove in Nate Pecota. Four runs in the fourth inning put the HarbourCats up 5-4, but the Bells pushed a run across in the ninth inning to tie the match. Haney finished the game with three hits, drove in three, and scored one. The winning run in the 10th inning was unearned as Chase Meidroth who had singled and stolen second base, crossed the plate on an error by the third baseman. Luka Green, who had come in to pitch in the eighth inning, shut the door on the Bells to preserve the victory. Branson Wilson was named WCL Pitcher of the week for his complete game on the road and his sparkling 1.19 ERA.

The HarbourCats played a home-and-home series against their cross-strait rivals, the Lefties. In the first game, the bats came alive, and they ended up on the right side of a 15-3 score. They pounded out seventeen hits, scoring in all but two innings. Gus Wilson had a three-hit night including a double, drove in three runs,

The HarbourCats played a home-and-home series against their cross-strait rivals, the Lefties. In the first game, the bats came alive, and they ended up on the right side of a 15-3 score.

and scored a run. Griffin Paxton also had a double among his three hits while Harrison Spohn also had a double, and Nick Adams hit a pair of homers to lead the offence. Hunter Omlid started for Victoria and allowed two runs on four hits with four walks and three strikeouts. Zach Swanson worked two innings of scoreless relief, Mikey Callia had one inning of work, and Griffin Paxton finished the game. In the second game, Victoria scored five runs in the top of the first and cruised to an 11-2 win. Reagan MacDonald pitched five innings and gave up two runs on two hits, with two walks and 11 strikeouts. Tyler Hilton worked three innings, and Tyler Pettit came in to work the ninth. Griffin Paxton went three-for-five at the plate, including two home runs to drive in five and score two. Kyle Sherick had a double among his three hits and scored two runs. Nick Plaia and Gus Wilson produced doubles in the offensive onslaught. Game three was a 9-0 shutout for the 'Cats. Mitch Lines got the start and worked five innings of two-hit ball with one walk and nine strikeouts while Chase Stewart, Mikey Callia, and Harrison Spohn came in to finish the game. Nick Plaia, Gus Wilson, Harrison Spohn, and Tanner Haney all had two hits, including a double, to lead the offence. With the sweep, the Lefties were eliminated from playoff contention.

The action switched back to Royal Athletic Park for the final series of the regular

> On Fireworks Night, a crowd of 4,172 watched the HarbourCats complete a 7-4 conquest of the Lefties.

season. The first game was a blowout win for the 'Cats as they bested the Lefties by a score of 22-5. Kyle Sherick had four hits with one home run and brought home four runs and scored two. Nick Plaia also had four hits, including a double and a homer; he scored four runs and had one batted in. Ty Schindel was the third HarbourCat with four hits, scoring three runs and driving in one. Other homers were hit by Liam Balance and Nick Adams, who had five runs batted in. Dakota Hawkins went three innings on the mound, giving up two runs on one hit, one walk, and five strikeouts. Jacob Potter got the win in relief as he worked three innings allowing two runs on six hits with one walk and five strikeouts. Fynn Chester threw the seventh and eighth innings and designated hitter Nick Plaia worked the scoreless ninth. On Fireworks Night, a crowd of 4,172 watched the HarbourCats complete a 7-4 conquest of the Lefties. With the visitors leading 3-1 in the third inning, the 'Cats bats came alive, and they recorded runs in the next four innings to secure the victory. Five players hit home runs: Nick Plaia, Griffin Paxton (with two), Tyson Hays, Harrison Spohn, and Kyle Sherick to account for the offence. Sherick, Hays, and Fynn Chester had stolen bases. Josh Laukkanen got the start and worked four innings with three runs on five hits, one walk, and two strikeouts. Tyler Hilton and Chase Stewart worked in relief. In the final game of the

THE HARBOURCATS CLINCH A PLAYOFF SPOT

WINNERS OF YEAR-END HONOURS

regular season, the 'Cats completed the sweep with a 6-0 shutout of the Lefties. Zach Swanson worked five innings of two-hit shutout ball, with three walks and five strikeouts for the win. Reagan MacDonald, Tim Holyk, and Hunter Omlid combined for four scoreless innings in relief. Tyson Hays had a double and a single, while Nick Plaia added two singles and a stolen base. Nick Adams added a double, and Harrison Spohn launched a home run. Ty Schindel stole two bases, with Harrison Spohn and Kyle Sherick stealing one each.

The offensive outburst in that game typified the 2019 season for the HarbourCats. They became the first team in West Coast League history to record more than 400 runs in a season, ending the campaign with 415 which eclipsed the old record of 360 runs which had been established in 2015 by the Bend Elks. After the game, Coach Haney reflected on how many players had left the team (10 to 15) and how others had filled in and made their contributions. This is how summer baseball

Griffin Paxton was named Player of the Year, while Luka Green and Dakota Hawkins were Pitchers of the Year, and Harrison Spohn won the Community Service Award.

VICTORIA HARBOURCATS 2019 TEAM PHOTO

works and is unlikely to change as the schools in the southern US start their seasons earlier than is done in Canada and the Pacific Northwest. One example was Gus Wilson from Duncan, who played nine games for the team and hit .381. Griffin Paxton was named Player of the Year, while Luka Green and Dakota Hawkins were Pitchers of the Year, and Harrison Spohn won the Community Service Award.

Now it was time for the playoffs with the first game in Wenatchee, with the second game and the third (if necessary) in Victoria. Proving that six-game winning streaks in the regular season mean nothing in the playoff, the AppleSox knocked off the HarbourCats in the first game 5-1. The Victoria bats that had been so prevalent through the regular season went quiet and only produced one run on six hits. The run by the 'Cats came in the ninth inning. With two out, Griffin Paxton doubled and came home on a Harrison Spohn double. Kyle Sherick grounded out to end the inning and halt the comeback. The action then shifted to Victoria, where the Victoria Junior Eagles, who had captured the BC Junior Premier Baseball League

Now it was time for the playoffs with the first game in Wenatchee, with the second game and the third (if necessary) in Victoria.

playoff title with a 5-0 postseason record, were honoured before the game. The 'Cats responded and secured a 7-2 win to tie the series and ensure a third game. Both teams scored in the first inning, and Wenatchee actually took a 2-1 lead in the third. However, that was the end of their offence, and Victoria scored three in the fifth and one in the sixth. Tanner Haney had a double, while Gus Wilson and Harrison Spohn hit home runs. The third game was a nail-biter as the team exchanged leads, and the series was decided in the ninth inning. Victoria scored in the first inning when Nick Plaia walked, advanced to second on a Gus Wilson single, and scored when Griffin Paxton singled. After Wenatchee scored twice in the fourth to take the lead, the 'Cats got one in the fifth to tie the score when Nick Adams, who had singled, scored on a Griffin Paxton single. They took the lead in the sixth when Nick Adams hit a towering home run which also plated Tanner Haney and Ty Schindel. With the HarbourCats up 5-3, Wenatchee roared back with four in the ninth to take the lead. It all came down to the bottom of the ninth and the home team walked it off with three to win the game. Nick Plaia walked to start the inning, advanced to second when Gus Wilson walked and scored on Griffin Paxton's double. Harrison Spohn then singled, driving in Wilson and Paxton. It was a fabulous ending to a great series from the perspective of the 2,019 fans who stayed to the end.

Now, it was on to the final against the powerhouse Corvallis Knights. The first game was played in Victoria, and it did not end well for the home team.

Now, it was on to the final against the powerhouse Corvallis Knights. The first game was played in Victoria, and it did not end well for the home team. Leading 3-1, Corvallis scored seven runs in the fourth inning to put the game out of reach. They continued their onslaught and defeated the HarbourCats 14-8. Harrison Spohn and Liam Balance had home runs to lead their offence. The second game was played in Corvallis, and the 'Cats bounced back to win 5-2. They got off to a good start with a run in the first inning when Harrison Spohn hit the ball over the fence. The Knights got two in their first inning to take the lead, but the HarbourCats showed their resilience by scoring three in the third to go back in front. Andrew MacCuaig started off with a single. He then advanced to second on a MacGregor Sharpe put out, made it to third on a Nick Plaia single, and scored

LOCAL FANS MEET THEIR TEAM AFTER THE FINAL GAME, 2019

on a wild pitch. After Ty Schindel walked, Kyle Sherick singled, driving in Plaia and Schindel. Reagan MacDonald took the mound for the first 3 1/3 innings and Hunter Omlid finished the game, holding the Knight scoreless for 5 2/3 innings. The whole season came down to one game and, unfortunately for Victoria fans, the Knights showed their power in an 11-1 drubbing. Their pitchers were masterful, allowing only one run on four hits. In the third inning, Nick Plaia doubled and advanced to third on Ty Schindel's single. He then scored on a Harrison Spohn sacrifice fly, but that was the end of the offence.

It was a disappointing end to the season, but several fans turned up to Royal Athletic Park to welcome their team home and celebrate their season. Everyone was excited about the prospects of retaining the core of the well-hitting team. How could we have known that the world would be turned upside down in a few months?

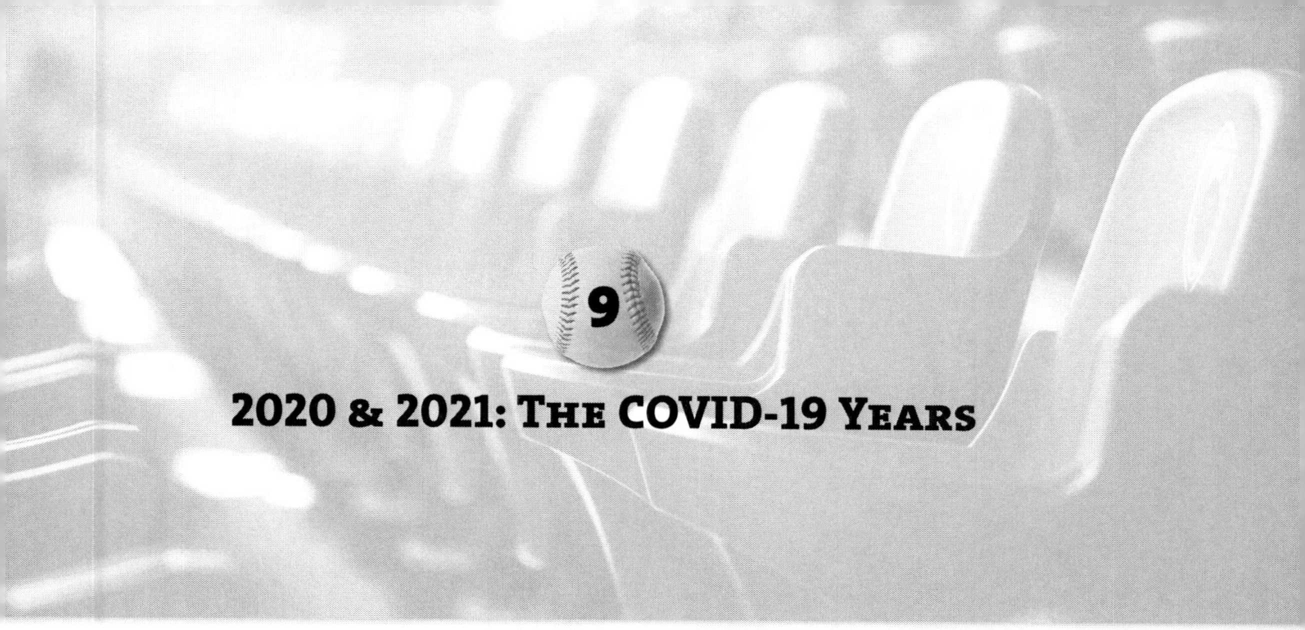

9

2020 & 2021: The COVID-19 Years

With no idea of what was about to happen worldwide, the HarbourCats signed players for the 2020 season. From the Texas Longhorns would come Thomas Burbank, Justin Eckhardt, Peter Gibb, and returnee Tanner Haney.

In early March, it was formally announced that the HarbourCats ownership group would also own a new franchise in Nanaimo in the 2021 season. The name would be chosen after a public contest, as had the Victoria franchise's name. The team would play in Serauxman Stadium, which would undergo significant upgrading, including new lights and a scoreboard. The historic stadium was opened in 1976 by former New York Yankees star Mickey Mantle, who was in Nanaimo for a fundraiser at the time and had a long history of community involvement.

On March 17, 2020, a public health emergency was declared in the province of British Columbia. Under the regulations, events with more than 50 people were banned.

On March 17, 2020, a public health emergency was declared in the province of British Columbia. Under the regulations, events with more than 50 people were banned. This directly affected sports franchises, including the HarbourCats, as without fans in attendance, the clubs cannot make money to survive. Individuals were instructed to get no closer to one another than six feet and were encouraged to wear masks. The Victoria Royals junior hockey team paused operations but hoped for the ability to play their playoffs at a later date. In the US, the NCAA shut down baseball operations – the source of players for summer ball here. At this early stage of the pandemic, the HarbourCats were still optimistic about being able to play in the summer.

In late March, the City of Victoria set up temporary shelters at additional locations, including Royal Athletic Park, with access to meals, bathrooms, and bathing facilities.

By early May, it was believed that some teams would be able to play in the summer but there would be no fans in the stands. This would not have worked financially for summer baseball as revenue from seat sales was required to cover operational costs. However, on May 9, 2020, the HarbourCats announced that

By early May, it was believed that some teams would be able to play in the summer but there would be no fans in the stands.

they were officially cancelling their season. With the US-Canada border closed to all but essential traffic, Canadian teams would be unable to stock their rosters with US players, so would be unable to assemble a team or the coaches who would guide them. Other sports were also cancelled, making for a strange summer season.

Of concern was the spinoff economic losses caused by a cancelled season. Beer sales of the branded beer from Red Arrow would plummet and hotels would lose the revenue from visiting teams even if they did bunk four to a room – estimated at 325 rooms per season. The Commissionaires, who handled security at the ballpark would not have jobs, nor would the City employees who would normally work selling tickets, taking tickets, and selling at the concessions. The numerous food trucks would lose an entire summer of sales and likely have to lay off employees. In addition, the City would lose the rent paid per game, and there would be no money from 50/50 draws to support charities and minor sports teams. Transportation companies would lose the cost of moving teams to and from games.

To bring some semblance of baseball to local fans, the HarbourCats held a couple of outdoor viewings of old games and fireworks shows with some food trucks there to feed the guests. They also made all prior games available on hcats.tv. There were also a few Zoom sessions with coaches and former players so season ticket holders could feel part of the team.

With all the bad news, it was good to hear something positive. Former HarbourCats players had signed Major League Baseball contracts. AJ Block inked a deal with the Kansas City Royals, and Carter Loewen did the same with the San Diego Padres. In August, the team extended Todd Haney's contract for another three years, to 2023.

By August, young players interested in playing baseball were able to return to training at the Victoria HarbourCats Players Club. At one session, the youngsters had a Zoom conversation with former HarbourCat AJ Lewis, who had just signed a minor league pro contract with the Colorado Rockies. He told them to work hard and explained how good things can come from that. The facility was working with the young players in small groups to comply with the new provincial return-to-play guidelines.

More positive news came when the coach of the new franchise, the Nanaimo NightOwls, was named: Greg Frady, who coached the Georgia State University Panthers for 13 seasons, and the German national team for 11 years. There would be a second new team in the West Coast League for the 2021 season, bringing the total number of teams to 14 with the addition of the Kamloops NorthPaws, who would play out of Norbrock Stadium. In September, the West Coast League announced another new Canadian team in Edmonton as the fifteenth franchise. Known as the Riverhawks, they would play in ReMax Field with new artificial field turf, a new scoreboard, and new lighting.

With restrictions being relaxed in September, the HarbourCats began to prepare for the 2021 season. The Canadian teams were determined to find homegrown players just in case the border was closed for longer than anticipated. Local players signed included Noah Takacs and Josh Walker from the Canadian junior national team and Eric Luchies, who played for St. Andrew's Secondary School. Later signings includ-

With restrictions being relaxed in September, the HarbourCats began to prepare for the 2021 season.

ed Coquitlam products Giordano Mezzomo and Steve Moretto, and Declan Dutton from Vancouver, who all played with the Canadian national junior team.

The HarbourCats announced the team's new indoor training facility on Cook Street in the former Cook Street Squash Club. Among the equipment available for players in the 5,000-square-foot centre, were batting cages, pitching machines, and pitching tunnels, as well as strength and conditioning areas. A second announcement was that the HarbourCats would sponsor a new team, Victoria Golden Tide, that would play in the Canadian College Baseball Conference. Other teams in the conference were Vancouver Island University, University of the Fraser Valley, Okanagan College, Thompson Rivers University, University of Calgary, Edmonton Collegiate Baseball Club, and Prairie Baseball Academy of Lethbridge. To play, players had to be registered as students at either the University of Victoria or Camosun College. The goal was to have some Golden Tide players work their way onto the HarbourCats roster.

The 2021 season schedule was released, and the 54-game plan had the HarbourCats opening on the road in Edmonton in the 9,000-seat ReMax Field, with the first home game on June 4 against the Port Angeles Lefties. Early December signings for the 2021 season included Liam Rocha, Spencer Bengard, David Martin, and Mitch Simon from the Cal Baptist Lancers.

The HarbourCats ended the year 2020 with a food drive to support the Mustard Seed. The event, co-sponsored by Arbutus RV, saw visitors fill a recreational

The 2021 season schedule was released, and the 54-game plan had the HarbourCats opening on the road in Edmonton in the 9,000-seat ReMax Field.

vehicle with food and other necessities. In accordance with current health rules, it was a drive-through event, with volunteers taking the donations from vehicles with minimal contact.

Early in 2021, the 'Cats signed more players for what they hoped would be the summer season. On the list were Matt Jew (Santa Clara), Tyler Best (University of Hawaii), Dustin Allen (University of San Diego), Devon Hawks (UC-San Diego), and Mason Palagyi (Tacoma Community College). The schedule assumed that the closed Canada-US border would open before June 1. Based on the mass vaccination timeline set to run from April to September, sports might be able to be played in the summer.

Additions were made to the HarbourCats' coaching staff in February 2021. Greg Swindell, who won the 2001 World Series with the Arizona Diamondbacks, was named as bench coach and Mark Petkovsek, who had played nine seasons of Major League Baseball, was named pitching coach. They both came out of the University of Texas Longhorns NCAA program, as did head coach Todd Haney.

Early in February 2021, Provincial Health Officer Dr. Bonnie Henry said that sport could return to the province in a limited form by the end of the month. It would all depend on the vaccination program and the number of active cases at the time. However, the HarbourCats had the additional issue of the closed US-Canada border, which made things difficult. The team was confident they could allow fans to enter and could provide a safe space, but the decision would not be made until later in the year.

In the meantime, they signed Victoria Eagles product Gavin Pringle. Teams were searching for Canadian players to stock their rosters in case the Canadian-based WCL teams could play a season amongst themselves. The team also signed pitchers Braden Gowdy and Micah Wallette from Chico State and AC Plum from Rice University. Tickets for single games were offered for sale as island sports teams were optimistic that the accelerated vaccine programme would allow some games to proceed in the summer season.

Finally, in mid-April, the HarbourCats announced that the 2021 season would have to be cancelled, as would the start of the new franchise in Nanaimo. The Kelowna Falcons had decided not to play earlier, and they were joined by the remainder of the franchises north of the border. As the American-based teams would be playing, not having to cross an international border, the decision had to be made to allow previously signed players to find a new team for the summer. The cancellation would have a ripple effect through the community as the team had generated

Finally, in mid-April, the HarbourCats announced that the 2021 season would have to be cancelled.

about $3.8 million per season. It would affect City operations, food vendors, and local charities, and would no longer be able to benefit from 50/50 draws and similar promotions.

The West Coast League accepted its 16th franchise in April 2021 when the Springfield Drifters became the fourth Oregon-based team. They would play that summer with the other US-domiciled teams. Former HarbourCat pitcher Will McAffer was named to the Canadian team for the Americas' Olympic qualifying tournament. He was then playing for the Single-A Vancouver Canadians, a Toronto Blue Jay farm team. Nick Pivetta, who had thrown the first pitch in franchise history, had found a home in Boston with the Red Sox and had started the 2021 season with a sparkling 5-0 record. He reflected on his early days in Victoria and how that time had made him a better player. In July, six former HarbourCats players were selected in the 2021 Major League Baseball draft. Shane McGuire, who had been the 2017 player of the year, was selected 278th overall by the Oakland Athletics. Others were Rowdey Jordan (New York Mets), Jack Neely (New York Yankees), Owen Sharts (Pittsburgh Pirates), Wyatt Young (New York Mets), and Luke Boyd (San Diego Padres).

The HarbourCats extended the contract of head coach Todd Haney for five years, up to the end of the 2026 summer season. He hoped to have his coaching staff return for the 2021 season. They included pitching coach Mark Petkovsek, bench coach Greg Swindell, hitting and catching coach Curtis Pelletier, and first base coach Troy Birtwistle. The first two played with coach Haney at the University of Texas, while the latter two are Vancouver Island products.

In July, we learned that the HarbourCats had been among the 72 successful applicants for provincial government pandemic relief. In order to qualify, teams had to prove 30% revenue loss during the pandemic. Amounts of the individual grants were not released because of confidentiality reasons. The 'Cats were able to weather the pandemic by being strategic in their spending and did not have to lay off any core staff. This grant ensured that operations continued undeterred. In addition, the majority of sponsors and season ticket holders who had prepaid had left the funds with the club, and that certainly helped the cash flow.

The Golden Tide era officially began in September with games at Royal Athletic Park. Among the players on the team were former Canadian junior national team infielder Brody Alexandre from Swift Current, Saskatchewan, and Ethan Keates from Calgary, while Tristan Bolger, Jacob Popadynec, and Nick Lee were all from the Island. Head coach Curtis Pelletier was optimistic about the program. He had assembled a stellar coaching staff, including Kyle Orr, Ethan Fox, and Ryan Haines.

Finally, the West Coast League announced its 2022 schedule. The HarbourCats would open on May 31 at home against the Port Angeles Lefties.

Finally, the West Coast League announced its 2022 schedule. The HarbourCats would open on May 31 at home against the Port Angeles Lefties with their first fireworks night on June 30. The season would also mark the debuts of the new franchises, Nanaimo NightOwls, Edmonton Riverhawks, Kamloops NorthPaws, and the Springfield Drifters. In November, the HarbourCats announced that assistant coach Curtis Pelletier had been promoted to General Manager. Former General Manager Jim Swanson would remain as managing partner of the local club and would become GM of the Nanaimo franchise.

In August, the HarbourCats announced that any coaches or players wishing to participate in their team would be required to be fully vaccinated. There would be no exceptions. These rules with also apply to the Nanaimo NightOwls summer ball franchise and the new Victoria Golden Tide team that would commence play in the Canadian College Baseball Conference in the fall.

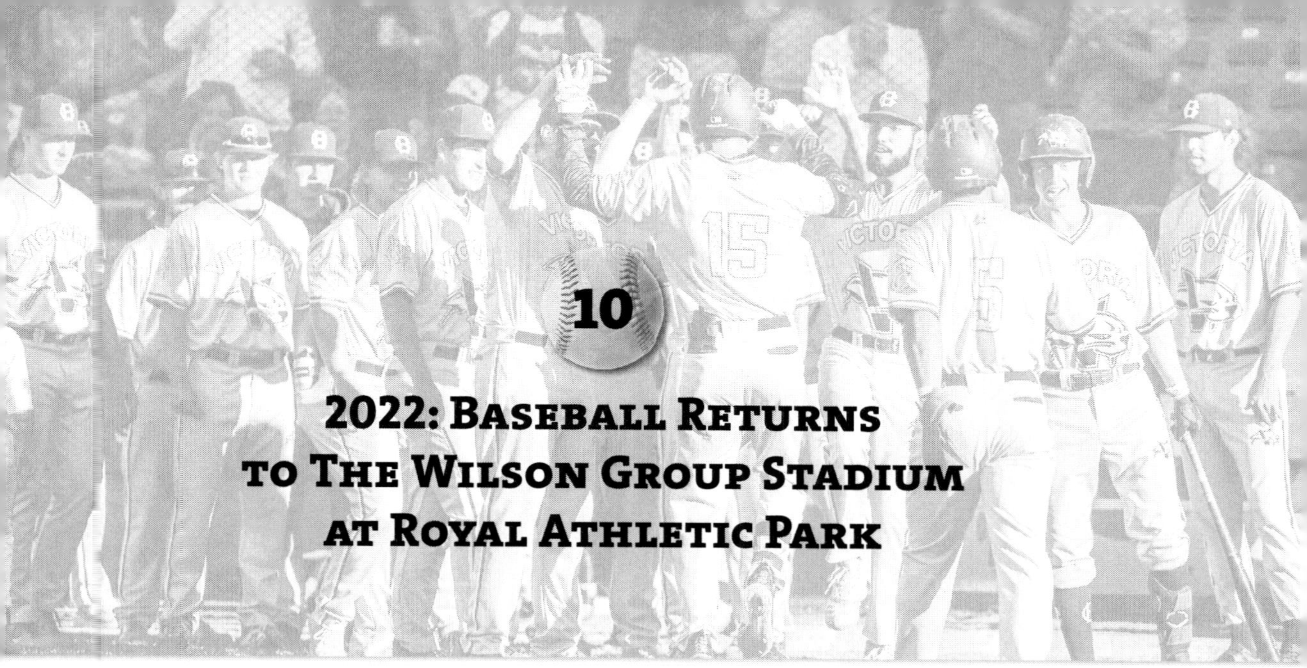

10

2022: Baseball Returns to The Wilson Group Stadium at Royal Athletic Park

For local baseball fans, the 2022 summer season was highly anticipated. At long last, the boys would be able to play at Wilson's Group Stadium at Royal Athletic Park after two summers of inactivity due to the COVID-19 pandemic.

Early in January 2022, the club signed Noah Takacs and Josh Walker (Sacramento State), Eric and Owen Luchies (Lower Columbia College) and Golden Tide players Haldon Craig, Jacob Popadynec, Jordan Bond, and Daniel Sawchyn. The league would be expanded to add Canadian teams Nanaimo NightOwls, Kamloops NorthPaws, and Edmonton Riverhawks.

In off-field news, the group that owned the HarbourCats and the NightOwls added new partners: Helen Edwards and Mike Macdonell of Victoria; Bob Swanson of Duncan; John Schnaderbeck of Vancouver, Washington; Victor Vendetti of Pittsburgh, Pennsylvania; and an unnamed investor.

Before plans could be made to start the season, it was announced that Victoria City Council was considering a pilot project to create an off-leash dog park at Royal Athletic Park. The argument used was that the park had not been used much in the previous year. Of course, there had been no baseball due to the pandemic, so

---

The 2022 home schedule was announced in late May with the first game to be played on May 31 versus Port Angeles.

---

that position was not valid. Fortunately, saner heads prevailed, and the project was never carried through.

The 2022 home schedule was announced in late May with the first game to be played on May 31 versus Port Angeles. To make a competition between the four BC teams in the West Coast league, a new trophy was created, called the BC Cup, to go to the team with the greatest number of wins in head-to-head contests between BC teams.

After 1,017 days between games, the 2022 season got underway. Jace Walker from Temple College in Texas was on the mound for the home opener. Liam Rocha from Cal Baptist was scheduled to get the assignment but couldn't get to Victoria on time. Jace worked four innings, giving up one run on four hits, one walk, and four strikeouts. Both teams scored single runs in the first inning. The score remained the same until the fifth inning when the HarbourCats sent nine men to the plate and counted five runs. Their offence was aided by two Lefties' errors, a walk, a stolen base, and a hit batter. The only other run came in the top of the ninth

After 1,017 days between games, the 2022 season got underway. Jace Walker from Temple College in Texas was on the mound for the home opener.

and made the score 6-2. Grady Morgan led the offence with three hits, including a double and a stolen base. Luke Cheng contributed one hit and three stolen bases. Flynn Ridley got the win in relief, working two innings, and Owen Luchies worked the last three innings.

The second game of the season was not as successful. The HarbourCats were leading 3-1 at the end of five innings when the Lefties' bats came alive. They notched two runs in the sixth and four in the seventh, with singles in the eighth and ninth to lead 9-3. A home team rally in the bottom of the ninth inning could only manufacture three runs, resulting in a losing score of 9-6. Luke Cheng continued his positive offence, going three for five at the plate, including a double. The HarbourCats used six pitchers, none of whom were particularly effective. Thousands of screaming schoolchildren attended the rubber match of the series the next day at 11 am. Their enthusiasm did not seem to help as the Lefties upended the 'Cats 4-1. Ironically, the home team scored the first run in the second inning when Russell Young singled, and Clark Henry, who had reached base on a fielder's choice, scored on an error by the pitcher. Port Angeles plated one run in the third, two in the seventh, and one in the ninth. Starting pitcher Loretto Siniscalchi worked four innings, and Hudson Shupe finished the game.

Then, it was on the road to Kelowna. The game scheduled for June 3 was postponed due to rain and became part of a doubleheader the following evening. Game one went to the home team by a 4-3 score. The Falcons scored twice in the first inning of game one, and the visitors could never catch up. Noah Takacs started for Victoria and worked three innings, with Dawson Hurford handling the last three. In the nightcap, the 'Cats rebounded in the to take it 5-2. They scored four runs in the first inning, giving starting pitcher Harry Deliyannis the lead he needed to gain the victory. Joseph Redfield was the offensive star for the game, going two-for-three at the plate and scoring one run. Kelowna won the rubber match 9-2 when the Victoria bats fell silent. After scoring first, the HarbourCats couldn't hold the Falcons off the scoreboard as they pounded out 11 hits off starter Jace Walker and relievers Owen Luchies, Haldon Craig, and Darius Opdam Bak.

June 7, 2022, was a historic day for Vancouver Island baseball. The HarbourCats played their first series against their Nanaimo cousins and defeated the NightOwls 7-6. It was certainly an exciting game with several lead changes. Victoria scored first with single runs in the first and second innings. However, Nanaimo tied it up in the third and notched four in the sixth to go ahead, 5-2. One run in the bottom of the seventh made the game closer, and the 'Cats took the lead for good in the eighth with four runs. They made use of timely hitting, hit-by-pitch, stolen bases, and wild

June 7, 2022, was a historic day for Vancouver Island baseball. The HarbourCats played their first series against their Nanaimo cousins and defeated the NightOwls 7-6.

pitches to get the runs with only two hits. Victoria used six pitchers, with Russell Hicks getting the victory and Flynn Ridley the save. Clark Henry had two hits, two runs scored, and two driven in. The second game was over almost before it had gone very far. The HarbourCats scored seven runs in their first at-bat and cruised to an 11-8 win. Luke Cheng had four hits, a walk, and a stolen base and drove in four runs. Jake Skipworth and Joseph Redfield had doubles, and Jordan Bond hit a home run. Starting pitcher Loretto Sinisalchi worked four innings, and Walker Bordovsky, Addison Sells, Haldon Craig, and Owen Luchies worked in relief. The third game of the series, scheduled for June 9, was rained out and would be played on July 7.

The homestand continued with three games against the Kelowna Falcons. In game one, the HarbourCats sent nine men to the plate in the second inning and scored five runs. They added three in the third and singles in the seventh and eighth for an 10-3 decision. Luke Cheng and Grady Morgan both had three hits and scored two runs. Joseph Redfield, Jake Skipworth, and Jordan Bond all added two hits. Clark Henry contributed a triple. Noah Takacs worked the first two innings, Harry Deliyannis worked four innings, and Jaxson Smith finished the game. The middle match was much closer. Kelowna took an early one-run lead and added three runs in the eighth. Victoria got one back in the eighth and a ninth inning rally fell one-run short as Kelowna won 4-3. Joseph Redfield was the only 'Cats player with more than one hit as the team only managed four in total. Cooper Crompton worked four innings and was tagged with the loss. The HarbourCats took the rubber match by a score of 6-1, making the most of doubles by Josh Walker and Russell Young and homers by Jake Skipworth and Colton Moore. Levi Abbott worked five innings for the win, with Jack Seward and Walker Bordovsky finishing the game.

Back on the road in Kamloops, the HarbourCats dropped a close 5-4 decision to the NorthPaws. They fell behind early, took a lead, and then surrendered the winning run in the ninth inning. Grady Morgan and Joseph Redfield hit triples, and Colton Moore added a home run and a double. Loretto Siniscalchi started the game and pitched four innings. Russell Hicks and Owen Luchies worked in relief. The next game was another one-run decision, with Kamloops again the victor. Victoria built up an 8-1 lead but failed to hold it and surrendered the winning run in the ninth inning to lose 9-8. Joseph Redfield, Colton Moore, Hudson Shupe, and Russell Young all had two hits. The HarbourCats won the third game with a convincing 8-3 decision. Scoring two runs in the first inning, they added singles in the fifth, sixth, and seventh and put the game on ice with three in the ninth. Colton Moore led the offence with three hits while Jake Skipworth added two. Michael Nunez worked 4 1/3 innings to gain the victory.

With a break in league play, the HarbourCats played three games against the senior Coquitlam Angels. This gave them a chance to rest regular players and let some newcomers get some game action. Roberto Gonzalez, who was born in Caracas, Venezuela, and lived in Houston, Texas, joined the team and impressed coach Todd Haney with his play. Newcomer Jesse Brown also played well.

League play resumed with a home series against Wenatchee. In a game that took almost 3 ½ hours to play, the visitors upended the 'Cats 8-6 in 10 innings. Tyler Pettit had a home run, while Joseph Redfield and Jake Skipworth had doubles. Flynn Ridley was tagged with the loss after working two innings in relief. The middle

With a break in league play, the HarbourCats played three games against the senior Coquitlam Angels. This gave them a chance to rest regular players and let some newcomers get some game action.

game went to the HarbourCats. They started slowly, scoring a run in the first and fifth innings and adding two in the sixth. A huge eight-run eighth inning put the game on ice. Colton Moore, Roberto Gonzalez, and Shane Jamison had three hits each, and Jesse Brown hit his first home run. Levi Abbott worked five innings for the victory with relief work by Sam Walbridge, Harry Deliyannis, and Haldon Craig. The final score of 12-2 reflected the calibre of play. Wenatchee took the final game of the series with a 9-4 decision. They scored six runs in the first inning and had a seven-run lead before the 'Cats got on the board. Nick Lee was tagged with the loss, working only 2/3 inning with relief work by Jace Walker, Addison Sells, and Jacob Popadynec. Jesse Brown hit his second home run while Michael Tsoukalas and Luke Cheng had doubles.

After a ferry trip and bus ride, the team arrived in Ridgefield for a three-game series against the Raptors. The opening game was a close 13-11 decision for the home team. The lead changed hands often. After three innings, the HarbourCats had a 7-3 lead but surrendered five runs in the fourth inning and two in the fifth. Both teams notched three runs in the sixth and the 'Cats scored the final run of the encounter in the eighth. Jesse Brown, Roberto Gonzalez, and Josh Rolling had three hits each while Grady Morgan had two. Noah Takacs started for the 'Cats and was relieved by Dawson Hurford, Sam Walbridge, and Flynn Ridley. In the next game, the Victoria bats went cold, and they were shut out 12-0. Luke Cheng had three hits in a losing cause. The HarbourCats managed a win in the final game of the series. They came from behind with a big five-run seventh inning the difference in an 8-7 victory. Joseph Redfield led the offence with three hits, driving in two runs. The team used five pitchers, with Sam Walbridge picking up the win in relief.

Back home, the HarbourCats entertained the Cowlitz Black Bears. The home team used a seven-run third inning to work their way to a 12-11 victory. Jesse Brown, Roberto Gonzalez, Michael Tsoukalas, and Josh Walker all hit doubles, while Colton Moore and Jake Skipworth hit homers. Cooper Crompton got the start and worked 4 2/3 innings. Jace Walker was credited with the victory, and Jack Seward and Flynn Ridley finished the game. The second game was also a one-run victory. After Cowlitz put two runs on the board in the fourth inning and four in the sixth, the HarbourCats got two in the sixth and added four in the seventh on a Jake Skipworth grand slam to tie the score. The game was won 7-6 in a walk-off when Jesse Brown singled, advanced to second on a Roberto Gonzalez single, and scored on a Joseph Redfield single. Redfield and Skipworth both recorded three hits, accounting for half of the team's production. Walker Bordovsky gained the victory in relief. The third game went 7-5 to the Black Bears. After Victoria took a one-run lead in the third inning, Cowlitz put up four in the sixth and two in the seventh to take a 6-1 lead. They added a single run in the eighth. The 'Cats counted three in the seventh, and the ninth-inning comeback fell one run short. Roberto Gonzalez had four hits to lead the offence while Jesse Brown added another home run. Noah Takacs got the start and worked five scoreless innings before being relieved by Josh Verdon, Sam Walbridge, Addison Sells, and Flynn Ridley.

Next on the schedule was a three-game series in Portland. On Canada Day, the Pickles built up a two-run lead and then held on for a 2-1 victory. Hudson Shupe, Michael Tsoukalas, and Josh Walker had the only hits for the 'Cats. Loretto Siniscalchi worked five innings while David Chase completed the game. The next evening, Portland won again, this time with a 5-2 decision. They built up a five-run lead and then limited Victoria to single runs in the fifth and eighth innings. Joseph Redfield and Colton Moore recorded two hits in a losing cause. Harry Deliyannis worked three innings before being relieved by Sam Walbridge, Owen Luchies, and Jack Seward. The Pickles swept the series with a 10-3 decision. It was a close game

Next on the schedule was a three-game series in Portland. On Canada Day, the Pickles built up a two-run lead and then held on for a 2-1 victory.

until the fifth inning when Portland scored seven runs. The road trip continued in Springfield and so did the losing streak. The Drifters took the first game in a walk-off, 5-4. Victoria had built up a 4-0 lead but couldn't keep their opponents off the board. Joseph Redfield, Roberto Gonzalez, and Colton Moore had two hits each, but the offence failed to produce when it was needed the most. On the following evening, Springfield built up a 3-0 lead and held on for a 3-1 decision. Roberto Gonzalez and Josh Rolling hit doubles but it was not enough. The losing streak came to an end in the final game of the series when the 'Cats used timely hitting

Back home, the 'Cats hosted the Nanaimo NightOwls in a game to make up the rained-out contest from June 9.

and stolen bases to take the game, 3-2. Jesse Brown and Hudson Shupe contributed two hits each and drove in two of the runs, while Josh Walker drove in the third run. The announced attendance at that game was only 200. At this stage of the season, the Victoria record was 12-17, a far cry from the record-setting pace of the 2019 season.

Back home, the 'Cats hosted the Nanaimo NightOwls in a game to make up the rained-out contest from June 9. The visitors built up a 4-0 lead before the 'Cats scored five to temporarily take the lead. Both teams scored once in the seventh inning, and Nanaimo won it with three in the ninth for a final score of 8-6. Colton Moore recorded four hits for Victoria, and Roberto Gonzalez had three. Next to come to town were the expansion team from Kamloops. It was a close game until the fifth inning when the NorthPaws counted three runs en route to a 5-4 decision. Hudson Shupe led the offence with two hits. Finally, the bats woke up, and Victoria defeated Kamloops 10-2 in the middle game of the series. They scored eight runs in the second inning and two in the third, then cruised to the victory. In the second, they sent 14 men to the plate, and took advantage of an error, a wild pitch, and walks, coupled with seven hits including a Russell Young three-run homer and good base running. The slump was over, and the team hoped to get on a winning streak. Newcomer Andre Duplantier II worked five innings for the win with relief from Addison Sells and Walker Bordovsky. The HarbourCats took the rubber match, 2-1, in a Sunday matinée event. After falling behind 1-0 in the seventh inning, the 'Cats scored two runs in the eighth for the victory. Starter Cooper Compton, who was later given WCL Pitcher of the Week honours, worked six innings of scoreless ball, but it was Sam Walbridge who gained the victory with his two innings of work, with Jack Seward earning the save. Roberto Gonzalez and Colton Moore had doubles for the winners.

Up next was the long-awaited series in Nanaimo. The opening match went to Victoria in a 7-3 result. The 'Cats scored runs in the middle innings for a 7-0 lead and limited the Owls to three runs. Roberto Gonzales again led the offence with three hits, including a double, while Joseph Redfield added a triple. Starter Owen Luchies worked five innings for the decision with relief from Josh Verdon,

ANDRE DUPLANTIER II IN ACTION

Andre Duplantier II, Haldon Craig, and Jace Walker. In the middle game, Nick Lee worked 3 1/3 innings of relief to gain the win, with Jack Seward recording the save. It was a close game, with the score tied 4-4 at the end of regulation play. The 'Cats won 6-4 with two runs in the twelfth inning, both coming on wild pitches. Roberto Gonzalez had three hits, including a double, while Jesse Brown and Grady Morgan contributed two hits each. The final game in the series was a one-sided affair, with the HarbourCats scoring 16 runs and only surrendering one. Grady Morgan, Jesse Brown, and Joseph Redfield had four hits each in the onslaught, during which the team had 23 hits in total. Andre Duplantier II spun five innings of one-run ball while Addison Sells and Jacob Popadynec worked four innings of scoreless relief. With the victory, the HarbourCats won the WCL Island series, 5-1, and the Re/Max Cup.

Back at home, the Yakima Valley Pippins came to town and upended the 'Cats 13-8. Joseph Redfield and Hudson Shupe led the offence with two hits each. Harry Deliyannis worked three innings and was given the loss. Jace Walker and Haldon Craig worked in relief. The Pippins extended their winning streak to seven games as they demolished the 'Cats 10-4. That was a special day for coach Todd Haney. When he played his first major league game in Montreal with the Expos, he did not get a jersey to keep. The team owners located a replica of that year's jersey, had it personalized, and put it in a shadow box. The presentation was made on the field before the game to a very surprised coach. Unfortunately, the team did not pick up on the positive vibes, and the only offensive highlight was a home run by Noah Sudyka. The HarbourCats finally won a game as the third game of the series went to the home team by a 6-3 score. Yakima scored two runs in the first inning to take the lead, but the 'Cats came back and plated five runs in the eighth to secure the victory. Loretto Siniscalchi pitched 4 1/3 innings, Sam Walbridge worked 2 2/3, and Jack Seward completed the game and got the "W." Four of the critical runs came on a grand slam homer by Russell Young that scored Josh Walker, Grady Walker, and Jesse Brown ahead of him.

The Bellingham Bells then came to town for a three-game series. The 'Cats were leading 4-1 when the Bells scored five runs in the fifth to take the lead for good. Two runs in the sixth was the rest of the Victoria offence. Grady Morgan had three hits, Jesse Brown had two, and Joseph Redfield had a homer in the 9-6 defeat. The second game was a win for the 'Cats. After four innings, the Bells had a 6-4 lead, but the teams exchanged runs, and Victoria tied the score with two runs in the ninth. They won the game when Noah Sudyka walked, stole second, advanced to third on a ground out, and scored on a Grady Morgan single. Addison Sells got the victory in relief. However, the third game was a disaster for the home team as they fell 16-6 to Bellingham. The Bells rode a six-run inning and a seven-run one

COACH TODD HANEY IS PRESENTED WITH A REPLICA OF HIS MONTREAL EXPOS JERSEY

JOSEPH REDFIELD IN ACTION

to cruise to the victory. Colton Moore was the offensive star for the 'Cats with three hits, including a homer, while Jesse Brown had a homer as well.

For the road trip to Edmonton, the team had to fly – the first time this mode of transportation had been used in their history. Game one was a 9-1 victory for the Riverhawks. They scored early and often and held the 'Cats to one run. Tyler Pettit and Josh Walker had a pair of hits for Victoria but that was about it for offence. Loretto Siniscalchi worked 5 2/3 innings and took the loss. The middle game of the series was another Edmonton victory, 12-3. Joseph Redfield, with three hits, and Josh Walker, with two, led the offence. Tristan Bolger worked three innings and

For the road trip to Edmonton, the team had to fly – the first time this mode of transportation had been used in their history.

Haldon Craig finished the game. In game three, Andre Duplantier II worked 7 2/3 innings, allowing only one run on four hits with one walk and five strikeouts. Flynn Ridley pitched the remainder of the contest. Hudson Shupe had three hits for the 'Cats, accounting for half of the offensive production. Victoria was helped by two Edmonton errors and some sloppy pitching.

With a break from league play, the HarbourCats played an exhibition series against the Northwest Honkers of the Pacific International League. Then, it was back on the road for games in Port Angeles. Sitting one back of a wild card playoff spot, this series could determine their fate. They helped their cause by winning game one 8-2 behind the pitching of Loretto Siniscalchi, Flynn Ridley, and Ryder Green. Grady Morgan and Joseph Redfield had two hits in the victory to lead the offence, with the scoring assisted by four Lefties' errors. The middle game was a complete reversal as the Lefties scored ten runs to Victoria's two. Roberto Gonzalez had two hits, accounting for 1/3 of the team's output. The HarbourCats got back to form in the final game of the series with a 13-4 defeat of the Lefties. Owen Luchies worked seven complete innings and was relieved by Sam Walbridge and Jackson Belanger. Grady Morgan led the offensive surge with three hits, while Jesse Brown, Joseph Redfield, and Roberto Gonzalez contributed with two each. On a day free from league play, the Cats hosted the Redmond Dudes and won the game easily 10-2.

A road series in Bellingham started well for the HarbourCats as they won the first game 8-6. Flynn Ridley got the start and was relieved by Sam Walbridge, Josh Verdon, and Ben Smedshammer. The game was close until the 'Cats put up six runs in the eighth inning using three hits, four walks, one hit batter, and one passed ball. A late drive by Bellingham fell short by two runs in the ninth inning. Game two was also a victory with the final score of 11-5. The 'Cats scored three in the first, one in the second, and four in the fourth before the Bells got on the scoreboard. Loretto Siniscalchi started and worked three innings while Nick Taylor, who pitched five innings, got the "W," and Andrew Gillion finished the contest.

THE HARBOURCATS CLINCH A PLAYOFF SPOT

WNNERS OF YEAR-END HONOURS

Josh Walker picked up four hits, including a double and a triple, in the game, while Roberto Gonzalez added three. Bellingham managed to win the third game of the series with an 8-3 win. The 'Cats couldn't overcome a four-run third inning by the Bells and never recovered. However, taking two games out of three put them closer to a playoff berth.

It would all come down to the final series – with the Edmonton Riverhawks in town. Game one was a close one, but the visitors emerged with a 9-8 victory. The winning run was scored in the top of the ninth inning and a 'Cats comeback fell one run short. Grady Morgan and Hudson Shupe had a pair of hits. The HarbourCats left 13 men on base when just one more run would have changed the game. The middle game was a real slugfest as the teams combined for 30 hits and produced 30 runs. Edmonton took a two-run lead in the second inning, but three consecutive big innings put the 'Cats ahead to stay. They scored five in the fifth, seven in the sixth, and five in the seventh, then watched while the Riverhawks put up seven in the eighth and four in the ninth. That result meant that the winner of the third game would secure the last playoff spot. The entire season came down to one game. Nick Taylor pitched six complete innings to secure the win with Ben Smedshammer and Jack Seward coming in to relieve. Russell Young and Nick Lee had two hits in the game, which ended with a 3-1 score in Victoria's favour.

In year-end honours, Joseph Redfield was selected as Player of the Year, Andre

> The big news of the off-season was that the West Coast League announced an agreement with Major League Baseball to "jointly pursue initiatives of mutual interest."

Duplantier II as Pitcher of the Year, and Jesse Brown as the winner of the Community Service Award.

The HarbourCats entered the playoffs as the number four seed and played the first-half winner Bellingham Bells. The first game was played in Victoria and resulted in an 8-2 decision for the Bells. With the game tied 2-2 in the fifth inning, the visitors scored three in the sixth and three more in the eighth and the 'Cats had no answer. Tyler Pettit and Russell Young had three hits, with Jesse Brown the only other hit for the home team. The second game was played in Bellingham. With the 'Cats holding a 2-1 lead, a misplayed ball in the outfield led to three Bellingham runs, and the game was over with a score of 4-2. The season was over, but it had been interesting, and there had been some great games. After having lost two summers due to the pandemic, it was heartening to see the fans come back to cheer their home team at the ballpark.

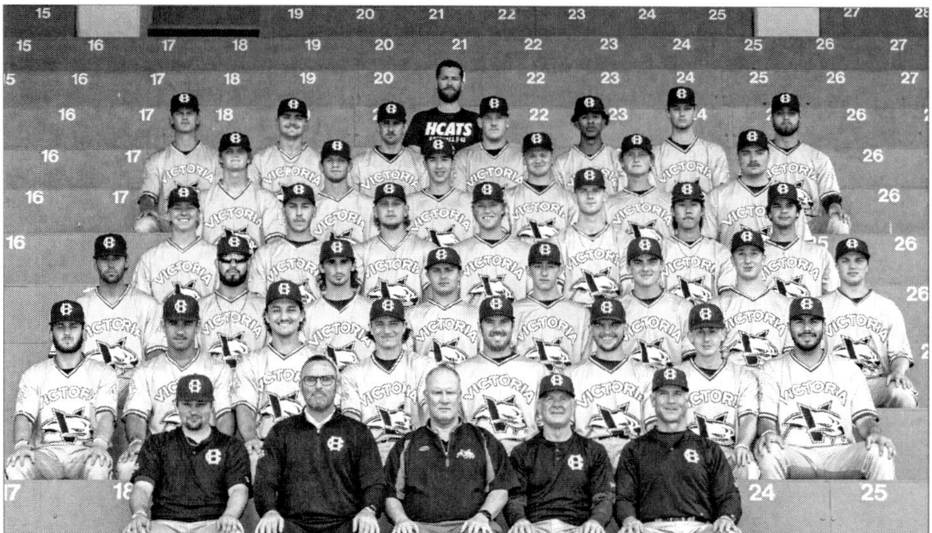

Victoria HarbourCats 2022 team photo

The big news of the off-season was that the West Coast League announced an agreement with Major League Baseball to "jointly pursue initiatives of mutual interest, including player and coach development, technology innovation related to scouting and fan experience." It was expected that specific details of the agreement would be announced over the next few months.

The WCL announced the 2023 schedule in November. The HarbourCats would open at home on June 2 against the Kamloops NorthPaws.

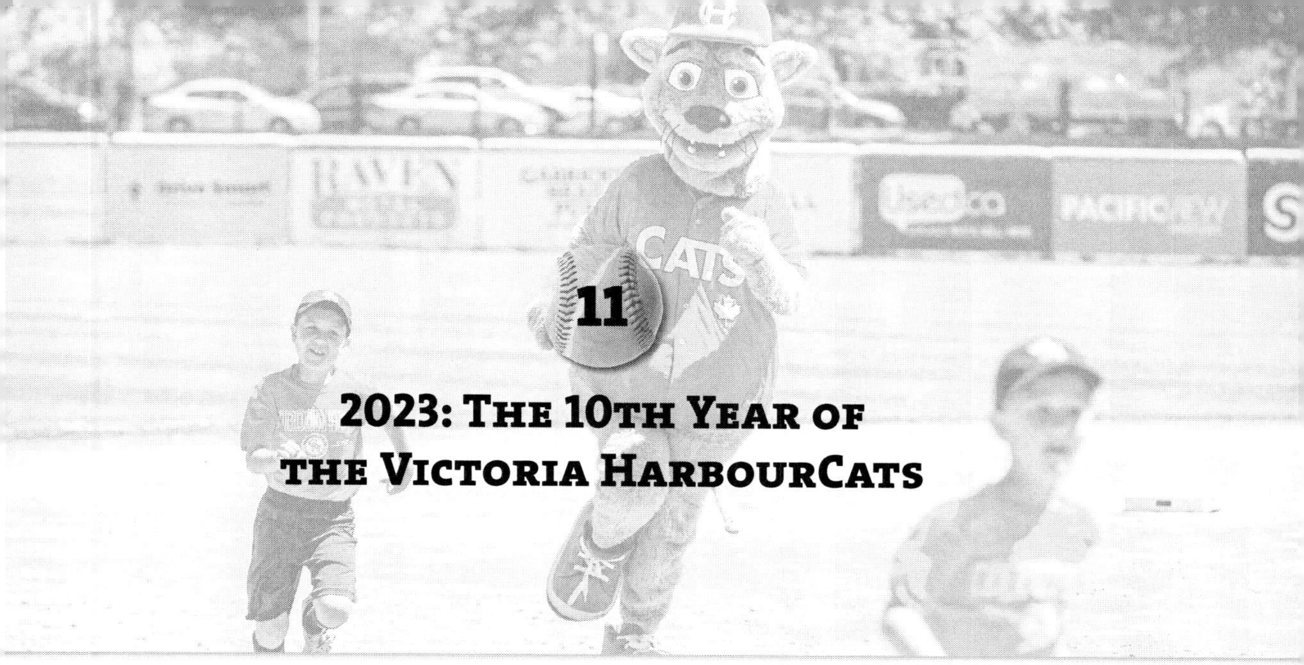

11

2023: The 10th Year of the Victoria HarbourCats

In early February, the HarbourCats announced the signing of three NCAA players for the upcoming season: Reece Usselman (Oregon Ducks), David Shaw (Texas Longhorns), and Max Clark (Washington Huskies). Also inked was Lee Grey from the Victoria Golden Tide. In the front office, Christian Stewart was named the new General Manager of the team.

The introduction of a pitch clock in Major League Baseball meant that the West Coast League had to come up with a strategy to have the clock at the college level. Lacking the necessary resources to install stadium clocks, the league decided that umpires would follow NCAA rules and have a "20-second action rule" between plays and a limit of two minutes between innings. Officials would use a stopwatch to determine the timing.

The opening game of the season was played on June 2, 2023 against the Kamloops NorthPaws. The team was still waiting for 10 to 12 players to come after their college season finished but were ready to play with those on hand. Jack Seward got the start and worked two innings, Dawson Hurford worked five, Brett Harvey pitched three, and Alan Dai threw the ninth inning. After Kamloops scored a single run in the second inning, the HarbourCats put up three in the fourth to take the lead. The NorthPaws tied the score in the fifth, but six runs in the bottom of the sixth put the game out of reach. The 'Cats added another four in the

The opening game of the season was played on June 2, 2023 against the Kamloops NorthPaws.

eighth for a 13-3 victory. Cam Caley, Ryan Magdic, and Kevin Shea had doubles, Bradden Kesey hit a triple, and Russell Young had a homer in the decisive victory. The good play continued in the second game of the series. It was closer than game one, but just as satisfying. Again, Kamloops took an early lead, but the 'Cats tied it in the fourth. They added two in the seventh only to see Kamloops tie the score

The HarbourCats stormed back with two runs in the eighth and added two more in the ninth for the win.

in the eighth. However, Victoria was not finished as they counted two runs in the eighth to win the game. Both teams were a bit rusty, committing two errors. Ryan Magdic hit a two-run homer, while Jack Johnson had two hits in the 6-4 victory. Starter Cam Caley worked four innings, Levi Abbott worked two, Josh Berenbaum pitched 1 2/3, and Jake Finkelstein got the "W" in relief. The series concluded with an afternoon matinée in which the home team narrowly defeated the visitors, 4-3. For the third game in a row, Kamloops took the lead and, in this case, were leading 3-0 after the top of the eighth. However, the HarbourCats stormed back with two runs in the eighth and added two more in the ninth for the win. Kevin Shea had two hits, including a double, and drove in two runs in the ninth with a single that scored Kai Gray and Bradden Kesey, who had reached base on a single and an error, respectively. The HarbourCats used five pitchers, with Tucker Christensen securing the "W" in relief.

Next to come to town were the Walla Walla Sweets. Victoria scored in the first inning and added runs in the third, fifth, sixth, and eighth to win the game 8-3. Kai Gray had two hits, including a triple, and drove in three runs; Jack Johnson had three hits, drove in two, and scored three runs; and Nick Dumesnil's two hits included a double while five runners stole bases to get into scoring position. Starter Benny Roebuck worked four innings, Dawson Hurford pitched the next three (and received credit for the victory), and Brett Harvey finished the game. The middle game of the series went much the same way as the opener. In this case, the Sweets scored twice in the third inning to take an early lead, but that was short-lived as the 'Cats brought home three in the fourth, two in the fifth, three in the sixth, and one in the seventh to win handily, 9-5. Kevin Shea, Marco Pirruccello, and Phoenix Sommay all had two hits, while Tyler Davis had a grand slam in his first game with the team. Sam Jordan took the win in relief. The final game of the series was the annual school field trip and was played before thousands of screaming youngsters, many of whom had never seen a baseball game before. The 'Cats certainly showed the students how the game is played as they cruised to a 12-1 victory. Three runs in the third inning got the home team off to a good start, and they added runs in every other inning except the seventh. Jack Johnson had a productive day at the plate, with a triple and a single, driving in four runs and scoring one. Marco Pirruccello had two doubles and scored twice, while Tyler Davis had four hits and drove in one run. Jack Seward started the game and worked four innings, then was relieved by Josh Berenbaum, who was credited with the victory. Chase Marshall, Loretto Siniscalchi, and Darius Opdam Bak worked the last three innings. With the series sweep, the HarbourCats were now 6-0 at home on the season as they prepared for their first road trip.

In Wenatchee, the AppleSox walked off the 'Cats in 10 innings. The game was tied 5-5 in the eighth when the Sox scored three to take the lead. Victoria managed to tie the score in the ninth but couldn't produce any more runs and suffered their first defeat on the season, 9-8. Nick Dumesnil had three hits, and drove in four runs and scored one, while Tyrus Hall had three hits and scored twice. Ryder Green was tagged with the loss in extra innings. In game two, the AppleSox were leading 6-0 before the 'Cats got on the board. The final score of 13-6 meant a second loss for the HarbourCats on the road. Nick Dumesnil was the offensive star of the game with three hits, including a three-run home run. Benny Roebuck started the game and was tagged with the loss. Loretto Siniscalchi, Carson Latimer, and Ryan Magdic worked in relief. The final game of the series also went to the home team.

Victoria managed to tie the score in the ninth but couldn't produce any more runs and suffered their first defeat on the season, 9-8.

Wenatchee won the pitching duel 3-1 to sweep the series. The sole Victoria run came in the eighth and was too little, too late. Michael Crossland had two hits, but the team could not cash in on them or the five walks, leaving 23 men on base. Sean Heppner started the game and worked four innings.

The next stop on the trip was in Port Angeles for a cross-strait series. The HarbourCats bats came alive in a 12-7 victory. Jack Johnson had three hits, while

Nick Dumesnil, Tyrus Hall, Cam Caley, Kyle Hepburn, and Bradden Kesey had two each. Sam Jordan was the winning pitcher, working three innings. The team was back on the winning track. Game two was a thrilling extra-inning win for the 'Cats. They took a 1-0 lead in the first inning when Nick Dumesnil was hit by a pitch, stole second, and scored after a Jack Johnson single on an error by the first baseman. After the Lefties tied the score in the fifth inning, Victoria scored single runs in the sixth and seventh innings, then surrendered two in the seventh. That was the end of the scoring until the top of the 10th when Cam Caley walked, advanced to second on a passed ball, and scored on a Marco Pirruccello single. Logan MacNiel got the 4-3 win in relief as he shut out the Lefties in the 10th inning. The HarbourCats swept the series with a 9-4 decision. Tyler Davis led the hit parade with three, including a home run, while Nick Dumesnil drove in two runs with a homer. Levi Abbott worked the first three innings, and Loretto Siniscalchi got the win in relief. Tucker Christensen and Flynn Ridley completed the match. The victory evened the team's road record at 3-3 and brought their season record to 9-3.

Back at home, the HarbourCats, with former Vancouver Canucks star goaltender Kirk McLean in attendance, continued their winning ways with a 12-2 defeat of the Yakima Valley Pippins. With a 1-0 lead, they unleashed three runs in the sixth inning and seven in the seventh to take an insurmountable lead. They had an impressive 17 hits, including doubles by Hudson Shupe, Marco Pirruccello, and

Former Vancouver Canuck goalender Kirk McLean after throwing first pitch to Kevin Shea. Joined by Harvey the HarbourCat.

Harrison Caley, and a homer by Brandon Green. The start of the game featured Cam Caley as a pitcher and his brother, Harrison, as a catcher. Dawson Hurford got the victory in relief, and Ryan Magdic and Dylan Osborne completed the game. The middle game also had a high score as the 'Cats outscored the Pippins

Father's Day did not go well for the home team. Their home win streak was snapped at eight games when the Pippins outscored them 6-3.

11-4. They started slowly with one run in the first inning but increased the lead with five in the third. Yakima put up three of their own over three innings, and the 'Cats responded with two more of their own. Father's Day did not go well for the home team. Their home win streak was snapped at eight games when the Pippins outscored them 6-3. The HarbourCats were leading the game 3-2 after six innings but gave up four runs in the eighth and could not recover. Yakima Valley pitchers allowed only four hits while Victoria pitchers surrendered 12. That was the difference in the game. Nick Dumesnil had two hits, accounting for half of the team's production.

Edmonton Riverhawks were the next visitors and the HarbourCats got back in the win column with a 7-4 decision. Trailing 3-2 after three innings, the home team scored single runs in the next five innings to secure the victory. Hudson Shupe and Dallas Macias had three hits each, including a double, while Nick Dumesnil hit a home run. Jack Seward got the start and worked 2 2/3 innings, being relieved by Logan MacNiel, Brett Harvey, and Ryan Magdic. In the middle game of the series, the 'Cats bats came alive, and they pounded out 15 hits. Michael Crossland had four hits, including a triple, while Tyler Davis had three, and Hudson Shupe and Dallas Macias had doubles. Dawson Hurford got the "W" for the home team. It was clearly not a pitchers' duel as the Riverhawks had 13 hits of their own. The series concluded with another home victory. This was a closer game, and it was tied twice before Victoria plated five runs in the sixth inning to take the lead for good. A ninth-inning comeback by Edmonton fell a bit short in a 9-7 decision.

Then it was back on the road for a series in Bellingham. The first game of the series was well-played, with an emphasis on good pitching and stellar defence. The HarbourCats scored one run in the first, and Bellingham matched that. The game continued tied until the 11th inning when the Bells pushed across the winning run on a Victoria error. It was a tough game to lose, but the 2-1 score reflected the level of play. Nick Dumesnil, Tripp Clark, and Lane Brewster each had a pair of hits for Victoria, who left 11 men on base. The second game also went Bellingham's way as they outscored Victoria 6-3. The HarbourCats took an early 3-0 lead but couldn't hold it and surrendered a total of five runs in the sixth and seventh innings to fall behind, and they could never recover a scoring touch. The 'Cats only managed five hits with Nick Dumesnil, Jack Johnson, Kyle Hepburn, and Michael Crossland all hitting doubles. Jake Finkelstein was tagged with the loss for his 1 2/3 innings of work. The Bells swept the series with a close 2-1 victory. All the scoring came in the fourth inning as the 'Cats had one run and the Bells two. Victoria had seven hits by seven different players but could not bring the baserunners home. Sean Heppner got the start and was relieved by Brett Harvey, Jed Decooman, and Carson Latimer.

Next on the agenda was a road trip to Kelowna. Victoria bats came alive again as they pounded out 11 hits and took advantage of four Kelowna errors in an 11-4 victory. Dallas Macias and Jesse Brown had three hits each to lead the hit parade; interestingly, all hits were singles. Max Grubbs started and was relieved after two innings by Davis Franklin, who worked three and was credited with the victory. Loretto Siniscalchi and Chase Marshall completed the game. The middle game of the series went to extra innings before the home team eked out a 5-4 victory. Only 491 fans were in attendance. Michael Crossland hit a grand slam homer in the sixth inning for the 'Cats' only runs. The rubber match went to the HarbourCats in an impressive 11-3 game. Both teams scored two runs in the first inning, and then Victoria's bats came alive. They scored one in the third, two in the fourth, four in the fifth, and two in the eighth to win handily.

The West Coast League announced a new feature, the WCL Spotlight. It was designed to showcase the talents of the top players in the league.

The West Coast League announced a new feature, the WCL Spotlight. It was designed to showcase the talents of the top players in the league, with a new list released every two weeks. On the first list, released on June 28, 2023, Dallas Macias was ranked number 12.

The next home series was a crucial one. The visitors were the Bellingham Bells who had just swept a series in their ballpark. With more than 4,000 fans in atten-

DAVIS FRANKLIN IN ACTION

dance for fireworks night, Victoria got off to a good start in game one and built up a six-run lead before the visitors hit the scoreboard. Tyler Davis had four hits and drove in three runs, while Michael Crossland had a double and drove in a run. Jack Seward started the game and worked five innings for the win. Dawson Hurford and Davis Franklin worked in relief in the 6-4 victory. The second game was a one-sided decision for the HarbourCats. Scoring six runs in the second inning, they cruised to an 11-1 win. Russell Young had three hits, including a home run, while Hudson Shupe contributed two hits with one home run. Five HarbourCats pitchers held the powerful Bells to six hits while striking out nine. Victoria completed the home sweep with an 8-2 win in a Sunday matinée. Five runs in the first inning got them off to a great start while their pitcher limited the Bells to two hits and struck out fifteen. Sean Heppner got the start and worked five complete innings before being relieved by Brett Harvey and Logan MacNiel. The season series was now tied 3-3, with both teams sweeping at home. Sean Heppner was named West Coast League's Pitcher of the Week for his efforts in the previous games.

After that successful series, the 'Cats travelled to Walla Walla to play the Sweets. They were down 9-0 before they got on the scoreboard, and then it was too little, too late. Kyle Hepburn was the hitting star with one hit, one run batted in, and one run scored. The Sweets took game two as well, this time by a 6-4 score. Nick Dumesnil and Marco Pirruccello had two hits each, including a double, and Russell

HUDSON SHUPE IN ACTION

Young had a double as well. Nick Taylor took the defeat after working four innings while Jake Finkelstein and Ben Smedshammer split the last four. Victoria took the final game of the series with a 9-5 decision that took over three hours to play. They scored single runs in the third and fourth innings, allowed the Sweets to tie in the fifth, and went ahead by two in the eighth, only to have the Sweets notch two of their own in the ninth to send the game to extra innings. The 'Cats sealed the victory with a big five runs in the 10th and then held their opponents to only one. Neither team played particularly well, as the 'Cats committed three errors and Walla Walla had four. Hudson Shupe raised his batting average to .446 as he had four hits and drove in three runs. Jack Seward started and was relieved by Davis Franklin. Jed Decooman got the win in relief.

Back at home, the HarbourCats faced the Port Angeles Lefties. In the opening game of the series, the 'Cats scored three runs in the first inning, aided by two Lefties' errors, and added one in the eighth for a 4-1 decision. Russell Young led the offence with three hits and drove in one run. Max Grubbs worked four innings, Jake Finkelstein got the win for his three innings work and Davis Franklin finished the game. The middle game was a one-sided affair with a final score of 11-2 in favour of the home team. Tyler Davis and Michael Crossland both had three hits and drove in two runs in a 14-hit effort. They scored three runs in the first inning and added six in the fourth and two in the fifth to win easily. Ben Smedshammer got the start while Ryan Magdic, Logan MacNiel, Daniel Gonzalez, and Josh Berenbaum were the relievers. The HarbourCats swept the series with a 13-4 victory. In this game, the score was tied 3-3 after three innings, and the 'Cats went ahead by one run in the fifth. Scoring eight runs in the fifth inning put the game on ice. Tyler Davis went two-for-three at the plate, including a home run, and drove in five

In the Major League Baseball draft, 2023 Most Valuable Player Joseph Redfield was selected by the Los Angeles Angels and former pitcher Derek Salata went to the Texas Rangers.

runs to lead the offence. Jed Decooman got the start and worked three innings and Loretto Siniscalchi for the win for his three innings of work. Cooper Crompton was announced as WCL Pitcher of the Week. In his 12 innings of work, he had allowed just one earned run and had 13 strikeouts.

In the Major League Baseball draft, 2023 Most Valuable Player Joseph Redfield was selected in the fourth round by the Los Angeles Angels and former pitcher Derek Salata went to the Texas Rangers in the 19th round. After the draft, former 'Cat Dakota Hawkins was signed as a free agent by the New York Mets.

Back in league action, the HarbourCats entertained the AppleSox, who had swept the series in Wenatchee earlier in the season. The first game went to the home team by a score of 8-4. After Wenatchee scored four runs in the top of the fifth, the 'Cats put up five in the bottom of the inning to take the lead for good. They

HARVEY THE HARBOURCAT AND THE KIDS' RACE

added a single run in the seventh and two in the eighth. Tripp Clark had three hits including a grand slam home run. Marco Pirruccello had a double, while Lane Brewster hit a triple. Starter Jack Seward worked 4 2/3 innings and was relieved by Tucker Christensen, who was credited with the win, while Carson Latimer finished the game. Game two was much closer, with the HarbourCats coming away with a 4-3 decision. Tyler Davis hit a home run and drove in two runs, and Dallas Macias

The final game of the series was another HarbourCats victory that pushed their home record to 20-1.

had two hits and drove in two runs. Hudson Shupe, who had earlier been named the top player in the second twenty-player WCL Spotlight, had a hit and walk in the game; with the hit, he raised his batting average to .418. Logan MacNiel got the decision in relief. The final game of the series was another HarbourCats victory that pushed their home record to 20-1. They started with two runs in the first inning, added single runs in the second and fourth and finished their scoring with two in the seventh. Dallas Macias led the offence with three hits and a walk in four plate appearances. Hudson Shupe and Tyler Davis had two hits apiece. Starter Flynn Ridley worked four innings and struck out six batters, and Brett Harvey got the win in relief while Cody Howard and Russell Derbyshire worked the last three innings of the 6-1 victory.

First baseman/catcher Tyler Davis was named the WCL player of the week for his hitting prowess as he went 12-for-22 and drove in 14 runs to extend his league-leading total to 39.

The Vancouver Island rivalry continued when the NightOwls hosted three games. In the series opener, the 'Cats prevailed 9-4 in a game that went to extra innings and took over 3 ½ hours to play. Victoria took a two-run lead only to see Nanaimo respond with four. The 'Cats tied the game with single runs in the fourth and sixth innings, and the score stayed that way until the 11th inning. Lane Brewster started the inning with a single. He advanced to second when Jesse Brown drew a walk. A Dallas Macias groundout advanced both runners to scoring position, and Hudson Shupe was intentionally walked. Tyler Davis then singled, scoring Brewster. Tripp Clark followed with a double, which scored Brown, Davis, and Shupe. Jack Johnson then singled to drive home Clark. The Owls were unable to score in

JESSE BROWN IN ACTION

their final inning. Max Grubbs, Ryan Magdic, and Jake Finkelstein worked the first nine innings and Carson Latimer the final two and was credited with the "W." The Victoria winning streak came to a crashing halt when Nanaimo upended them 5-3. The lone hitting highlight was Hudson Shupe's double as the team's bats went silent. Nick Taylor was tagged with the loss. The rubber match went to Nanaimo as they outscored Victoria 6-5. Russell Young had three hits and Jesse Brown had two in a losing cause. The HarbourCats used four pitchers, with Davis Franklin being tagged with the loss.

On the road in Kamloops, the 'Cats won the first game, 2-0, by scoring single runs in the seventh and eighth innings. Tripp Clark had three hits, and Jesse Brown had the fourth: both hit doubles. Cody Howard worked the sixth and seventh innings and got the credit for the victory. The second game went to the NorthPaws by a score of 6-3, who scored consistently and effectively shut down the potent offence. Dallas Macias, Jesse Brown, Ryan Magdic, and Jack Johnson all had two hits, but the team left ten men on base. Jed Decooman got the start and took the loss. The third game was rained out and was never replayed. In the third WCL Spotlight, Ryan Magdic was on the list at number 10 and Michael Crossland at number 20.

Back at home, the HarbourCats kept their home win streak alive with a 5-0 shut out of the Kelowna Falcons. Doubles by Hudson Shupe, Tripp Clark, Jack Johnson, Jesse Brown, and Ryan Magdic powered the 'Cats to victory. Starter Levi Abbott struck out five in his four innings of work. Ben Smedshammer pitched three innings and was credited with the "W." Brett Harvey and Dustin Davidson worked in relief. A crowd of 4,135 watched the next game go the HarbourCats' way as well as they outscored, Kelowna 12–2. Victoria had a narrow 3–2 lead after the top of the fifth inning but then scored three in the fifth, four in the sixth and singles in the seventh and eighth to win the hand. Ryan Magdic had a double and a triple, while Brandon Green had a home run. Jesse Brown had the hit of the game, a massive grand slam in the sixth inning that put the game on ice. Daniel Gonzalez got the start and worked 4 1/3 innings and was then relieved by Cody Howard, who received credit for the victory. Logan MacNiel and Darius Opdam Bak worked the last two innings. The fireworks during the game were matched by the final fireworks game of the season after the play was over. The final game of the series was unusual as the giveaway was a free funeral. Unfortunately, the HarbourCats were dead in the water and were shut out 11-0. Over the course of the game, they managed only two hits—by Tripp Clark and Jesse Brown. They used six pitchers, and none was very successful. This was not a good birthday gift for coach Todd Haney. With their home record now at 22-2, the team was determined to get back on track as they qualified for the playoffs as a wild card.

The Vancouver Island rivalry heated up for the last time in the 2023 season as Nanaimo came to town. Russell Derbyshire got the start for the HarbourCats in the first game and worked 3 1/3 innings. Josh Berenbaum, Zak Johnson, Dustin

The Vancouver Island rivalry heated up for the last time in the 2023 season as Nanaimo came to town.

Davidson, Skyler Manelski, Ryudai Watanabe, and Brett Harvey all worked in relief in an 8-6 victory for the home team. Marco Pirruccello had two hits and scored two runs, while Jesse Brown contributed two runs, drove in one, and scored one. Game two also went to the 'Cats. With the 9-5 victory, they set a West Coast League record for home wins in a season. They had previously been tied with the 2016 HarbourCats and the 2009 and 2019 Corvallis Knights. After falling behind 3-0, the 'Cats got their offence in gear and scored a run in the third when Michael Crossland singled, advanced on a Marco Pirruccello single, and scored on a Hudson Shupe single. They took the lead in the fourth inning when Jesse Brown, Dallas Macias, and Lane Brewster had singles, and Marco Pirruccello hit a triple. Tripp Clark launched a two-run homer in the fifth to put the team ahead to stay. The team used 17 position players in the game while six pitchers worked over the

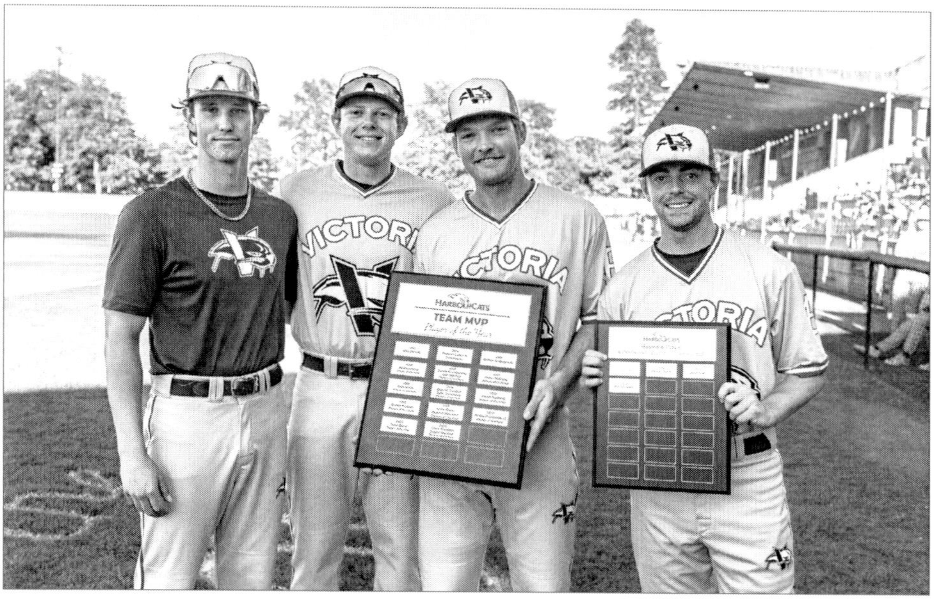

WNNERS OF YEAR-END HONOURS

course of the contest. The HarbourCats swept the series with a 4-1 win in the final game. Dallas Macias had two hits and a stolen base to lead the offence. Levi Abbott worked five innings for the victory, with Ryan Magdic and Sam Jordan completing the match. The HarbourCats finished the home season with a 25-2 record, losing only on Father's Day and coach Todd Haney's birthday.

The team announced their year-end awards. Logan MacNiel and Davis Franklin were named Pitchers of the Year; Tyler Davis, Player of the Year; and Brandon Green won the Community Service Award.

The final regular season road games were in Edmonton. Playing before a crowd of 5,402 on "Christmas in August Night," the HarbourCats scored five big runs in the eighth inning to win the game 7-2. Hudson Shupe had four hits, including a triple that drove in three runs to maintain his high batting average at .372. Josh Berenbaum got the win in relief. Game two was a much closer event. Trailing 1-0 after four innings, the 'Cats put up three in the fifth and cruised to a 4-1 decision. Dallas Macias had two hits, including a double, and stole a base. HarbourCats pitchers combined to strike out 14 Riverhawks while allowing only two walks. Logan MacNiel got the win in relief. Victoria swept the series with a 3-0 shut out in an afternoon matinée. Jack Johnson had two of the team's seven hits, drove in a run, and scored one. Ryan Magdic was credited with the win, and Brett Harvey with the save. The series sweep gave the team an impressive 38-15 record for the season, with one game rained out and never made up. They also clinched the Northern Division second-half title, which gave them a home-field advantage in the first two rounds of the playoffs.

The playoffs opened in Wenatchee, with the second and third (if necessary) games of the opening-round series to be played in Victoria. The 'Cats got off to a great start in game one with three runs in their first at-bat, taking advantage of wild pitches and hit batsmen along with a Jesse Brown single. He led the offence with two hits, driving in two runs. Tyler Davis also had two hits, including a double, and scored two runs in the 6-2 victory. Daniel Gonzalez started and worked four innings and was relieved by Dustin Davidson, Cody Howard (who was credited with the victory), and Logan MacNiel. After a long bus ride back from Wenatchee, the teams met at Wilson's Group Stadium at Royal Athletic Park. With 2,353 fans in attendance, the 'Cats took a three-run lead in the sixth inning and rode it to a 4-2 victory. Marco Pirruccello started the inning with a triple and was driven home by Hudson Shupe's double. He then crossed the plate after Tripp Clark's home

Bellingham Bells had defeated Kelowna Falcons in their semi-final series, so the title would be decided in one game, winner-take-all in Victoria.

run. Victoria added one run in the seventh and allowed the visitors only two in the ninth for the satisfying win that sent them to the North Division Championship game.

Bellingham Bells had defeated Kelowna Falcons in their semi-final series, so the title would be decided in one game, winner-take-all in Victoria. It wasn't easy, nor was the best baseball ever played, as the HarbourCats fell behind 5-0 early but bounced back to win the game 7-6 and secure their place in the league final. Two runs in the second inning made the score 5-2 for Bellingham, but the 'Cats managed to plate five runs in the fourth to take the lead for good. They took advantage of walks, wild pitches, hit batters, and sacrifice flies, along with singles by Tripp Clark and Dallas Macias. The Bells comeback fell one run short, and the jubilant crowd of 3,672 celebrated their home team's win. Logan MacNiel struggled early and was replaced by Jake Finkelstein, who worked 5 1/3 innings of scoreless ball. Josh Berenbaum, Dustin Davidson, and Brett Harvey completed the game for the 'Cats.

Then it was back on the bus for the trip to Corvallis to meet the Knights who

FANS ON THE UPPER DECK EXPERIENCE BUS

had defeated Portland in their one-game series. It was so hot at game time that the start was pushed back to 8 pm. Even then, it was very hot in the stands and even hotter on the artificial playing surface. Playing before a disappointing announced crowd of 1,097 which included several Victoria supporters who had made the trip, Corvallis shut out the 'Cats, 5-0 to win the title. Ironically, if the game that had been rained out had been replayed and Victoria had won, they would have had an identical record to Corvallis, and the site of the title game would have been decided by a coin toss. If the game had been held in Victoria before a much larger crowd, it is likely that the HarbourCats would have won. Such is the world of sport, where chance can influence decisions, and there are always "if only" events.

Nevertheless, the HarbourCats could hold their heads up high, having set a record for home wins and played a terrific season. Their home fans appreciated their effort and look forward to the day when the championship comes to Victoria.

In year-end awards, Logan MacNiel was named to the First-Team All-WCL Team, while Tyler Davis, Hudson Shupe, and Davis Franklin made the second team. Honourable mention was made to Dallas Macias, Nick Dumesnil, Jack Seward, Jack Johnson, Russell Young, and Michael Crossland. To top the season off in style, Todd Haney was named Coach of the Year.

In the final WCL Spotlight, Cody Howard made the list at 11 and Dallas Macias at 17.

HarbourCats fans are so proud of their former players who have played at least one game in the major leagues. Nick Pivetta, Andrew Vaughn, Alex De Goti, and Nathan Lukes had all played before this season. This season, we can add Cade Smith and Davis Wendzel to the list. I am sure the list will get longer as time goes by.

12

10th Anniversary Videos

A book about a baseball team would only be complete with comments from former players, coaches, executives, and other interested parties. Several former players and coaches were asked to provide short videos to recognize our 10th year in operation. The feedback was heartening, and those comments are included in this section. I also attempted to talk with as many persons as possible with mixed results; sometimes, our schedules did not allow interviews. For those who spoke with me, I am eternally grateful as you gave me "behind the scenes" information I could never have obtained elsewhere.

Visit https://hcats.tv/10th-anniversary-player-messages/ to see the players as they present their messages.

Nick Pivetta

From Victoria – first MLB player in HarbourCats history

Hi everybody, Nick Pivetta here, Boston Red Sox, just wishing the Victoria HarbourCats a happy 10th anniversary. I think one of my fondest of being a part of that organization was being able to start the (very first) home opener (in 2013) in front of all my friends and family. Always grateful for every opportunity and wishing everyone there with the organization nothing but health and success moving forward. Thank you so much – and GO HARBOURCATS!

Caleb Rickets, C

University of San Diego and Philadelphia Phillies organization

Hello everybody, Caleb Rickets here, I just wanted to take a moment and congratulate the HarbourCats on an amazing 10 years. I played for the

HarbourCats in the summer of 2018 and had an incredible time there that summer, and a lot of great memories, especially how great the fans were and how many people came out to support us and it was an awesome place to play for the summer.

Alex Rogers, RHP

North Dakota State (from Nanaimo)

Hey HarbourCats supporters, this is Alex Rogers, just wanted to say congratulations on the 10-year anniversary of the team. I was a member for the summer of 2014 and half of the summer of 2015, and what I remember most is all the bus rides and hotel stays with the team, that's always a favourite part about those teams. I also remember the trip travelling to Klamath Falls, Oregon, and that being a whirlwind experience, only to have the WCL all-star game rained out, and then drive all the way back. They are lasting memories I will never forget and again, congratulations on 10 years and GO HARBOURCATS!

Zach Swanson, RHP

Park-Gilbert (from Victoria, former team batboy)

What's up HarbourCats fans? It's Zach Swanson here, I was a batboy for the HarbourCats a bunch of years ago, and played for the HarbourCats in 2018 and 2019, and most recently the play-by-play guy for the HarbourCats in 2022. I'm just thankful for the 10 years of the HarbourCats, excited to watch more good baseball, and one of the things I remember most about playing with the HarbourCats was the atmosphere, I got a chance to start the first game of the 2019 West Coast League final against Corvallis. Thankful to be able to do that and the fan atmosphere was amazing. Go Cats!

Austin Russell, OF

First year team, from Victoria

Hey, it's Austin Russell here. I want to give my congrats to 10 great years of HarbourCats baseball. I was on the 2013 team, the inaugural season, Connor Russell, Nick Pivetta and I were the first three signees in team history, and we did not know what we were in for. But that first year seemed to lay the groundwork for what it is today, and it was a major success, and many more good years to follow!

Joseph Redfield, OF

NOW WITH THE ANAHEIM ANGELS ORGANIZATION

Hey everyone, I'm Joseph Redfield and I played for the Victoria HarbourCats in 2022. The thing I remember most about playing there was just how awesome of a baseball environment it was, from the fans showing up to all of our games; the fireworks nights were awesome, the coaches were great, and I loved all my teammates. I have nothing but good things to say about the whole organization – congrats on 10 years, and I'm super happy for the organization as a whole and keep doing your thing, Victoria!

Griffin Andreychuk, 2B

FROM NANAIMO, WAS AT SEATTLE UNIVERSITY

Hey everyone, it's Griffin Andreychuk here, a second baseman from 2014 to 2016; I just wanted to say a big congratulations to the HarbourCats on 10 awesome seasons. It gets me thinking back to the 2016 season when we had 40 wins as a club and a 19-game winning streak and broke a few records that year. Congratulations, it's an awesome place to play, the fans are absolutely the best – Go Cats!

Adam McKillican, RHP

UBC AND NOW IN COLORADO ROCKIES ORGANIZATION

Hi, it's Adam McKillican here; happy 10 years to the HarbourCats and 10 years of West Coast League baseball in Victoria. I was a member of the 2017 HarbourCats and we came second, lost to the Corvallis Knights in the final. My favourite memory would be starting the first game of that series at home and winning that game via walk-off style, thanks to Bernie Po Hao Huang, with the walk-off double.

Jason Leone

ASSISTANT COACH FOR 2017, 2018 AND PART OF 2019

What's up HarbourCats! Congrats on 10 years, an amazing accomplishment, I look forward to following the team and hopefully I get back there one day. Go Cats!

Brian Chen

LHP in 2018, now a translator in the Philadelphia Phillies organization

What's up HarbourCats? Brian Chen from Taiwan and I was with the HarbourCats in the 2018 summer and the HarbourCats really brought me a new baseball view worldwide, and now I'm a translator for Mandarin with the Phillies. I want to congratulate the HarbourCats on 10 years! Happy birthday!

Alejandro Ortega Lopez

My friend Adriel Pena and I played for you guys in 2018. We were the first Cubans to play with you, and we want to congratulate you on your 10 years in the industry.

Mikey Wright, RHP

2014 and 2015 teams

Hey everyone, Mikey Wright here—part of the 2014 and 2015 HarbourCat teams. I wanted to congratulate everyone in the HarbourCats organization, especially the fans, on 10 years of being an amazing organization. My favourite part every summer was all the friendships I would make with the players we had, the host families, and the fans that made every single one of us feel like we were back at home—we appreciated it all!

Nick Plaia, OF

Cal Baptist, 2018 and 2019 teams

What's up HarbourCats? Nick Plaia here, aka Baby Shark. Happy 10-year anniversary! Big shout out to (all the people in the organization), Coach Haney and Coach Birt – moments at that field I will cherish for a lifetime, best fans in the whole WCL!

Wyatt Young, SS

Pepperdine, 2016 team, now in NY Mets organization

Hey Victoria! This is Wyatt Young of the New York Mets organization. I just wanted to say congratulations on the 10-year anniversary. I played in Victoria back in 2016, and I really enjoyed my time there, and I hope to be back soon.

Sid Lacy, RHP

Chico State, 2019 team

Hey, HarbourCats! Sid Lacy, I was a right-handed pitcher for Victoria in 2019; I want to congratulate you guys on your 10-year anniversary. The atmosphere was electric and the coaches were great, my teammates were great, and we made a tremendous amount of memories.

Alan Baldwin, C/OF

2014 team, University of Hawaii and Tampa Bay Rays draft pick

Hey, HarbourCats fans, Alan Baldwin here, University of Hawaii, from Kailua, Hawaii. I played on the 2014 HarbourCats. It's kind of crazy to think it's been that long ago, and it makes me feel really old. Victoria's always going to have a really special place in my heart, It was one of the best summers of my life; the team was pretty stacked, with a lot of really good players. The people were great and the atmosphere was great, the experience just in general was amazing and one I'll never forget.

Harrison Spohn, IF

2018 and 2019 teams, Cal Baptist,
now in Florida Marlins organization

This is Harrison Spohn from California Baptist University, now with the Miami Marlins organization. I played for the HarbourCats in 2018 and 2019, and those were the two most fun summers I've had in my entire life. I miss everything about it; I miss the coaches, my host parents, Nick and Colleen, and a shout-out to everyone who gave me a chance to play in Canada for those two summers. Todd, Ian, Jim, and everyone who was involved, thank you so much and congrats on 10 years.

Ben Polshuk

Cal Poly, 2015 and 2016 teams

What's up HarbourCats fans? Ben Polshuk here. I wanted to wish everyone a huge congrats on the 10-year anniversary of the team for the best place in the world to play baseball. I was lucky enough to play two summers for the team, 2015 and 2016, and truly, every day, I still miss the atmosphere, the team, the ballpark, and the fans; it's still the greatest feeling in the world to be part of the organization. I'm excited to keep cheering everybody on and look forward to seeing what the next 10 years brings.

Zachary Fraser

former GM of Yakima and Walla Walla

I want to congratulate Jim and his team in Victoria, his family and his partners, for coming up on their 10-year anniversary. I remember well the early years and the struggles that the organization went through and to see how well they have progressed and what an essential part of the success of the West Coast League they have become. What a great thing to look back on and realize I had the ability to experience that both as a partner and as a competitor and as a fan and I want to congratulate the HarbourCats and can't wait to see what the next 10 years holds.

Logan Lombana

2013 and 2014 teams, Long Beach State, pitched for Minnesota Twins organization

I want to congratulate the Victoria HarbourCats on their 10-year anniversary. I played in the summers of 2013 and 2014 and the things I remember most about playing in Victoria was playing in front of some amazing fans and the lifelong relationships I was able to create with the front office, my teammates, and the French family as well. Go HarbourCats!

Josh Mitchell

played 2015 and 2016

HarbourCats fans, what's up? It's Josh Mitchell. I'm a former HarbourCat and current Minnesota Twin. I was lucky enough and blessed enough to be able to play for two years in Victoria in 2015 and 2016, and I just want to reach out and say congratulations on the 10-year anniversary. That is such an amazing accomplishment, a huge accomplishment, and it couldn't have happened to a better City, better organization, and better fan base. I was lucky enough to play for two years, and it'll go down forever as the two best Summers of my life and just one of my favourite places to play. The stadium, the front office, the management, the coaching and the fans it was just phenomenal. At 10 years, guys, that's an amazing accomplishment. I'm happy for you, I'm proud of you. I'm looking to come back and visit sometime soon. Go, Cats!

Alex De Goti

Mr. HarbourCat, 2013-2014-2015 teams, played in MLB with Houston Astros, been with Astros, Marlins, Twins and Rangers organizations

What's up everyone, Alex De Goti here, with the Minnesota Twins, and I can't believe it's been 10 years since the first game was played there at Royal Athletic Park as the Victoria HarbourCats. I still remember going out there and playing in that first game with a full stadium and the fans were cheering us on like it was Game 7 of the World Series. It's a true testament to the front office, the players, and the fans for bringing that great energy and great product to that amazing and beautiful city of Victoria – I miss you guys and hope to reunite with all of you guys in the near future.

Austin Dondanville, RHP

2015 and 2016 teams, Cal Poly

Hi, this is Austin Dondanville. I pitched in Victoria in 2015 and 2016, and I just wanted to congratulate the Cats on 10 years. Those were two of the best summers of my life by far, and I will never forget the atmosphere up there. Thank you to you all who were involved. Here's to 10 more!

PJ Floyd, IF

2015 and 2016, Sacramento State

What's up, everyone? This is PJ Floyd from the 2015 and 2016 HarbourCats; just wanted to say congrats on the 10-year anniversary – hope everyone is doing well and Go Cats!

Griffin Paxton, IF

2019 Player of the Year

Congratulations to the Victoria HarbourCats on the 10-year anniversary! I was the 2019 HarbourCats player of the year, and my favourite memory was Todd Haney's Canada Day locker room speech, and for those who were there, they will never forget it. Being around the community and how much support they gave us; it was truly a wonderful place to be and I will never forget it and can't wait to go back. Go Cats!

Matt Amrhein, RHP
closer, 2019 team, Cal Baptist

This is Matt Amrhein from Cal Baptist. I just want to give a huge shout out to the HarbourCats for their 10-year anniversary. Playing for the HarbourCats and playing in Canada was one of my fondest memories in my entire college career, and I'm super thankful I got to experience it.

John Grimsley, OF
2014 team

What's going on y'all? John Grimsley from Houston, Texas, a proud member of the 2014 Victoria HarbourCats, and let me tell you one thing – southern hospitality is definitely a thing in Canada; you're all sweet as pie but tough as nails. Go get 'em, Cats!

Graig Merritt
Head Coach 2015 and 2016, WCL coach of the year 2016 (and the villain of Big Brother Canada in 2016)

Victoria, what it is! HarbourCat baseball fans, you are the most passionate, loyal, committed and most knowledgeable fans in all of Canada. Graig Merritt here, 2015 and 2016 Head Coach – and 2016, oh what a year! Franchise record in wins with 40, 19 straight wins, which is still a West Coast League record, the most magical summer of my life. I just want to say Happy Anniversary to the HarbourCats, to the owners, to the players, to the fans, to the entire community of Victoria, and to the 10th anniversary. I miss you guys.

Hunter Vansau, OF
2017 and 2018 teams, all-time home run record holder, Mississippi State

What's going on HarbourCats fans? Former outfielder Hunter Vansau here from the 2017 and 2018 HarbourCats, I want to congratulate you guys on your 10th anniversary as a ball club, it's a huge milestone and testament to the hard work of all you guys in the front office do, day in and day out for the team. You guys provide the players with the absolute best experience, and I know you give the best experience to the fans, who are electric at every single game and it's so fun to play for you guys. The best memory I have playing with y'all is back in 2017, I hit a grand slam that allowed us to go into the West Coast League playoffs! Really miss you guys, love my family up north, and Go HarbourCats!

Ian Sanderson

Pitching Coach, 2018, 2019 teams

This is Ian Sanderson, I was the pitching coach up in Victoria, and I'd like to congratulate everybody in Victoria on 10 years, and thanks for some of the greatest times I've had in summer baseball and some of the greatest people I've met. Thank you for everything you've done and all the memories you've given me.

Bernie Po-Hao Huang, IF

Taiwan, 2017 team, now in Taiwan's top pro league

Hi everyone! My name is Bernie. Victoria HarbourCats fans, long time no see! I'm playing baseball right now in the Taiwan Major League. I was very happy to get the chance to travel to Canada and meet everybody, and I will find the time to go back to Canada and see everyone. I wish the HarbourCats a happy 10th-year anniversary (then breaks into his signature song, Happy Birthday!).

DJ Porter, OF

2017 team, Cal Baptist

Hey, HarbourCats! I just want to say congratulations on your first 10 years of being an organization and thank you for the time I was able to spend there. I was part of the 2017 team, and it was the three best months of my life that I wish I could go back to all the time; you guys were so awesome, all the personnel. I miss the road trips with you guys, and a special shout-out to the greatest host family anyone could ever ask for the Chamberlains. I miss you guys, and hopefully, you can host my little man here when you guys are in year 28. Congratulations!

Holden Lyons, RHP

2016 team

Hi, this is Holden Lyons. I was a relief pitcher for the HarbourCats in 2016, and I just remember having an absolute blast that summer. I went on a crazy run and won something like 19 games in a row and broke the record for most wins in league history. Hopefully, it still stands, but good luck to everyone, and congratulations on 10 years. We'll be following you along the way.

Connor Russell

Original 2013 team and an All-Star that year, from VIU, RHP

"What's up HarbourCats fans? This is Connor Russell from your 2013 Victoria HarbourCats baseball team – and I just want to congratulate the best West Coast League organization on a successful 10-year anniversary. You guys do so much for the community and City of Victoria, and I know how much people enjoy coming out each summer to take in some great HarbourCats baseball. My favourite memory and moment with the HarbourCats has to have been getting the opportunity to play in front of my hometown crowd, and I can't wait to get out to the ballpark this summer to cheer you guys on. Good luck, and Go, Cats!"

Todd Haney

Head Coach 2019-22-23-24, Assistant Coach 2018, former MLB player with Expos, Cubs and Mets, and proud Texadians!

"Hey HarbourCats! Happy 10th anniversary – Coach Haney here! What an amazing summer of 2023, our 10th anniversary – 27-2 at home, thanks to your support and your enthusiasm, your passion for the team. We look forward to bringing home the championship in 2024 for you guys. We love you guys. Kira and I are so proud to be Texadians. Let's go HarbourCats – GTW!"

Jason Willow

from Victoria, played in the 2015, 2017, and 2019 seasons

Hey, HarbourCats fans, it's Jason Willow. I'm just congratulating the HarbourCats on their 10-year anniversary. Being a Victoria kid, born and raised, it's been super cool to see the team grow over the last 10 years. It was even more special to play two seasons in 2018-2019. Both summers were super unforgettable with memories. Playing in front of a great crowd, good teammates, coaches, front office, everything was great. Can't wait to see what the next 10 years look like.

Cade Smith

from Abbotsford, BC, played in 2019,
now with Cleveland in the American League

Hi, my name is Cade Smith. I was with the HarbourCats in 2019. I'm currently with the Akron River Ducks. Just wanted to say congrats on 10 years.

Larry Quigley

Bus Driver

Hey, HarbourCat fans and the HarbourCats. It's Larry, the bus driver. I've been driving for the HarbourCats for almost 10 years now and am looking forward to another great season, although I'll be a spectator. I want to wish everybody a happy 10th anniversary for the team. This is our year. We're going to get them this year. Good luck, guys.

13

From a League Perspective

It's hard to think back to a time when the Victoria HarbourCats weren't a part of the West Coast League. Or even when Royal Athletic Park had all those other teams, or was silent. In fact, those involved in the WCL itself, which has been around since 2005, have a hard time thinking back that far.

That's the case for Tony Bonacci, the President of the WCL and owner of the Cowlitz Black Bears (who debuted in 2010), and Ridgefield Raptors, who first set foot in the WCL in 2019. Bonacci, like the group that owns and operates both the Victoria HarbourCats and Nanaimo NightOwls, has one of the three situations in the WCL where one group owns two teams.

"A lot of Victoria's story parallels the league's story in terms of its progression. Victoria was right in the middle of it at very exciting times as we brought in new

> "A lot of Victoria's story parallels the league's story in terms of its progression. Victoria was right in the middle of it at very exciting times as we brought in new teams."

teams. The individuals behind all the teams are committed, and it makes for a pleasant experience at every level, from the players to the fans and even for those of us who are involved at the league level," said Bonacci, an attorney from Scottsdale, who has been to Victoria a couple of times to feel the energy of Wilson's Group Stadium at RAP.

When the HarbourCats joined the league, it was just the second foray into a BC/Canadian market—the Kelowna Falcons, playing out of Elks Stadium near the shores of Lake Okanagan, were a charter member. Now, of course, there are five Canadian entries, with Victoria and Nanaimo on the Island, Kelowna and the Kamloops NorthPaws in the interior, and the Edmonton Riverhawks, the northern outlier in Alberta.

When the HarbourCats joined the league, it was just the second foray into a BC/Canadian market.

"The area we play in is one of the nicest parts of the world in the summer and is a great place to play baseball," said Bonacci. He felt Victoria was an attractive market for the West Coast League as it had a history of baseball, and the fans were knowledgeable and very supportive. On the other side of the equation, players love to come to Victoria as there are huge crowds, and some of them had never played before more than a few spectators. There is a benefit to the short season, as you never get a chance to be bored, as there is always something exciting happening. He added that the league's travel alone is a preparatory tool for players who look to move to the pro level. The various iterations of pro leagues the Vancouver Canadians have played in are in the same footprint and essentially mimic the travel demands minor leaguers face at the formative levels. In addition, the coaches are, for the most part, former major leaguers who can give the young players insight into what could lie ahead," he added.

I interviewed John McLean, owner of the team until late 2014. He got it all started – no McLean, no HarbourCats. His most telling comment on the game of baseball is, "It is a game where it is social, and it is one that it doesn't matter down to the last pitch, the game's not over. Whereas in most other sports, if you're down 6-0 in hockey and there are 40 seconds left in the game, you're not winning. It's kind of the same thing with football, but in baseball, you can be down 6-0 with one batter left – two out and you're in the bottom of the ninth, and you can come back and win."

"After examining other alternatives, I decided on Victoria as the ideal location for summer college baseball," said McLean, who lives in Vancouver. "The baseball team, at that time, was probably the most joyous part of my life," he added.

McLean's love of sports is well known – a sports management graduate whose son played a high level of baseball, coached by his dad in many of those younger years. Arm fatigue halted his son's progression, but not before great experiences in tournaments as far away as Egypt.

McLean fully believes in the college development model that fuels the WCL. He told me a story about a sports agent who thinks baseball should follow the example of football and basketball and use college rather than minor pro leagues to develop players drafted out of high school.

From the "Nothing Is Ever Easy" file, the story of the very first HarbourCats game, played at home at Royal Athletic Park on June 25, 2013, is one for the ages. A bus breakdown kept the Kelowna team from making the assigned ferry time, but some help from transportation guru John Wilson helped the Falcons get rolling again – and a ferry was held to ensure the club would arrive. "I'll never forget the visiting team walking across the field. Some of them had their pillows under their arms," he said. Anyone who has ever been on a minor sports road trip can imagine this scenario.

That first year will always involve the name Jones—first team GM Holly Jones and late staff addition Brad Norris-Jones, who was with the team for seven years. The hiring of Holly Jones was seen as ground-breaking, in fact. McLean tells his story about Holly Jones. "The media were expecting a male GM and at the team announcing her hiring as General Manager, a communications firm went out and did the press release and got little bags of popcorn for everybody there. The media knew we were going to announce a general manager, and there was a group of

From the "Nothing Is Ever Easy" file, the story of the very first HarbourCats game, played at home at on June 25, 2013, is one for the ages.

people standing around, and the press was there. When her name was announced, it was almost met with disbelief," he adds. Jones would be named the league's top executive at season's end.

Brad Norris-Jones—no relation, in case anyone was wondering—started selling tickets and then moved into corporate partnerships. With the collapse of so many teams prior and baseball's instability, it wasn't smooth sailing from the start, as this baseball team-come-lately wasn't exactly trusted off the start to end the futility of the recent past.

The zenith of the first season was hosting the all-star game, but in reality, the real win was getting through the inaugural summer and being in position to repeat it all again in 2014 – even though Holly Jones left, her spot filled by Jim Swanson in November of 2013.

For Norris-Jones, his memories bring a smile— seeing Andrew Vaughn in a Victoria uniform and playing a key role in the addition of Claire Eccles, still the only female to compete in the WCL.

Vaughn's promise was evident, and he would go on to be the third-overall pick in the 2019 MLB draft. Norris-Jones recalls, "I'm out on the field with them, and I said to Andrew when he was taking batting practice if you hit three home runs, I'll buy everybody lunch or dinner today. He hit two home runs, and he's got three balls left, and the pressure's on now: everyone's watching. And his last one, he didn't hit a home run." However, they got dinner anyway.

Nothing beat having his son Kelly Norris-Jones, a draft pick of the Toronto Blue Jays, both play and coach for the HarbourCats – 2014 as a catcher, 2016 as staff on the record-setting 40-14 team. "That was fun watching him, said Norris-Jones. "He had a pretty good career, but when he got all those concussions, it was pretty well over, and that was pretty special to have him there," he added.

"The travel of the WCL is not for the faint of heart, something the fans likely can't ever fully appreciate."

"The travel of the WCL is not for the faint of heart, something the fans likely can't ever fully appreciate," said Norris-Jones. He also recalled those crazy road trips that the team took. "I still remember being in Bend, driving home right after the game, getting to the ferry at 5 a.m., and sleeping for an hour. And then I would go, we'd get back to the park, and I would go work the whole day because we had a game that night," he notes.

There's no one better to talk about the process of even having the team land in Victoria than former mayor Dean Fortin, who recognized that the West Coast League model was the one that could break the curse of baseball teams past. He still remembered the folding of the Victoria Seals when the Golden League collapsed. "However, it gave me an idea of how a sports team could help define the capital city," said Fortin, mayor of Victoria from 2008 to 2014. He felt that the West Coast League would be a good league to operate in Victoria.

The location of Royal Athletic Park definitely fed into the opportunity to be successful. A short walk from downtown and so many neighbourhoods, the historic facility is part of the fabric of the north section of the city.

He recalls the opportunity presented by John McLean and the league commissioner and held meetings with them. They negotiated a deal after considerable discussions with the local community. He wanted to know their concerns and endeavoured to deal with the issues and make the end product successful.

It wasn't about politics for Fortin, it was about community, and he sensed this format would win the hearts of people and provide a strong economic spin-off—which certainly has been the case. "The HarbourCats are very successful in the community, and a spin-off effect is an economic boost for the city," said Fortin, a noted basketball coach and regular attendee of HarbourCats games.

The location of Royal Athletic Park definitely fed into the opportunity to be successful. A short walk from downtown and so many neighbourhoods, the historic facility is part of the fabric of the north section of the city.

He was the one who got the old wooden fence boards along Cook Street taken down. That meant that people passing by could see there was action on the field. Despite others saying that people would stand there and not pay to go in and watch, that was not the case. "I attended a game with my friends where two older ladies were sitting not far away. They were giving the umpires a hard time, and when we went to talk with them, we discovered that they used to be umpires. They were having the time of their life," said Fortin.

He would attend the Canada Day game and throw out the first pitch. With all his duties as mayor, he had few opportunities to view games. However, he now has time to enjoy the games.

Fortin is eager to see the team win the last game of the season, as close as the HarbourCats have been, falling in the final outing three times (2017, 2019, 2023). "It's only a matter of time before the city has a winner," he says.

14

Coaches

The HarbourCats have been blessed with outstanding head coaches and talented assistant coaches, but none have meshed more with the city than Todd Haney, who was named WCL coach of the year in 2023 after leading his team to a record 25-2 home record.

Todd Haney

I interviewed coach Haney on April 4, 2024. Todd joined the HarbourCats as an assistant coach in 2018 and was named head coach in 2019. When asked what it was like to coach in Victoria, he responded that there are many amazing things about Victoria. The people and the fans are just amazing people. They love the team and enjoy coming out and supporting the team. There is also joy in coming each day to the field, knowing that you're going to have a great day because of the atmosphere. He feels our operation is top-notch with amazing owners, which continues throughout the organization.

He wants the players to have an unforgettable experience here, despite where they are from. He is excited about the 2024 season because of the returning players who are fired up to win a championship. The new players will recognize the culture of the team and work together. He told me about the Northern Division Championship game last season against Bellingham. With the HarbourCats down five runs, he went to the mound to talk with Logan MacNiel, and the assembled players told him, "We're good. We averaged seven runs a game. If we hold them here, we're good." What a prophetic statement.

Ethan Fox

I interviewed Ethan on April 15, 2024. He has a unique experience in that he played for the HarbourCats organization and is now coaching. He and Kelly Norris-Jones are the only ones who can say that. In the fall and spring, he coaches the Golden Tide and looks forward to it every year. When it comes to the summer and the HarbourCats, he feels it's like a little window into what professional ball feels like where you show up at three, you get your practice in, and then you take the field, and there are thousands of fans, and it's pretty amazing. He appreciates having the opportunity to work with many highly skilled baseball players from different races, countries, and just all walks of earth.

When he was playing for the HarbourCats, he had probably never played in front of more than 50 people, and there were always immense crowds here. He talked about pitching in 2017 during the playoffs and said that when he pitched, he would get tunnel vision, so focussed on the game that he heard nothing else. However, as soon as the inning ended, he could enjoy the enthusiastic crowd. Considering he never played professional baseball, to be on a coaching staff with former major leaguers and be respected, not in the same way perhaps, but to be valued, is pretty exciting. He likes to look back and think about his former teammates who are playing professional baseball in the minor or major leagues. He likes the mixture of Division One players and ordinary players and wants to bring our Canadian players up to the same high standard.

15

FROM BAT BOY TO PITCHER AND BEYOND

ZACH SWANSON

I interviewed Zach on April 9, 2024. Born in Prince George in Jan 2000, he made national news when he was 2 for singing US and Canada anthems for a WHL game in Prince George. He moved to Victoria when his father began working for the HarbourCats and graduated from Lambrick Park Secondary School. He played for both the Victoria Eagles and Mariners and started college baseball at San Diego Christian in 2018. He pitched the 9th inning of his very first college game in an 8-4 win on January 25, 2019, the day his grandfather Harold Swanson died. He transferred to Park-Gilbert, also an NAIA school, for his third year and earned his business degree in four years. COVID gave him an extra year of eligibility, so he stayed and played for former MLB catcher Kelly Stinnett (who coached Edmonton and Cowlitz in WCL) and used that fifth year to attain his MBA.

ZACH SWANSON WORKS AS A BAT BOY

ZACH SWANSON IN ACTION

He had a unique view of the organization as he started out as a bat boy at age 14. He absorbed information from the coaches and watched how the players went about their business. He felt the experience was invaluable, and he would not have the level of baseball understanding he has today without his early experiences. It was exciting to play for the team, given his early connections. He was a right-handed pitcher as well as an outfielder. And he sang anthems for a couple of Victoria HarbourCat games. He was named to the original Nanaimo team for 2021, but his season was cancelled because he was dealing with an injury. In 2022, he was the 'Cats play-by-play guy while rehabbing a torn right tricep.

He notes that you never stop learning about the game – and it's a wonderful perspective for life in general. When you stop learning, there is something wrong. Although he understands the game well, he learns from his fellow coaches and the young players. He is thrilled when young men who were his teammates with the HarbourCats make it to the major leagues.

Zach is currently coaching a baseball team and tells his players to remain positive even when beaten badly.

16

Made it to the "show"

Nick Pivetta

Victoria native Nick Pivetta is best known for being the starting pitcher in the first HarbourCats game and then becoming our first alumnus to make it to the major leagues. He attended Lambrick Park Secondary School but missed his senior year due to an injury. He also pitched for the Victoria Eagles. As a member of the Canadian National Junior Team from 2009-2012, he pitched in the 2010 18U World Championship. He attended the New Mexico Junior College on a scholarship, graduating in 2013. He was thrilled to be able to pitch in his hometown and said in a *Times Colonist* interview, "I loved coming out to watch the (former Victoria pro franchises) Capitals and Seals play. It's nice to have a summer league team (HarbourCats) here now." On June 7, 2013, he was drafted in the fourth round, 136th overall, by the Washington Nationals. He would pitch one more game for Victoria before turning pro and leaving for pro ball with the Gulf Coast Nationals of the Rookie Gulf Coast League.

On July 28, 2015, he was traded to the Philadelphia Phillies for Jonathan Papelbon. He played in their farm system, taking a break to play for Team Canada in the 2017 World Baseball Classic. He made his major league debut on April 30, 2017, for the Philadelphia Phillies. On August 21, 2020, Nick was traded to the Boston Red Sox and made his debut for them that day against the Baltimore Orioles. He remains with that organization as a starting pitcher.

ANDREW VAUGHN, T-MOBILE PARK,
SEPTEMBER 6, 1922, WITH THE AUTHOR

ANDREW VAUGHN

I was privileged to interview Andrew Vaughn in the Chicago White Sox dugout at T-Mobile Park in Seattle on September 6, 2022. He was more than willing to share his experiences with the HarbourCats and to provide suggestions to young players on the way up. He wished he could have played more games for the 'Cats, but that was not possible. However, he will never forget his time here, from seeing whales on the BC Ferries to the huge crowds that cheered every play that the team made. He loved playing in Victoria. His statement on the game of baseball made quite an impact on me. He said that baseball is actually a very simple game. "You go out every day and do the same things, but every game is different because of many factors: how you feel on the day, your opponent's skill, the weather, etc."

Born in California, he attended Maria Carrillo High School in Santa Rosa. He enrolled at the University of California, Berkeley and won Pac-12 Conference Freshman of the Year in 2017. The following year, he was named Pac-12 Conference Baseball Player of the Year and received the Golden Spikes Award. He was drafted third overall in the 2019 draft and made his major league debut with the Chicago White Sox on April 2, 2021. He hit his first major league home run on May 12 of that year.

He has played left field and first base. Watching him play in three games in Seattle was a thrill for me, especially right after the interview when incredulous Chicago fans wondered how I got the autographed ball and the autograph on my t-shirt. He is still playing with Chicago and will likely remain there for years.

We continue to follow his career with interest.

Alex De Goti

Alex played with the HarbourCats for three seasons, from 2013 to 2015, and is affectionately known as "Mr. HarbourCat." He played his college ball at Long Beach State, moving to the Barry Buccaneers in 2016. He was drafted by the Houston Astros in the 15th round of the 2016 amateur draft and played his first professional ball game in 2016 for the Tri-City ValleyCats. He made his way up the baseball ladder and made his major league debut on April 16, 2021, for the Houston Astros and recorded his first hit off Yusei Kikuchi of the Seattle Mariners. He ended that game 2/4 with 1 RBI.

After playing in the minor leagues for Houston, he elected free agency in 2022. On December 1, 2022, he signed a minor league contract with the Miami Marlins. He was traded in 2023 to the Minnesota Twins and played for their Triple-A team. He was released on August 3 and then signed a minor league contract with the Texas Rangers on January 26, 2024.

He had a great career in Victoria, batting .287, .296, and .294 in his three seasons here. He was very popular with local fans and made a point of talking with young fans, which they appreciated and will remember for the rest of their lives. It is relatively rare to have players with the HarbourCats for three seasons, as their college coaches often want them to play elsewhere for different types of exposure. To recognize his contribution to the team, he was added to the Ring of Honour in 2016.

When asked about his time in Victoria, he provided amazing details. "Playing in Victoria for 3 seasons was some of the most fun I have had playing baseball. Let's start with the incredible attention to detail the whole organization had with incoming players. I felt like I was being taken care of before I even set foot into the country. For a young athlete to go play baseball in a different country isn't something so easy to do, but the HarbourCats organization made me feel at home. I was set up to live with an amazing woman, Brittany French (now Wilson). This wonderful soul welcomed my college roommate, Logan Lombana, and me into her home, which was the first time we had ever done such a thing. The transition was easy because we dealt with a special person and family. Brittany and the French family became my second family. This family made me feel at home and was always attentive to Logan and me. The constant attention and love they expressed to us made playing baseball easy even though we were teenagers living in a different country for the summer. I will forever be grateful for the French family because they made three summers in Victoria some of the best moments of my life.

Furthermore, playing summer baseball in Victoria is arguably the best set up for college players looking to improve their game. From the front office personnel to the coaching staff, I always felt like they were helping my teammates and I improve our game and also learn how to win. From a player's standpoint, that is everything and more. To top that off, the atmosphere at Royal Athletic Park was electric every single night. Playing in front of so many fans that love the game of baseball made coming to the yard exciting.

Lastly, but certainly not least, I want to thank the Swanson family. This family also took time out of their days to make me comfortable in a different country. They would invite me over to their home for dinner frequently because they were genuinely trying to get to know me. I felt that connection, and that is why Jim and I still have frequent communication to this day.

Quite simply, the Victoria HarbourCats are a first-class organization. I would recommend playing summer baseball there to any young aspiring athletes because they will be provided with the best people who are willing to make the experience as best as possible.

Nathan Lukes

Nathan was born in Portland, Oregon, and attended Center High School in Antelope, California. He played at Sacramento State for three seasons and was named All-Western Athletic Conference in 2014. That summer, Nathan played for the HarbourCats. He returned to school and finished his career as Sacramento State's all-time hit leader with 244. He was drafted by the Cleveland Indians in the seventh round of the 2015 draft and assigned to their A-affiliated team, the Mahoning Valley Scrappers. In 2016, he was traded to the Tampa Bay Rays and played in their minor league system, reaching the Triple-A level. He was named to the Rays' 2021 Spring Training Roster and spent the entire season with Durham. On November 29, 2021, he signed a minor league contract with the Toronto Blue Jays and played 111 games for the Triple-A Buffalo Bisons. He made his major league debut with the Blue Jays on March 30, 2023, entering the game as a pinch runner; he would eventually score on a Matt Chapman single. He would play 29 games at that level. He is currently playing for Buffalo.

Cade Smith

When I started writing this book, there were only four former HarbourCats who had played in the majors. It was with pleasure that I learned that Cade had made his debut with the Cleveland Guardians on March 30, 2024. He pitched for the Victoria HarbourCats in 2019. Born in Abbotsford, Cade attended Mennonite Education Institute Secondary School in Abbotsford, then travelled to study at the University of Hawaii. He was the opening day pitcher for Victoria, continuing the tradition of having Canadian products have that honour. He worked 29 innings in six games, yielding 17 runs, 14 of which were earned, allowing only one home run, striking out 27, and walking 7. He was drafted by the Minnesota Twins in the 16th round of the 2017 draft but did not sign. He was signed by the Cleveland Indians and played his first pro game in 2021. He worked his way up the Cleveland system, progressing every year until this year when he made the major league roster. He led the player development system in saves, with 15 in 2023 and 13 in 2022. He competed in the 2023 World Baseball Championship, yielding two earned runs across two outings.

Davis Wendzel

Much to the delight of HarbourCats fans, we were able to add another name to our list of former players who made it to the majors. Davis Wendzel made his debut with the Texas Rangers on April 25, 2024. I was watching my favourite team, the Seattle Mariners, when his name was announced as a pinch hitter. He then proceeded to get a base hit, his first one in the majors. His first home run, a two-run effort, was hit on April 27, 2024, against the Cincinnati Reds, making him the second former HarbourCat to homer in the big leagues.

He was a member of the HarbourCats in the 2017 season, logging time at both shortstop and third base. He played in 10 games with 12 hits in 39 at-bats but hurt his knee and had to leave the team. After he left here, he played college baseball for the Baylor Bears. After the 2018 season where he started 58 games at third base and won several accolades, Davis was selected by the Boston Red Sox in the 37th round but did not sign. The Texas Rangers selected him the 2019 draft and he signed a professional contract. He began playing at the rookie league after rehabbing a thumb injury that he had suffered at college. He gradually made his way up the Rangers system and made his major league debut on April 9, 2024. We will continue to follow his progress as we do for all of "our boys."

17

From Vancouver Island to Professional Baseball

Adam McKillican

I interviewed Adam on April 17, 2023. Born in Courtenay, he played here in 2017. He has many memories of that season with Andrew Vaughn, who made an impact while he was here, and that talented team. He talked about the hit by "Bernie" Po-Hao Huang that won game one of the final. He noted that Bernie was not a flashy player, so it was good for him to get that attention. Adam thinks playing for the HarbourCats was a pretty big turning point in his career because up to then, he hadn't played at the high level of college baseball where there were Division One players from the US and some of the best. This was his chance to play against and with a lot of guys who were going to go on to be draft picks. He was playing at UBC, which is an NAIA school, and there are good players there, but the level of depth just isn't the same as those Division One teams. However, he earned Academic All-Canada honours in 2019. So, for him to play in Victoria and do what he did: have a really good year and win Pitcher of the Year, really put him on the radar not only of some Division One teams, but it put him in touch with the man who is now his agent in pro ball.

He said it was tough to be a baseball player on Vancouver Island as there are neither a lot of scouts nor a lot of opportunities. When he was in high school, he had to drive 50 minutes to practice in Parksville, where he played for the Royals. Unfortunately, he ran into injury problems and required Tommy John surgery and couldn't come back to the HarbourCats in 2018. In 2021, he moved to Georgia Gwinnett College when Canadian teams were shut down, and his team won the NAIA national championship, posting a 51-10 record. Adam had a 7-3 record that year in 12 starts, with 34 walks and 69 strikeouts in 61 2/3 innings. After he finished his college career, he didn't get drafted, so he played Independent ball for the Québec Capitales of the Frontier League before the Texas Rangers signed him as a free agent. After he was released by the Rangers, he signed nine days later with the Colorado Rockies where he was an organization all-star.

He played one season for the 2022-23 Adelaide Giants of the Australian Baseball League. Of course, their season corresponds to North America's off-season, so it would mean he had to play right through. However, after discussing it with left-hander Evan Rutckyj, a Capitales teammate who had played in Adelaide in 2019, he jumped at the chance to get more baseball time. The bonus was that he and a couple of teammates were given a luxurious house on the beach to live in as well as a vehicle. There were some ex-big leaguers there and the bonus was that they ended up winning the league championship. He is currently in the Colorado Rockies organization.

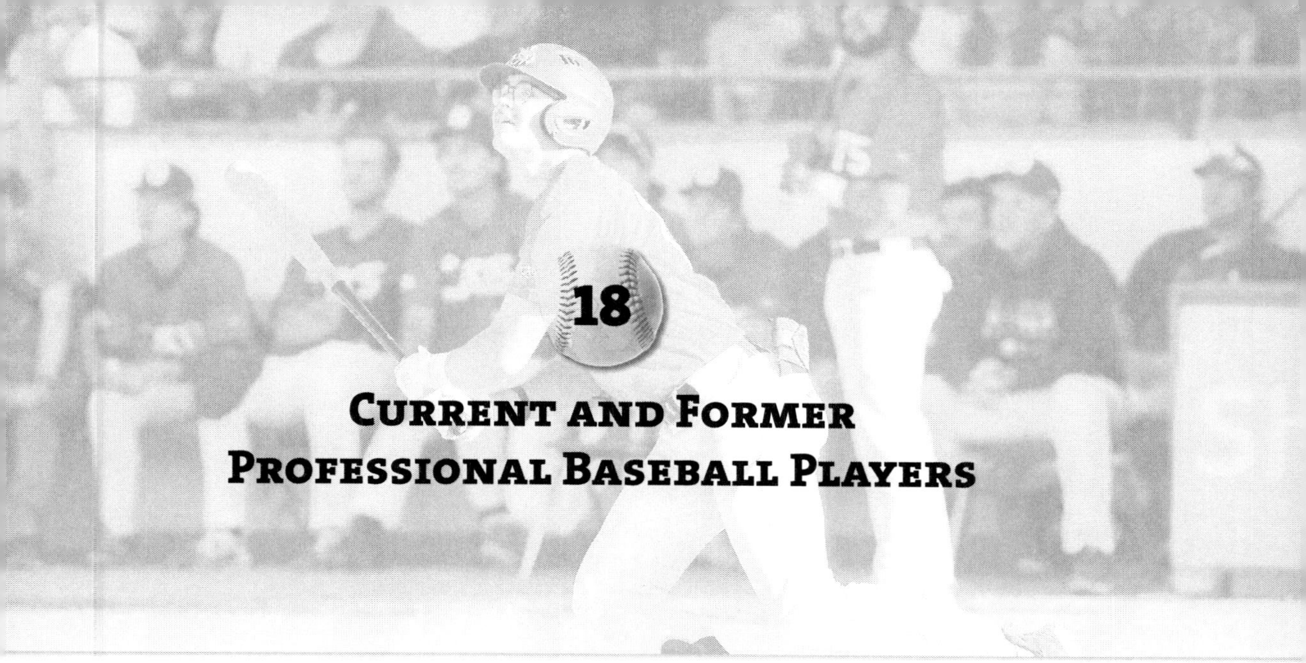

18

Current and Former Professional Baseball Players

Joseph Redfield

I was able to interview Joseph Redfield in person on April 17, 2023, the day before he left the team. He is from Waco, Texas and has lived there all his life. His father played in the major leagues, and he feels he just inherited the baseball gene. His ambition is to be like his Dad. He started out with Little League and was overlooked by high school recruiting scouts. So, he found a home at Temple College, which is only half an hour away from Waco, so he could see his parents often. It was a pride check going to junior college instead of to a big-name school, but it proved to be beneficial, and he feels that is the biggest part of his journey to becoming who he is today as a baseball player.

He ended up with the HarbourCats because Coach Haney seemingly knows everybody in Texas who plays baseball. He was the coach of the Waco Storm organization and when Joseph played for that team for a couple of years, he got to know him even more. He was more than happy to come to Victoria and play for our awesome fans and to create new relationships. He talked about the Edwards Family Training Centre and how the young baseball players who come to learn about the game of baseball idolize the HarbourCats because they are the "big guys." As to his future, he will be attending Sam Houston in the fall and hopes to be drafted the following year. At the game that evening, he was named Most Valuable Player for the season. He played one season with Sam Houston University and was then drafted in the fourth round of the 2023 draft by the Los Angeles Angels and signed a pro contract.

Harrison Spohn

I interviewed Harrison on April 15, 2024. He felt very lucky to have played for the HarbourCats in 2018 and 2019. He still talks with friends about those two summers. Friends he plays with now who played on a different team in the same league are very jealous that he played in Victoria. He credits the coaching staff with reinvigorating his baseball career. His goal was to pick coach Todd's brain and create a good relationship with him. He learned a lot from him that helped him gain confidence about how to go about baseball the right way. As far as the city of Victoria playing there in general, he absolutely loved Victoria. He thinks it was probably one of the most beautiful cities he's ever been to. He is still in contact with many of his former coaches and teammates from that time.

2019 was his last year of playing Summer ball and, of course, COVID cut the next season. He did five years of college at California Baptist University and used the extra year of eligibility. If it wasn't for that fifth year, he probably wouldn't be playing professionally right now. After that 2022 college season, he signed as a free agent with the Miami Marlins. He feels that his experience with the long road trips for the HarbourCats prepared him for minor league baseball. Some of the players are close to home, but for him, home is the other side of the country. He loves to look at old videos and pictures of the HarbourCats and to remember the happy times he had here.

AJ Alcantara

I interviewed AJ on April 1, 2024. Before coming to play for the HarbourCats, he played one summer in Wenatchee. When he came to Victoria the next year, he noticed a huge scene change. He loved playing here. The team was breaking attendance records, and the atmosphere was unbelievable. Victoria was like a perfect baseball environment. The stands were full, and the fans cheered every play. He considered himself an offensive player and Royal Athletic Park was a hitter's park. After his first year when his coach asked him where he wanted to play for the second year, he said he wanted to return to Victoria. After his college career, he coached baseball at Citrus Junior College for four or five seasons. He got a job opportunity to work as a children's social worker with LA County and it was too good to turn down. He had just become engaged, so he needed job security.

Josh Mitchell

I interviewed Josh on April 12, 2024. Until he came to Victoria to play, Josh had never played in front of a sellout crowd, or even a large one. He thought it was great that the fans were so baseball savvy and actually understood the game. It was some of the best baseball he got to experience at that age and definitely a home-field advantage. He considered it a pleasure and an honour to play in the city of Victoria and spent two summers here. He felt the city treated players like they were superstars. Whether they were playing well or had just lost five in a row, they were treated the same. It was very warming and welcoming. Playing in Victoria had a definite effect on his later baseball activities. He had been having arm trouble at school, and the university had actually pulled his scholarship. So, to be able to go out and play like he did that season, with a 9-0 record and a 1.87 ERA, was unbelievable. He set a wins record for Victoria and the West Coast League. The team ended up winning 40 games and had a 19-game win streak. When he went back to the university, he ended up being the Friday night starter, which is the ace of the staff.

He got drafted that year and feels that he wouldn't have played professional baseball for another eight years without the HarbourCats, so they turned his career around. They gave him a love for the game again, and it was just a beautiful opportunity. He loved playing for coach Graig Merritt, who was a fiery guy who made him want to win. Right now, he has retired from baseball after injuries ended his career. However, he's in the business of training as a pitching coordinator, and he trains young athletes, high-level pitchers, and athletes in sports performance. In other words, he's passing on the skills that he learned from his coaches to the next generation of baseball players.

Nick Plaia

I interviewed Nick on April 20, 2024 and present his comments here. I played in Victoria for two summers. I had the same host family for two summers (Nick and Colleen Grant). Yeah, well, I mean, players are living together. It's not like we're all in the hotel room, all separated. My experience is that Harrison [Spohn], my buddy Matt [Amrhein], and I were in a basement with three beds, and that's where we lived for the entire summer.

I played in Yakima the year before I was in Victoria, which was a different experience. Hands down, nothing will come close to the experience I had in

Victoria, and I could not have asked for a better experience. On a multi-different level, it's just the coaching staff, the front office, the fans, people that work at the stadium, a lot like teammates, and all that. It's just all in one, just made the experience one of the best things in my life. Definitely I'm very grateful and thankful for the experience I got out there. I honestly miss it to this day. Just a fun experience. It's the ballpark, the surroundings, just having the fans there no matter what each game, always cheering for us. And if we lost, it wasn't like they would get mad at us or anything. Then we were out the next game, and they were just excited to be out there watching us and cheering us on.

And so, it just felt very welcoming that we were such a big part of the Victoria community, at least for the summer. We felt really engulfed into the culture out there, and we became a part of Victoria's family, and everyone welcomed us in. So, I went home, and then COVID happened; I was in talks with Jim about going back out there to play, but then, obviously, that never happened. I went and trained in Arizona with one of my good buddies who played professional baseball and went back to school; ended up getting my master's in business administration because of COVID, so it was a blessing in disguise. My team that year ended up winning the WAC championship, so we won the WAC title. We were still in the five-year ban for playoffs, so unfortunately, we couldn't go to the playoffs.

After college, I hung up the cleats, and I officially just started working, getting into the everyday life as an adult. Currently, I'm working in medical sales for a company called Karl Storz. I'm a sales associate there for all specialties. I've just been doing that for the last couple of years and it's been great. Definitely, the experience of playing baseball and everything has helped me. It's very competitive because it's sales and being competitive in anything is definitely a must for us. Even if it's a game of horseshoes, I may have never played before, but I can tell the person I'm playing that I'm trying to win.

It's the competitiveness that's been built in me since a very young age and even grew more when I was in Victoria. I can thank Todd Haney for that. He was a great mentor to me. He gave me many stories and many lessons and just was always there to talk to even after I was there. I would text him on the side so it wasn't like you're in Victoria for this amount of time and then you'll never hear from these individuals again. You're in Victoria for this amount of time, but because you played in Victoria, you get engulfed in that family.

That was a heartbreaker for me in that last year there, being in the championship and losing to Corvallis.

I think, hands down, Victoria has been the best fan experience I've ever been around. Just the atmosphere itself. Even if it's raining, the stands are still packed. You pull a bunch of kids from all over the country from let's say Mississippi, Florida, kids from New York, and you get kids from California like myself, kids from Washington, Montana, Nevada, you go and pull like kids from all over just different cultures, different families, different groups of people, and then you just put them all in one spot in Victoria and it's like everybody has that same goal where it's like, well, we want to bring a championship to Victoria. The best part, too, is that, yeah, the coaching staff has been in the majors, and they have many, many triumphs and accomplishments. But the thing that is so great about them is that they'll never rub that in your face.

He said, "I've been talking to Jim and one of these summers, in the future, I'll come up and do some coaching. I do want to experience that." I told Nick that we would love to have him come back and work with the team.

19
Host families

The heart of a successful college program is the families who step forward to billet players for the summer. As described on the HarbourCats website, a "host family provides a 'home away from home' for player(s) during the HarbourCats season. In return, you gain a memorable summer experience and, most likely, a long-lasting friendship. Host families often refer to their players as an adopted member of their family, as you form a bond that will last far beyond the end of the season. But it is so much more."

Current Host Family Coordinator Cindy Kent provides comments on her experience as a host family and as the coordinator, following in the footsteps of Karen Russell, Brittany Wilson, and Katrinka Green.

Hosting

Having a son who played baseball and being involved with the ballparks he played at made hosting a player an obvious choice for our family. Watching our 'summer kid' play at the college level makes the games even more enjoyable. One of our most memorable players was our first, Hunter Mercado-Hood (I think he still holds a number of team records); he left two of his wood bats for our son when he was 11. We would also host our players' families when they would come to visit their son in Victoria. We have also remained in contact with several of our players and their families.

Coordinating

Being the Host Family Coordinator has been a great experience. As someone who is an organizer at heart and enjoys helping, being the host family coordinator was the natural fit for me after spending many years volunteering with local youth baseball organizations. Getting to know so many local families who are now part of the HC family has been great as well as all the players and their families. Being told directly by the players and their parents how thankful they are for the work that the 'Cats do to make their summer experience enjoyable and fun is worth all the hard work.

Author's notes

I could not write this section without commenting on my involvement with the host family program. With my children grown up and having left home years ago and me being widowed just before COVID, I welcomed the opportunity to welcome young players into my now-empty home. The pandemic postponed the events until the 2022 season, but it was certainly worth the wait.

I started with three pitchers from Texas. Having never visited there, I knew nothing. It didn't take long before I learned so much about that state and their food. I learned to bake jalapeño cheese bread and how to roast ribs. With the games ending so late at night, I became very good at preparing meals that could be reheated easily, like chili and tacos, or roasted for hours in the oven, like ribs or lasagna. I enjoyed talking baseball with the players and learned what it was like to be successful at the game. As is common in summer baseball, players leave and get replaced by others. They were always welcome here. Last year was also a pleasure. It was nice to have position players as my billets so I could learn more about baseball. I particularly enjoyed meeting the players' parents, brothers, sisters, and girlfriends. I made a point of taking them out to dinner so we could chat.

I have formed bonds that will last for years and have visited with some of the players when I have travelled to their regions. It is an experience that I will never forget – and I look forward to meeting new players this season.

Comments from some of my billets

Kevin Shea – 2023 season

The HarbourCats was one of, if not the most fun, baseball experiences I have had. The community embraced us like major leaguers, and Victoria felt like home. Every day, I woke up excited to get to the field and put on my jersey. I now play baseball at the University of San Francisco.

HELEN EDWARDS WITH JESSE BROWN AND BEN SMEDSHAMMER

ZAK JOHNSON – 2023 SEASON

Thank you for including me in this great book. I am very honoured to be a part of the HarbourCats history! Playing for the HarbourCats was more than just going to the field to play baseball. I felt like I was a part of something bigger. The team was a group of brothers and the crowd felt as if they were our family with their constant cheers and support. I truly felt like I was in a baseball town and that I had to do my best to honour the town with how I played. The coaches were amazing and helped me to improve my pitching abilities and my character. They truly cared for me and my teammates.

JESSE BROWN – 2022 AND 2023 SEASON

I absolutely loved playing in Victoria for two summers. I fell in love with the people, the city, and the baseball. I'm grateful for the lifelong memories I made there and for the baseball experience I gained. Victoria has a special place in my heart, and I will always think of it as my happy place.

Addison Sells – 2022 season

My experience in Victoria British Columbia was one of the best 3 months of my life. I stayed with Helen Edwards, and she was the sweetest lady and best host mom I've had in a long time! She would always offer to cook and take us to get food after games at times, and the food there was great. Everyone was so nice and happy to welcome us to the Harbour Cats plus the fans were great. We had the best fans out of the whole West Coast League, I believe, as well as the coaching and owners! Everyone got along and enjoyed their time there. I loved going to the beach on some days and just relaxing. It was so beautiful there and peaceful. The water was a little cold, but then you get used to it. The whole city was so cool and unique, as it was very different than my hometown. It was so beautiful the buildings were very unique and nice. I really enjoyed my time, and I cannot thank Helen Edwards enough for letting me stay with her and taking me in like family! She was awesome, and we loved having long talks in the kitchen about whatever it may be, but most of all, she made my stay very welcoming and comfortable! I will never forget my time staying there and meeting all the new friends I've made there, and I plan on coming to visit soon! Thank you, Helen!

20 Getting from One Place to Another

Larry Quigley – bus driver

I interviewed Larry on April 13, 2024. No summer baseball college team would be successful without a great bus driver, and Larry Quigley was that man for years. From the first road trip in 2013, until ill health forced him to give up the job, Larry was the team's driver, making sure they arrived at their destination safely. On one trip in the US, Nick Plaia got a spider bite, and his arm swelled. Larry got him onto the bus and drove to the hospital, found a parking spot, and took him in for treatment. On another trip, they had a tire blowout and had to try to fix it – in the heat under less-than-optimal conditions. He made sure that after games, the bus was ready with the air conditioning on, so the players didn't have to wait around after they were finished. He said some players sleep on little mats on the floor and some just stay in their seats. Getting rest is important as they often have to play a game when they reach their destination.

He always gave a speech to the boys at the beginning of the season when they were crossing the border to tell them to be respectful and just answer the questions with no joking around. As he explained it, border personnel don't need to hear silly jokes about hand grenades and bombs and stuff like that. Each coach has his own personality, but Larry got to know them all, and they all became like a huge family. He made fans very happy when he used to broadcast away games via Facebook before all games were live-streamed. Of course, his games featured interviews with players and other items that never appear now. For him, the most touching story was when the widow of the bus driver for the Humboldt

Broncos came to town and was recognized at the ballpark. He was able to talk with her and reflected on the fact that he has a million miles under his belt and what happened to that bus is a bus driver's worst nightmare. In addition to the HarbourCats, he also drove the Victoria Royals junior hockey team and UBC's baseball team, who travelled to southern California and played there. He noted that many drivers don't want to drive for sports teams because there are no tips, but he'd rather go and watch sports. As he says, "It's a terrible job having to drive around, watching baseball, being put up in a hotel, getting food, and a paycheque on top." He taught himself sports photography, so he'd take pictures during the road games and give them to the players, and they really appreciated his efforts. He went out of his way to take care of the team and if they wanted to go to a shopping mall or movie, he would load up the bus and drive them there. I have heard that he was the best at parking a bus in the tightest spots. He is still watching games, this time from a season ticket location to the left of home plate.

HarbourCats Records, 2013–2023

SINGLE SEASON

OFFENCE

At bats	Hunter Mercado-Hood, 2014	200
Batting average	Shane McGuire, 2017	.451
Hits	Hunter Mercado-Hood, 2014	77
Runs	Harry Shipley, 2017	46
Doubles	Kevin Collard, 2015	13
Triples	Kevin Collard, 2015	4
	Harry Shipley, 2017	4
	Joseph Redfield, 2022	4
Home runs	Gabe Clark, 2014	8
	Hunter Mercado-Hood, 2014	8
	Colton Moore, 2022	8
Runs batted in	Hunter Mercado-Hood, 2014	46
Walks	Hudson Shupe, 2023	29
Hit by pitch	Harry Shipley, 2017	14
	Nick Dumesnil, 2023	14
Stolen bases	Joseph Redfield, 2022	27

PITCHING

Appearances	Travis Kuhn, 2017	24
Starts	Dominic Topoozian, 2015	11
Complete games	Three tied with 2	
Innings pitched	Dominic Topoozian, 2015	73 2/3
Strikeouts	Josh Mitchell, 2016	61
Wins	Josh Mitchell, 2016	7
Saves	Travis Kuhn, 2017	9

CAREER RECORDS

OFFENCE

Games	Alex DeGoti, 2013-2015	134
At bats	Alex DeGoti, 2013-2015	514
Hits	Alex DeGoti, 2013-2015	150
Runs	Griffin Andreychuk, 2014-2016	81
Doubles	Alex DeGoti, 2013-2015	28
Triples	Alex DeGoti, 2013-2015	5
	Kevin Collard, 2015 and 2017	5
Home runs	Hunter Vansau, 201-2018	14
Runs batted in	Alex DeGoti, 2013-2015	70
Walks	Griffin Andreychuk, 2014-2016	68
Hit by pitch	P J Floyd, 2015-2016	16
Stolen bases	Nick Plaia, 2018-2019	37

continued

CAREER RECORDS, CONTINUED

PITCHING

Appearances	Cameron Schneider, 2014 and 2016	29
Starts	Alex Rogers, 2014-2015	15
	Logan Lombana, 2013-2014	15
	Austin Dondenville, 2015-2016	15
Complete games	Logan Lombana, 2013-2014	2
	Ty Provencher, 2013	2
Innings pitched	Austin Dondenville, 2015-2016	110
Strikeouts	Josh Mitchell, 2015-2016	84
Wins	Austin Dondanville, 2015-2016	10
Saves	Travis Kuhn, 2017	9

FRANCHISE RECORDS

WCL Attendance leaders, 2014-2019

Single game attendance record - 5,240 (June 2, 2018 vs. Wenatchee AppleSox

2013 WCL All-star Game host - record attendance - 4,210

Wins	40	2016
Runs scored	416	2019
Hits	518	2019
Doubles	105	2017
Triples	15	2019
Home runs	55	2019
Team batting average	.293	2017 and 2019
Stolen bases	150	2023
Walks	297	2019
Runs batted in	339	2019
Total bases	877	2019
Slugging percentage	.442	2019
At bats	1,986	2019
On base percentage	.391	2019

HarbourCats coaches, 2013–2023

NAME	POSITION	YEAR(S)
Ben Jackson	Assistant Coach	2013, 2014
Bob Miller	Head Coach	2013
	Head Coach	2014
Dennis Rogers	Head Coach	2013
Alec Adame	Pitching Coach	2015
Joe Meggs	First Base Coach	2015
	Assistant Coach	2016
Graig Merritt	Head Coach	2015, 2016
Jerry Pena	Assistant Coach	2015
Andrew Wilson	Bullpen Coach	2015, 2016
Joe Fabre	Pitching Coach	2016
Kelly Norris-Jones	Bench Coach	2016
Jason Leone	Assistant Coach	2017, 2018, 2019
Brian McRae	Head Coach	2017, 2018
Mike Spears	Pitching Coach	2017
John Schnaderbeck	Assistant Coach	2018, 2019, 2022, 2023
Ian Sanderson	Pitching Coach	2018
Troy Birtwistle	First Base Coach	2017, 2018, 2022, 2023
	Assistant Coach	2019
Todd Haney	Head Coach	2019, 2022, 2023
	Assistant Coach	2018
Curtis Pelletier	Assistant Coach	2018, 2019
Ian Sanderson	Pitching Coach	2019
Mark Petkovsek	Pitching Coach	2022
Greg Swindell	Bench Coach	2022
Ethan Fox	Assistant Pitching Coach	2022
	Bullpen coach	2023
Scott Anderson	Pitching Coach	2023
Tanner McGaw	Physiotherapist	2015-2023
Steve Sinclair	Assistant Coach	2023
Jaxon Williams	Bench Coach	2023

HarbourCats players, 2013–2023

NAME	NO.	POSITION	HOMETOWN	SCHOOL	YEAR(S)
Will Ballowe	37	Pitcher	Danville, CA	University of Washington	2013
Nick Pivetta	27	Pitcher	Victoria, BC	New Mexico Junior College	2013
Bryan Conant	20	Pitcher	Alta Loma, CA	Riverside Community College	2013
Emilio Foden	16	Pitcher	Abbotsford, BC	Central Washington University	2013
Ryan Keller	31	Pitcher	Castaic, CA	University of San Diego	2013, 2014
Daniel Koo	27	Pitcher	Abbotsford, BC	University of British Columbia	2013
Scott Kuzminsky	17	Pitcher	Puyallup, WA	University of Hawaii	2013
Logan Lombana	34	Pitcher	Newark, CA	Long Beach State	2013, 2014
Joe Navilhon	28	Pitcher	Antioch, CA	Cal State Fullerton	2013
Tyler Rowe	33	Pitcher	Rancho Cucamonga, CA	University of New Mexico	2013
Connor Russell	30	Pitcher	Victoria, BC	Vancouver Island University	2013
Alex Real	14	Catcher	Anthem, AZ	University of New Mexico	2013
David Schuknecht	19	Catcher	Palm Desert, CA	Riverside Community College	2013
Evan Willow	18	Catcher	Victoria, BC	McPherson College	2013, 2015
Alex De Goti	24	Infielder	Miami, FL	Long Beach State	2013-2015
Dylan LaVelle	32	Infielder	Lake Stevens, WA	Everett Community College	2013
Timmy Richards	13	Infielder	Long Beach, CA	Cal State Fullerton	2013
Ty Russell	9	Infielder	Victoria, BC	Marshalltown Community College	2013
John Schuknecht	15	Infielder	Palm Desert, CA	Cal Poly San Luis Obispo	2013
Jordan Ellis	8	Outfielder	Garden Grove, CA	Cal Poly San Luis Obispo	2013
Chris Lewis	6	Outfielder	Newark, CA	Sacramento State	2013
Austin Russell	10	Outfielder	Victoria, BC	Southern Polytechnic State University	2013
Brandon Smith	26	Outfielder	Irvine, CA	Grand Canyon University	2013
Brett Urabe	22	Outfielder	Huntington Beach, CA	UCLA	2013
Mike Darr	12	Outfielder	Corona, CA		2013
Daryl Blaskovich	16	Infielder	Brentwood Bay, BC	Marshalltown Community College	2013
Robby Nesovic	33	Pitcher	El Cajon, CA	University of California Santa Barbara	2013
Nick Rutckyj	11	Outfielder	Surrey, BC	Cuesta College	2013 *signed for 2014 but never played*
Justin Burba	11	Outfielder	Wichita, KS	University of Oklahoma	2013
Greg Fettes	40	Catcher	Madison Heights, MI	University of Kentucky	2013
Jack Graham	22	Infielder	Cranberry Township, PA	Youngston State University	2013
Zach Storm	16	Infielder	London, KY	University of Kentucky	2013
Brendon Magee	12	Outfielder	Victoria, BC	Jamestown Community College	2013
Ryan Adkins	11	Infielder	Victoria, BC	Jamestown Community College	2013
Jackson McCuaig	37	Outfielder	Victoria, BC	Vancouver Island University	2013
Chase Cuckovich	7	Outfielder	Victoria, BC	Riverside Community College	2013
Gunnar Swanson	*n/a*	Pitcher		Everett Community College	2013
Clark McKitrick	31	Pitcher	Idaho Falls, Idaho	Linn Benton Community College	2013
Ty Provencher	23	Pitcher	Long Beach, CA	Long Beach State	2013
Joe Record	35	Pitcher	Placentia, CA	University of California Santa Barbara	2013
Cameron Cuneo	18	Pitcher	Thousand Oaks, CA	University of California Santa Barbara	2013
Tanner Kiest	27	Pitcher	Yucaipa, CA	Riverside Community College	2013
Danny Moore	31	Pitcher	Victoria, BC	Thompson Rivers University	2013
Darren Honeysett	11	Outfielder	Port Coquitlam, BC	Central Washington University	2014
Hunter Mercado-Hood	16	Outfielder	Brentwood, CA	University of San Diego	2014
Nathan Lukes	30	Outfielder	Sacramento, CA	Sacramento State	2014
Sean Watkins	41	Pitcher			2014

NAME	NO.	POSITION	HOMETOWN	SCHOOL	YEAR(S)
Kelly Norris-Jones	5	Catcher	Victoria, BC	University of Illinois Champaign	2014
Alex Baldwin	8	Catcher	Kailua, HI	University of Hawaii	2014
Wyler Smith	33	Outfielder	Vista, CA	University of Utah	2014
Gabe Clark	20	Infielder	Riverside, CA	Oregon State University	2014, 2015
Aaron Barnett	12	Catcher	Mission Viejo, CA	Pepperdine University	2014
Bryce Greager	7	Infielder	Fountain Hills, AZ	University of Nevada Reno	2014
Jacob McAdams	28	Pitcher	Scottsdale, AZ	University of Arizona	2014
Cole Kreuter	29	Infielder	Miami, FL	University of California Irvine	2014
Jake Lesinski	14	Catcher	Huntington Beach, CA	Cal Poly San Luis Obispo	2014
Danny Collier	36	Outfielder	Albuquerque, NM	University of New Mexico	2014
Ted Boeke	18	Infielder	Lewisburg, PA	Loyala Marymount University	2014
Noah Cummings	15	Infielder	Alpine, CA	Oral Roberts University	2014
John Grimsley	6	Outfielder	Tomball, TX	University of San Diego	2014
Devin Carter	31	Outfielder	Temecula, CA	Pepperdine University	2014
Gunner Pollman	35	Catcher	West Linn, OR	California State Sacramento	2014
Alex Fagalde	23	Pitcher	Sacramento, CA	University of California Riverside	2014
Preston Ryan	38	Pitcher	Tempe, AZ	University of New Mexico	2014, 2015
Angel Delgado	9	Pitcher			2014
Brandon Feldman	9	Pitcher	Victoria, BC	Otero Junior College	2014
Drew Davidoff	9	Pitcher	Victoria, BC		2014
Mikey Wright	13	Pitcher	Elk Grove, CA	San Jose State University/ Cosumnes River College	2014, 2015
Alex Garcia	39	Pitcher	Whittier, CA	University of California Santa Barbara	2014
Quintin Torres-Costa	10	Pitcher	Hilo, HI	University of Hawaii	2014
Carson Schneider	37	Pitcher	Albuquerque, NM	University of New Mexico	2014
Dallas Patterson	10	Pitcher	Compton, CA	California State San Bernardino	2014
Riley Edmunds	19	Pitcher	Victoria, BC	Otero Junior College	2014, 2015
Don Sullivan	32	Pitcher		California State San Bernardino	2014
Dylan Stowell	17	Pitcher	Mission Viejo, CA	California Baptist University	2014
Andrew Nelson	40	Pitcher	Omaha, NE	Kentucky	2014
Tim Peabody	27	Pitcher	Tustin, CA	Loyola Marymount University	2014
Mark Marinch	29	Pitcher	Las Vegas, NV	Utah Tech University	2014
Eric Hegadoren	45	Pitcher	Victoria, BC	University of Victoria	2014, 2015, 2018
Shawn Anderson	14	Pitcher			2015
Matt Bryan	12	Outfielder	Victoria, BC	McPherson College	2015
Morgan Varley	10	Infielder	Victoria, BC	Thompson Rivers University	2015
Matt Blais	29	Pitcher	Half Moon Bay, CA	University of California Davis	2015
Kyle Francis	17	Pitcher	Redmond, WA	Everett Community College	2015
Pikai Winchester	35	Infielder/ Pitcher	Kapolei, HI	University of Hawaii	2015
Reno Rankin	7	Outfielder	West Hills, CA	Los Angeles Mission College	2015
Dane Fujinaka	21	Catcher	Aiea, HI	Sacramento State	2015
Kevin Amezquita	11	Outfielder	Covina, CA	East Los Angeles Junior College	2015
Jovan Ewusie	33	Infielder	Vancouver, BC		2015
Jonathan Buckley	35	Pitcher	Chino Hills, CA	St. Marys College of Minnesota	2015
Connor Suing	14	Pitcher	Keizer, OR	Western Oregon University	2015
Luke Manuel	32	Pitcher	Delta, BC	Northeastern Oklahoma A	2015, 2018
Calvin Christiansen	11	Pitcher			2015
Austin Dondanville	42	Pitcher	Walnut Creek, CA	Cal Poly San Luis Obispo	2015, 2016
Brett Irvine	17	Pitcher	Victoria, BC		2015
Shawn Kennedy II	16	Pitcher	San Dimas, CA	Georgetown College	2015
Sean OTolle	9	Pitcher	Huntington Beach, CA	St. Marys College of California	2015
Henry Omana	34	Pitcher	Walnut, CA	Cal Poly Pomona	2015
Alex Rogers	22	Pitcher	Nanaimo, BC	Trinidad State Junior College	2014, 2015

NAME	NO.	POSITION	HOMETOWN	SCHOOL	YEAR(S)
Nick Seginowich	1	Pitcher	Victoria, BC		2015
Dominic Topoozian	27	Pitcher	Clovis, CA	Fresno State University	2015
Zane Takhar		Infielder	Victoria, BC	Northeastern Oklahoma A	2015
Tei Vanderford	32	Pitcher	Glendale, CA	University of Tennessee	2015
Josh Walker	18	Pitcher	Chino Hills, CA	Orange Coast College	2015, 2016
Jason Willow	22	Pitcher/ Infielder	Victoria, BC	Santa Barbara Community College	2015, 2017, 2019
Nick Woitysiak	36	Pitcher	Scottsdale, AZ	Paradise Valley Community College	2015
Zach Bonneau	33	Catcher	Spokane, WA	University of Washington	2015
Nick Meyer	14	Catcher	Mission Viejo, CA	Cal Poly San Luis Obispo	2015
Jackson Thoreson	28	Catcher	San Jose, CA	St. Marys College of California	2015
Griffin Andreychuk	21	Infielder	Nanaimo, BC	Seattle University	2014, 2015, 2016
PJ Floyd	15	Infielder	Rocklin, CA	Sacramento State	2015
Torin Goldstein	12	Infielder	Irvine, CA	Fresno State University	2015
Michael Gretler	20	Infielder	Booney Lake, WA	Oregon State University	2015
Scott Jarvis	5	Infielder	San Jose, CA	UCLA	2015
Chase Lambert	25	Infielder	Malibu, CA	Pepperdine University	2015
Brady Rogers	2	Infielder	Nanaimo, BC	Trinidad State Junior College	2015
AJ Alcantara	30	Outfielder	Alta Loma, CA	University of California Irvine	2015, 2016
Kevin Collard	37	Outfielder	Vista, CA	University of San Diego	2015, 2017
Chris	23	Outfielder	Victoria, BC	Salt Lake Community College	2015
Austin Guibor	10	Outfielder	Campbell, CA	Fresno State University	2015, 2016
Ben Polshuk	26	Outfielder	Clayton, CA	Cal Poly San Luis Obispo	2015, 2016
Jake Pries	41	Outfielder	San Juan Capistrano, CA	UCLA	2015
Colin Ashworth	24	Pitcher	Placentia, CA	Orange Coast College	2016, 2017
Greg Casper	27	Pitcher	Pocatello, ID	South Dakota State University	2016
Casey Costello	23	Pitcher	La Quinta, CA	Orange Coast College	2016
Indigo Diaz	44	Pitcher	North Vancouver, BC	Iowa Western Community College	2016. 2017
Blake Hannah	39	Pitcher	Vacaville, CA	University of California Davis	2016, 2017
Holden Lyons	35	Pitcher	Edmond, OK	Oklahoma University	2016
Will McAffer	16	Pitcher	North Vancouver, BC	South Dakota State University	2016
Josh Mitchell	40	Pitcher	Ridgway, PA	University of Pittsburgh	2015, 2016
Kyle Mora	19	Pitcher	Los Alamitos, CA	UCLA	2016
Cameron Schneider	45	Pitcher	Concord, CA	Cal Poly Pomona	2016
Nick Seginowich	12	Pitcher	Victoria, BC		2016
Ethan Skuija	34	Pitcher	Victoria, BC	UBC	2016, 2017
Jack Wolger	37	Pitcher	Folsom, CA	University of California Berkeley	2016
Riley Guntrip	9	Catcher	Camrose, AB	Siena Heights University	2016, 2017
Hayden Jaco	7	Catcher	Coquitlam, BC	Vernon Regional Junior College	2016, 2018
Joe Prior	8	Catcher	Los Alamitos, CA	Fresno State University	2016
Dakota Dean	22	Infielder	Crestview, FL	University of New Orleans	2016
PJ Floyd	15	Infielder	Rocklin, CA	Sacramento State	2016
Tommy Jew	5	Infielder	San Ramon, CA	University of California Santa Barbara	2016
Kobe Morris	0	Infielder	Victoria, BC	Alabama	2016
Brad Pluschkell	11	Infielder	Pleasanton, CA	University of California Davis	2016
Tyler Schindel	6	Outfielder	Victoria, BC	San Diego Christian College	2016, 2019
Lucas Soper	10	Infielder	Vancouver, BC	UBC	2016
Ryan Anderson	32	Outfielder	Pleasanton, CA	University of California Davis	2016
Matt Lautz	41	Outfielder		Concordia	2016
Jarron Silva	14	Outfielder	Stockton, CA	UCLA	2016
Matt Smith	25	Outfielder	Placerville, CA	Sacramento State	2016
Cody Snider	0	Outfielder	Napa, CA	Chico State	2016
Jake Stone	17	Outfielder	Carlsbad, CA	Fresno State University	2016

NAME	NO.	POSITION	HOMETOWN	SCHOOL	YEAR(S)
Justin Bundy	5	Infielder	Edgewood, TX	Northeastern Texas Community College	2016
Wyatt Young	19	Infielder	Honolulu, HI	Pepperdine University	2016
Cameron Cannon		Infielder	Chandler, AZ	University of Arizona	2016
Matt Warkentin	28	Infielder	Leamington, ON	University of San Francisco	2016
Justin Brown	32	Infielder	Lake Stevens, WA	University of Portland	2016
Brayden Resch	8	Infielder	Saskatoon, SK	North Dakota State University	2016 *only on roster for 3 games*
Domenic Colacchio	6	Infielder	Aliso Viejo, CA	Long Beach State	2016
Codi Guillory	41	Catcher	Colorado Springs, CO	Colby Community College	2016
Creed Smith	34	Pitcher	Chico, CA	Sacramento City College	2016
Ryan Steindorf	38	Pitcher	Chico, CA	University of California Davis	2016
Dalton Erb	44	Pitcher	North Terrance, CA	California State Chico	2016
Cody Ahlgrimm	20	Pitcher	Colorado Springs, CO	Pacific University	2016
James Kannenberg	12	Pitcher	Littleton, CO	University of San Francisco	2016
Skyler Henderson	13	Pitcher	South Padre, TX	Vernon Regional Junior College	2016
Nick Woitysiak	36	Pitcher	Scottsdale, AZ	Paradise Valley Community College	2016
Ethan Fox	16	Pitcher	Campbell River, BC	Avila University	2017, 2018
Wyatt Boone	29	Pitcher		Seattle University	2017
James Bradwell	20	Pitcher	Roberts Creek, BC	UBC	2017
Claire Eccles	8	Pitcher	Surrey, BC	UBC	2017, 2018
Matt Kent	43	Pitcher	Fort Wayne, TX	Xavier University	2017
Travis Kuhn	23	Pitcher	Norco, CA	San Diego	2017
Cole Masik	35	Pitcher	North Vancouver, BC	Seton Hill	2017
Adam McKillican	33	Pitcher	Courtney, BC	UBC	2017
Mikey Musselwhite	5	Pitcher	Victoria, BC	Edmonds Community College	2017, 2018
Jack Owen	0	Pitcher	Coto de Gaza, CA	Auburn	2017
Noah Prewett	6	Pitcher	Woodland, CA	San Diego	2017
Taylor Prokopis	32	Pitcher	Sandu, UT	Colorado Mesa University	2017
Garrison Ritter	18	Pitcher	West Linn, OR	St. Martin's College	2017, 2018
Garinder Sarana	40	Pitcher			2017
Zach Swanson	7	Pitcher	Victoria, BC	San Diego	2017, 2019
Radd Thomas	36	Pitcher	Newcastle, CA	University of California Santa Barbara	2017
Dylan Thorp	19	Pitcher	North Vancouver, BC	Bellevue University	2017
Stephen Wade	28	Pitcher	Victoria, BC	College of Southern Idaho	2017
Tyson Abbott	2	Catcher	Victoria, BC	Prairie Baseball Academy	2017
Jayden Cull	0	Catcher	Victoria, BC	Lyon College	2017
Shane McGuire	16	Catcher	Renton, WA	San Diego	2017
Harrison Bragg	27	Infielder	Lakewood, WA	Mississippi State	2017
Tucker Johnson	11	Infielder	China Springs, TX	Baylor University	2017
Justin Orton	1	Infielder	Essex, ON	UBC	2017
Andrew Shaps	17	Infielder	Paradise Valley, AZ	William Jessup	2017
Harry Shipley	13	Infielder	Fishers, IN	Purdue University	2017
Cole Weiss	26	Infielder	Winston-Salem, NC	University of North Carolina Wilmington	2017
Sam Cachola	15	Outfielder	Irvine, CA	University of California Berkeley	2017
Po-Hao Huang	14	Outfielder	Kaohsing City	National Taiwan Sports University	2017
DJ Porter	42	Outfielder	Rancho Cucamonga, CA	Cal Baptist	2017
Hunter Vansau	26	Outfielder	Crawford, TX	Mississippi State	2017, 2018
Connor Whitney	22	Outfielder		Park University	2017
Riley Zayicek	31	Outfielder	Mount Ulla, NC	University of North Carolina Wilmington	2017
Nick Moroney	7	Infielder	Danville, CA	University of California Santa Barbara	2017
Davis Wendzel	5	Infielder	San Clemente, CA	Baylor University	2017
Kekai Rios	21	Catcher	Oahu, HI	University of Hawaii	2017
Tanner Rempel	18	Catcher	Abbotsford, BC	Colorado Mesa University	2017, 2019

NAME	NO.	POSITION	HOMETOWN	SCHOOL	YEAR(S)
Andrew Vaughn	99	Catcher/ Infielder	Santa Rosa, CA	University of California Berkeley	2017
Bryce Bonner	10	Catcher	Katy, TX	Purdue University	2017
Nick Bellafronto	29	Infielder	San Jose, CA	Stanford University	2017
Jake Garella	28	Infielder	Edwardsville, IL	St. Louis University	2017
Kyle McComb	7	Infielder	Surrey, BC	UBC	2017
Will LaRue	7	Outfielder	Evansville, IN	Xavier University	2017
Ryan Ricci	19	Pitcher	Greencastle, PA	George Mason University	2017
AJ Block	20	Pitcher	Bellevue, WA	Washington State	2017
Isaac Mullins	40	Pitcher	North Bend, WA	Washington State	2017
Luke Boyd	35	Pitcher	Ojai, CA	Baylor University	2017
Liam Steigerwald	38	Pitcher	San Ramon, CA	University of California Santa Barbara	2017
Kyle Stubbins	10	Pitcher	Surrey, BC	UBC	2017
Chavez Fernander	38	Pitcher	Grand Bahama	Polk State College	2017
Jack Tagget	30	Pitcher	Frankenmuth, MI	Kalamazoo College	2017
Mason Shaw	17	Pitcher	Ferndale, WA	Yakima Valley College	2018
Owen Sharts	38	Pitcher	Simi Valley, CA	Nevada	2018
Justin Solt	29	Pitcher	Spokane, WA	Lower Columbia Junior College	2018
Alejandro Ortega Lopez	97	Pitcher	Cuba	Union de Reyes	2018
Adriel Quesada Pena	75	Pitcher	Cuba	Union de Reyes	2018
Aidan Goicovich	36	Pitcher	Gilroy. CA	Cal Poly	2018
Ryan Rutherford	47	Pitcher	Corona, CA	University of California San Bernardino	2018
Tyler Yoshihara	18	Pitcher	Saratoga, CA	Pomona-Pitzer	2018
Landon Anderson	49	Pitcher	Bellflower, CA	Cal State Fullerton	2018
Kayden Beauregard	13	Pitcher/ Catcher	Abbotsford, BC		2018, 2019
Tyler Thomas	31	Pitcher		Baylor University	2018
Gunner Friend	35	Pitcher	Webcity, MT	Avila University	2018
Tyler HIlton	16	Pitcher	Mesa, AZ	Benedictine University	2018, 2019
Nathan Walker	40	Pitcher	Mountain View, CA	San Diego	2018
Cade Brown	48	Pitcher	Berkeley, CA	San Diego	2018
PIng-Chun Ho	11	Pitcher	Taichung, Taiwan	Barry University	2018
Po-Jui Huang	15	Pitcher		National Taiwan Sports University	2018
Carter Loewen	45	Pitcher	Abbotsford, BC	Hawaii	2018
Lawson Humphries	12	Pitcher	Americus, GA	Georgia Southern	2018
Garrett Goodall	20	Pitcher	Nanaimo, BC	Embry-Riddle (Florida)	2018, 2019
Luke Manuel	37	Pitcher	Surrey, BC	Eastern New Mexico University	2018
Ryan Green	7	Catcher		Fraser Valley	2018
Nicky Gibbs	53	Catcher	Barlow, FL	Florida Southern	2018
Matt Clayton	34	Catcher	Yuba City, CA	Nevada-Las Vegas	2018, 2019
Caleb Ricketts	44	Catcher	Newport Beach, CA	San Diego	2018
Adam Imwalle	5	Infielder	Sarasota, FL	State College of Florida	2018
Trey Bigford	25	Infielder	Burkburnett, TX	Cameron University	2018
Sam Nastari	*n/a*	Catcher		Jackson State	2018 *Only played two games*
Aharon Modlin	54	Infielder	Atlanta, GA	Pepperdine University	2018
Joe Casey	54	Outfielder			2018
Ryan Ober	9	Infielder	Mesa, AZ	Oregon State University	2018
Rowdey Jordan	3	Infielder	Auburn, AL	Mississippi State	2018
Brodan Bydeweg	92	Infielder	Langley, BC	Vancouver Island University	2018
Blake Wagenseller	51	Outfielder	La Jolla, CA	Cal Poly San Luis Obispo	2018
Silas Grinstead	27	Catcher	Palm Coast, FL	Florida State College	2018
Colton Peha	23	Outfielder	Spokane, WA	Saint Martin's University	2018
AJ Lewis	4	Infielder	Chicago, IL	Eastern Kentucky	2018

NAME	NO.	POSITION	HOMETOWN	SCHOOL	YEAR(S)
Gio Villanueva	75	Infielder	Chula Vista, CA	Academy of Art	2018
Nathan Flores	36	Infielder			2018
Jake McDonald	27	Catcher			2018
Jeremy Jess	72	Pitcher	San Luis Obispo, CA	Pomona-Pitzer College	2018
Chang-Chi Yeh	34	Infielder			2018
Trevin Reynolds	90	Outfielder	Las Vegas, NV	Colorado Mesa University	2018
Connor Nantkes	22	Pitcher	Aurora, CO	Washington State	2018
Po-Yen Chen	94	Pitcher	Taoyuan City, Taiwan		2018
Clark Streby	36	Pitcher	Selah, WA	St. Martin's College	2018
Michael Stovman	37	Pitcher	Maple Ridge, BC	Indian River State College	2018
Garrett Stevens	79	Pitcher		University of the Ozarks	2018
Samuel Brunning	18	Pitcher		Embry-Riddle University	2018
Dustin Demeter	10	Infielder	Santa Barbara, CA	Hawaii	2018
Harrison Spohn	6	Infielder	Upland, CA	Cal Baptist	2018, 2019
Tanner Haney	2	Infielder	Waco, TX	Texas	2018, 2019, 2022 *Wore #4 in 2022*
Jack Smith	13	Infielder	Mercer Island, WA	Washington State	2018
Jaxxon Fagg	32	Infielder	Murietta, GA	Georgia Southern	2018
Jeddediah Fagg	33	Infielder	Murietta, GA	Georgia Southern	2018
Nate Pecota	3	Outfielder	Lee Summit, MT	Cameron University	2018, 2019
Mike Malinchak	50	Outfielder	Delray Beach, FL	Pepperdine University	2018
Dustin Miller	39	Outfielder	Clayton, CA	Chico State	2018
Nick Plaia	23	Outfielder	Santa Clarita, CA	Cal Baptist	2018, 2019
Ethan Lopez	28	Outfielder	Whittier, CA	University of Hawaii	2017, 2018
Mikey Callia	53	Pitcher	Renton, WA	Western Nebraska	2019
Aaron Celestino	91	Pitcher	Houston, TX	University of Incarnate Word	2019
Fynn Chester	5	Pitcher	Victoria, BC	Cal State Fullerton	2019
Luka Green	18	Pitcher	Austin, TX	Pomona-Pitzer College	2019
Dakota Hawkins	29	Pitcher	Chehalis, WA	Lower Columbia Junior College	2019
Tim Holyk	36	Pitcher	Nanaimo, BC	Miles Community College	2019
Josh Laukkanen	32	Pitcher	Nanaimo, BC	Cloud County Community College	2019
Mitch Lines	11	Pitcher	Battle Ground, WA	Lower Columbia Junior College	2019
Reagan MacDonald	47	Pitcher		Dallas Baptist University	2019
Hunter Omlid	55	Pitcher			2019
Jacob Potter	31	Pitcher	Victoria, BC	Allen County Community College/ Southeastern Oklahoma State	2018, 2019
Derek Salata	38	Pitcher	Westchester, IL	Illinois State University	2019
Chase Stewart	4	Pitcher	Abbotsford, BC	University of Cincinnati	2019
Calvin Turchin	90	Pitcher	Federal Way, WA	University of Hawaii	2019
Branson Wilson	12	Pitcher	Fort Worth, TX	Baylor University	2019
Jon Gale	19	Catcher	Victoria, BC	University of Victoria	2019
Kyle Harper	51	Catcher	Houston, TX	Baylor University	2019
Tyson Hays	10	Catcher	Denver, CO	Illinois State University	2019
Frankie Niemann	27	Catcher	Sanford, FL	Tulane University	2019
Tyler Pettit	28	Catcher	Round Rock, TX	University of Incarnate Word/ Trinity University	2019, 2022 *Wore #35 in 2022*
McGregor Sharpe	17	Catcher	North Vancouver, BC	Douglas College	2019
Liam Ballance	39	Infielder	Parksville, BC	Vancouver Island University	2019
Parker Bramlett	25	Infielder	Bullard, TX	Angelo State University	2019
Jayden Cull	45	Infielder	Victoria, BC	Lyon College	2019
Chase Meidroth	14	Infielder	Manhatten Beach, CA	University of San Diego	2019
Emilio Nogales	35	Infielder	San Jose, CA	Fresno State University	2019
Griffin Paxton	33	Infielder	West, TX	University of Texas San Antonio	2019
Gus Wilson	15	Infielder	Duncan, BC	University of Science and Arts of Oklahoma	2019

NAME	NO.	POSITION	HOMETOWN	SCHOOL	YEAR(S)
Nick Adams	9	Outfielder	Peoria, IL	Yavapai College	2019
Andrew MacCuaig	52	Outfielder	Lacombe, AB	Vancouver Island University	2019
Nate Pecota	3	Outfielder	Lee Summit, MT	Camden County College	2019
Kyle Sherick	54	Outfielder	Ravensdale, WA	Seattle University	2019
Chase Wehsener	52	Infielder	San Diego, CA	Baylor University	2019
Trevor Paro	96	Infielder	Hot Springs, MT	Lower Columbia Community College	2019
Matt Turner	37	Outfielder	Broomfield, CO	Colorado Mesa University	2019
Chase Frady	14	Infielder	Evans, Georgia	Georgia State University	2019
Joe Butler	26	Infielder	Kankakee, IL	Illinois State University	2019
Grayson Jones	26	Pitcher	Dallas, TX	James Madison University	2019
Zach Horne	54	Pitcher			2019
Hunter Hennigh	50	Pitcher	Almeda, CA	Pomona-Pitzer College	2019
Matt Amrhein	55	Pitcher	Upland, CA	Cal Baptist	2019
Jack Hyde	53	Pitcher	La Mesa, CA	University of San Diego	2019
Sid Lacy	17	Pitcher	Fresno, CA	Chico State	2019
Connor Barison	32	Pitcher	Redmond, CA	Washington State	2019
Ryan Watson	15	Pitcher	Sugar Hill, GA	Georgia State University	2019
Jack Neely	41	Pitcher	San Antonio, TX	Ohio State	2019
Cade Smith	31	Pitcher	Abbotsford, BC	Mennonite Educational Institute	2019
Dylan Larson	39	Pitcher	Ellensburg, WA	Virginia Tech University	2019
Joseph Brandon	16	Pitcher	Loganville, GA	Georgia State University	2019
Jaiden Beck	44	Pitcher	Troy, TX	Paris Junior College	2019
DJ Peters	5	Pitcher	Mesa, AZ	Scottsdale Community College	2019
Josh Gessner	77	Pitcher	Sydney, Australia	Tulane University	2019
Jackson Belanger	14	Pitcher			2022
Levi Abbott	52	Pitcher	Lethbridge, AB	Canisius College	2022, 2023
Walker Bordovsky	23	Pitcher	Victoria, TX	San Jacinto College North	2022
Haldon Craig	40	Pitcher	Victoria, BC	UVic	2022
Cooper Crompton	29	Pitcher	Langley, BC	Iowa Western Community College	2022
Harry Deliyannis	14	Pitcher	Bloomington, IN	Pomona-Pitzer College	2022
Russell Hicks	36	Pitcher	Reno, NV	University of Nevada	2022
Nick Lee	38	Pitcher	Victoria, BC	UVic	2022
Owen Luchies	9	Pitcher	Victoria, BC	Lower Columbia Community College	2022
Michael Nunez	34	Pitcher	Stevenson Ranch, CA	Loyala Marymount University	2022
Jacob Popdynec	12	Pitcher	Victoria, BC	UVic	2022
Flynn Ridley	18	Pitcher	Burnaby, BC	Ottawa University	2022, 2023
Addison Sells	32	Pitcher	Helotes, TX	Temple College	2022
Jack Seward	16	Pitcher			2022
Loretto Sinisalchi	37	Pitcher	Burnaby, BC	Washington State/ Yavapai College	2022, 2023
Jaxson Smith-Peterson	27	Pitcher	Victoria, BC		2022
Noah Takacs	25	Pitcher	Victoria, BC	Sacramento State	2022
Jace Walker	2	Pitcher	Robinson, TX	Temple College	2022
Ryan Dominguez		Pitcher	Hesperia, CA	Riverside City	2022
Andre Duplantier II	19	Pitcher	Humble, TX	University of Texas Austin	2022
Sam Walbridge	47	Pitcher	San Antonio, TX	University of Texas Austin	2022
Josh Verdon	39	Pitcher	San Diego, CA	California State Chico	2022
Michael Tsoukalas	27	Catcher	Arlington, WA	Seattle University	2022
Colton Moore	6	Catcher	Amarillo, TX	University of Arizona	2022
Russell Young	13	Catcher	Surrey, BC	UBC	2022, 2023
Aidan Aguilar	53	Infielder	Little Elm,TX	Loyala Marymount University	2022
Jordan Bond	10	Infielder	Victoria, BC	Camosun College	2022
Noah Sudyka	20	Infielder	Aliso Viejo, CA	UC San Diego	2022
Luke Cheng	22	Infielder	Olney, Maryand	Illinois State University	2022

NAME	NO.	POSITION	HOMETOWN	SCHOOL	YEAR(S)
Roberto Gonzalez	53	Infielder	Houston, TX	University of the Incarnate Word	2022
Eric Luchies	33	Infielder	Victoria, BC	Lower Columbia Community College	2022
Lane Roggensack	28	Infielder	Wainright, AB	Victoria Golden Tide	2022
Josh Rolling	7	Infielder	Reno, NV	Sacramento State	2022
Hudson Shupe	17	Infielder	West Richland, WA	Gonzaga University	2022, 2023
Ignacio (Nacho) Alvarez Jr.		Infielder	Fontana, CA	Riverside Community College	2022
Johnny Ceccoli		Infielder	Tyler, TX	McLellan Community College	2022
Jake Skipworth	35	Infielder	Riverside, CA	Cal Baptist	2022
Josh Blount	54	Outfielder	De Pere, WI	Illinois State University	2022
Jesse Brown	3	Outfielder/ Catcher	Seattle, WA	UC Santa Barbara	2022, 2023
Clark Henry	17	Outfielder	Houston, TX	University of Texas San Antonio	2022
Grady Morgan	31	Outfielder	Laguna Beach, CA	University of California Chico	2022
Joseph Redfield	15	Outfielder	Waco, TX	Sam Houston	2022
Daniel Sawchyn	11	Outfielder	Victoria, BC	Camosun College	2022
Tyler Attal	22	Outfielder	Los Angeles, CA	Bates	2022
Josh Walker	41	Outfielder	Victoria, BC	Sacramento State	2022
Jaydon Malinowski	33	Outfielder	Victoria, BC	Galveston College	2022
Shane Jamison	4	Infielder	Bellingham, WA	Seattle University	2022
Trent Lenihan	91	Infielder	White Rock, BC	UBC	2022
Kyle Hepburn	76	Catcher	Richmond, BC	St. Ambrose University/ Johnson County Community College	2022, 2023
Tristan Bolger	10 2/3	Infielder	Victoria, BC	Camosun College	2022, 2023
Jack McLaren	50	Pitcher	Victoria, BC		2022
Ryder Green	34	Pitcher	Victoria, BC	Park University	2022, 2023
Aidan McCann	26	Pitcher	Seattle, WA	Linfield College	2022
Ben Smedshammer	36	Pitcher	Lorena, TX	Paris Junior College	2022, 2023
Nick Taylor	64	Pitcher	Kirkland, WA	Edmonds Community College	2022, 2023
Henri Draper	2	Pitcher	Seattle, WA	Olympic College	2022
Brett Harvey	1 4/11	Pitcher	Auburn, WA	University of Puget Sound	2022, 2023
David Chase	55	Pitcher	Manhatten Beach, CA	Loyala Marymount University	2022
Andrew Gillion	17	Pitcher	Surrey, BC	Douglas College	2022
Mitsuki Shimonishi	23	Pitcher	Kobe, Japan	Dakota State University	2022
Dawson Hurford	19	Pitcher	Victoria, BC	Western Nebraska Comm. College/ Southern Arkansas University	2022,2023
Josh Berenbaum	38	Pitcher	Richmond, BC	University of Fraser Valley	2023
Mason Chamberlain	49	Pitcher	Victoria, BC	Okanagan College	2023
Dustin Davidson	44	Pitcher	Haida Gwaii		2023
Jed Decooman	20	Pitcher	Vancouver, BC	University of California Santa Barbara	2023
Russell Derbyshire	50	Pitcher	Leamington, ON	University of Louisana Monroe	2023
Jake Finkelstein	33	Pitcher	Richmond, BC	Montana State University Billings	2023
Jack Finn	28	Pitcher	Victoria, BC	Illinois State University	2023
Davis Franklin	14	Pitcher	Saammamich, WA	University of Puget Sound	2023
Daniel Gonzales	19	Pitcher	Marrieta, CA	University of Louisana Monroe	2023
Brett Harvey	1 4/11	Pitcher	Auburn, WA	University of Puget Sound	2022, 2023
Sean Heppner	62	Pitcher	Point Roberts, WA	UBC	2023
Cody Howard	25	Pitcher	The Woodlands, TX	Texas State University	2023
Zak Johnson	16	Pitcher	Shiner, TX	Temple	2023
Sam Jordan	35	Pitcher	Victoria, BC	Thompson Rivers University	2023
Tucker Christensen	54	Pitcher	Norwalk, Iowa	Sam Houston State University	2023
Carson Latimer	60	Pitcher	Delta, BC	Cloud County Community College	2023
Logan MacNiel	40	Pitcher	Vancouver, BC	New Mexico Junior College	2023
Ryan Magdic	29	Pitcher/ Infielder	Beamsville, ON	Florida Southern	2023

NAME	NO.	POSITION	HOMETOWN	SCHOOL	YEAR(S)
Skyler Manelski	55	Pitcher	Shoreline, WA	Linfield College	2023
Chase Marshall	45	Pitcher	Vancouver, BC	University of Utah	2023
Wyatt McDonald	26	Pitcher	Victoria, BC		2023
Cam Caley	20	Pitcher	The Woodlands, TX	Baylor University	2023
Darius Opdam Bak	51	Pitcher	White Rock, BC	Camosun College	2022, 2023
Jack Seward	16/61	Pitcher	Port Moody, BC	San Jacinto College North/ Central Arizona College	2022, 2023
David Dressendorfer	15	Pitcher	Round Rock, TX	Angelo State University	2023
Max Grubbs	26	Pitcher	Arlington, TX	Texas State University	2023
Benny Roebuck	51	Pitcher	Bryan, ON	Kent State University	2023
Alan Dai	6	Pitcher	Vancouver, BC	Amherst College	2023
Ruydai Watanabe	54	Pitcher	Harrisburg, IL	Coffeyville Community College	2023
Dylan Osborne	26	Pitcher	Vancouver, BC	University of Washington	2023
Harrison Caley		Catcher	The Woodlands, TX	Baylor University	2023
Tripp Clark	31	Catcher	Waco, TX	Angelo State University	2023
Tyler Davis	48	Catcher	Fresno, CA	Fresno State University	2023
Jaxson Cordle	47	Infielder	Victoria, BC	Camosun College	2023
Brandon Green	5	Infielder	Olds, AB	Camosun College	2023
Max Clark	31	Infielder	Mercer Island, WA	University of Washington	2023
Tyrus Hall	39	Infielder	Victoria, BC	Bossier Parish Community College	2023
Jack Johnson	32	Infielder	Thousand Oaks, CA	Baylor University	2023
Phoenix Sommay	9	Infielder	Temecula, CA	California State San Marcos	2023
Dallas Macias	12	Infielder	Parker, CO	Oregon State University	2023
Marco Pirruccello	4	Infielder	Rockin, CA	Fresno State University	2023
Kevin Shea	15	Infielder	San Francisco, CA		2023
Lane Brewster	2	Outfielder	League City, TX	Sam Houston	2023
Michael Crossland	10	Outfielder	Roosevelt, WA	University of California, San Diego	2023
Kai Gray	22	Outfielder	Victoria, BC	Trinidad State Junior College	2023
Kieper Pate	23	Outfielder	Bentonville, AR	San Jacinto College North	2023
Bradden Kesey	28	Outfielder	Manahans, TX	Grayson County College	2023
Nick Dumesnil	22	Outfielder	Huntington Beach, CA	Cal Baptist	2023
Rei Kimura		Outfielder	Japan	College of Idaho	2023

INDEX

N

O

P